ALIVE IN CHRIST

GRADE 5

The Seven Sacraments

aliveinchrist.osv.com

OurSundayVisitor

Alive in Christ Parish Grade 5 Student Book
ISBN: 978-1-61278-014-6
Item Number: CU5104

3 4 5 6 7 8 9 10   015016   21 20 19 18 17
Webcrafters, Inc., Madison, WI, USA; July 2017; Job# 132565

Contents at a Glance

Contents In Detail

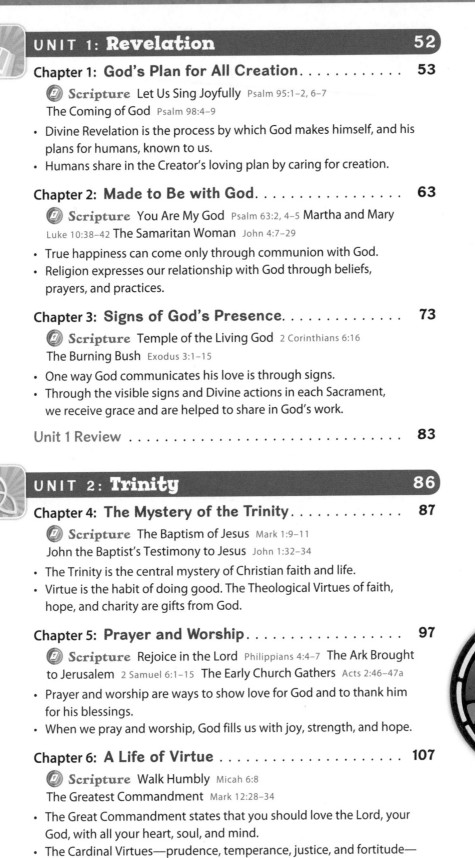

Catholic Social Teaching Live Your Faith

*These pages introduce you to important teachings of Jesus and the Church
that help us live Jesus' new commandment to love as he loved.*

Our Catholic Tradition Reference Section .. 304

*This reference section presents information on our Creeds, Sacraments,
prayers and practices of our Catholic faith.*

© Our Sunday Visitor

A New Year

 Let Us Pray

Leader: Holy God, we gather in prayer to give thanks for you and your presence in our lives.

Sing to the LORD a new song;
    sing to the LORD, all the earth.
Sing to the LORD, bless his name;
    proclaim his salvation day after day. **Psalm 96:1–2**

All: We thank you for sharing your life and love with us. Amen.

 **Scripture**

Or are you unaware that we who were baptized into Christ Jesus were baptized into his death? We were indeed buried with him through baptism into death, so that, just as Christ was raised from the dead by the glory of the Father, we too might live in newness of life.

For if we have grown into union with him through a death like his, we shall also be united with him in the resurrection. **Romans 6:3–5**

? What Do You Wonder?

- What does union with Jesus look and feel like?
- How does God share his life and love with us today?

Fifth Grade

What is the year going to be like?

You've started another year and taken another step in learning and living your Catholic faith. What can you expect this year?

This symbol lets you know the story or reading that follows is from the Bible. In every lesson you will spend time with God's Word in Scripture. Through these stories you will learn more about God's immense love for us, his faithfulness, and his desire for us to have new life in him.

You will join others in beginning and ending each lesson with a prayer. Each time you are together, you have the chance to thank God, ask his help, pray for the needs of others, and praise God for being God. God the Holy Spirit helps you pray.

You will sing songs to praise God and celebrate our faith. During the year, you'll explore the feasts and seasons of the Church year, and you will meet many Saints, heroes of the Church.

Every chapter has exercises to help you better understand what's being taught. You may be underlining, circling, writing, matching, or more.

Living as Jesus' Disciples

During this year, you will be looking closely at the Church's special signs and celebrations known as the **Seven Sacraments**. The Sacraments point to God and to his love. Christ himself acts in the Sacraments, and they become sources of grace and new life. As you learn, important Catholic Faith Words are **highlighted** in yellow to focus your attention.

You'll grow in your understanding of the Son of God, who was sent to bring salvation and new life. You'll learn about the Church's role in salvation and the Holy Spirit who unites the Church in Jesus. And, you'll explore how the Sacraments are celebrated and the ways the grace of the Sacraments deepen your relationship with Christ and strengthen you to follow him.

Three times a chapter you'll see green words like the ones below. You'll take a break to think about your faith and special people in your life; make connections to what you do at home, with friends, at Church; and see how living your faith can make a difference.

1. Underline why the Son of God was sent.
2. Circle who unites the Church.

Share Your Faith

Reflect What does the Catholic Church celebrate?

Share In small groups discuss what and how the Church celebrates. Write one way you can take part.

_____

_____

_____

_____

© Our Sunday Visitor

Catholic Faith Words

The **highlighted** words appear here again with their complete definitions.

Seven Sacraments effective signs of God's life, instituted by Christ and given to the Church. In the celebration of each Sacrament, there are visible signs and Divine actions that give grace and allow us to share in God's work.

God's Word

Sacred Scripture is the inspired Word of God written by humans. The canon of Scripture is the list of books of the Bible accepted by the Church as the inspired Word of God.

The word *canon* comes from an ancient Sumerian word for a reed used for measuring. Canon can also mean a collection or a list. The Catholic Church accepts a biblical canon of 73 books—46 in the Old Testament and 27 in the New Testament.

The Old Testament is the first part of the Bible, about God's relationship with the Hebrew people before Jesus was born. It includes the laws, history, and stories of God's People.

The New Testament is the second part of the Bible. It tells of God's love for people after the coming of Jesus. It is about the life and teaching of Jesus, his followers, and the early Church.

Scripture in the Liturgy

Bible readings are important in all liturgies.

- Words from Scripture are found in many prayers in the liturgy.
- Songs and hymns can often contain phrases and images from the Bible.
- The Bible readings and phrases and images express the faith of the people. They remind all people of God's mighty deeds.

The Old Testament

The first part of the Bible includes the laws, history, and stories of God's People.

The Pentateuch	Genesis, Exodus, Leviticus, Numbers, Deuteronomy
The Historical Books	Joshua, Judges, Ruth, 1 Samuel, 2 Samuel, 1 Kings, 2 Kings, 1 Chronicles, 2 Chronicles, Ezra, Nehemiah, Tobit, Judith, Esther, 1 Maccabees, 2 Maccabees
The Wisdom Books	Job, Psalms, Proverbs, Ecclesiastes, Song of Songs (Ecclesiasticus), Wisdom, Sirach
The Prophetic Books	Isaiah, Jeremiah, Lamentations, Baruch, Ezekiel, Daniel, Hosea, Joel, Amos, Obadiah, Jonah, Micah, Nahum, Habakkuk, Zephaniah, Haggai, Zechariah, Malachi

The New Testament

The second part of the Bible tells of God's love for people after the coming of Jesus. It is about the life and teaching of Jesus, his followers, and the early Church.

The Gospels	Matthew, Mark, Luke, John

The Acts of the Apostles

The New Testament Letters	Romans, 1 Corinthians, 2 Corinthians, Galatians, Ephesians, Philippians, Colossians, 1 Thessalonians, 2 Thessalonians, 1 Timothy, 2 Timothy, Titus, Philemon, Hebrews, James, 1 Peter, 2 Peter, 1 John, 2 John, 3 John, Jude

Revelation

Connect Your Faith

Scripture on Scripture Unscramble the letters in the words below to find out what the Bible tells us about the importance of Scripture.

SEUJS SI HET RODW FO ODG

☐☐☐☐☐ ☐☐ ☐☐☐ ☐☐☐☐ ☐☐ ☐☐☐

Our Catholic Life

Each chapter in your book has an Our Catholic Life section. It builds on what's in the chapter and focuses in a special way on what it means to be Catholic. Text, images, and activities help us better understand how to grow closer to Jesus and the Church.

Match the ways we grow as disciples of Jesus in the left column with the descriptions in the right column.

Growing as Disciples of Jesus

Know more about our faith	•	•	Understand and live the Beatitudes and the Great Commandment
Understand and take part in the Sacraments	•	•	Participate in the mission and community life of your parish
Live as Jesus calls us to	•	•	Understand and pray in adoration, praise, thanksgiving, petition, and intercession
Talk and listen to God in prayer	•	•	Spread the Gospel through how we live and act with our families, friends, and others
Be an active member of the Church	•	•	Celebrate the Eucharist and participate in Reconciliation
Help others know Jesus through our words and actions	•	•	Learn about God's plan for us all through Sacred Scripture and Sacred Tradition

People of Faith

You will also be introduced to People of Faith, holy women and men who loved God very much and did his work on Earth. They are officially recognized by the Church as Venerables, Blesseds, or Saints.

Live Your Faith

Choose one of the Seven Sacraments and answer the questions.

Who can you ask about this Sacrament? _____

What is one question you will ask this person? _____

Let Us Pray

Pray Together

Every chapter has a prayer page. Over the course of the year, you'll talk and listen to God using different prayer forms. You may listen to God's Word read from the Bible, pray for the needs of others, call on the Saints to pray for us, and praise God the Father, Son, and Holy Spirit in words and songs.

Gather and begin with the Sign of the Cross.

Leader: Blessed be God.

All: Blessed be God forever.

Leader: Let us pray.

Bow your heads as the leader prays.

All: Amen.

Leader: A reading from the holy Gospel according to John.

Read John 3:1–5.

The Gospel of the Lord.

All: Praise to you, Lord Jesus Christ.

▶ Sing "Alive in Christ"
We are Alive in Christ,
We are Alive in Christ
He came to set us free
We are Alive in Christ,
We are Alive in Christ
He gave his life for me
We are Alive in Christ,
We are Alive in Christ

FAMILY+FAITH
LIVING AND LEARNING TOGETHER

YOUR CHILD LEARNED >>>

This page is for you, the parent, to encourage you to share your faith and identify the many ways you are already live the faith in daily family life.

In this section, you will find a summary of what your child has learned in the chapter.

Scripture

 This introduces you to the opening Scripture, and provides direction for more reading.

Catholics Believe

• Bulleted information highlights the main points of doctrine of the Chapter.

People of Faith

Here you meet the holy person featured in People of Faith.

CHILDREN AT THIS AGE >>>

This feature gives you a sense of how your child, at this particular age, will likely be able to understand what is being taught. It suggests ways you can help your child better understand, live, and love their faith.

How They Understand Children this age like to be challenged and are capable of learning abstract concepts. Your child may ask more critical thinking questions about faith and beliefs than he or she has asked before. This is a normal process of trying to understand and find out to what you believe. When your child asks questions, answer simply and honestly.

• Fifth graders are often capable of sacrificing their own self interests for others or for the common good. Their peer group is very important to them.

• They are usually aware of both their gifts and their limitations and can view their actions and motives objectively.

• They find comfort in rules and guidelines and need to know what the rules are and what the consequences are for breaking the rules.

• Fifth graders generally love clubs and all of the rituals and items that members of a club share. Use this inclination and participate in the rituals, actions, and symbols of our faith and Sacraments.

CONSIDER THIS >>>

A question invites you to reflect on your own experience and consider how the Church speaks to you on your faith journey.

LET'S TALK >>>

• Here you will find some practical questions that prompt discussion about the lesson's content, faith sharing, and making connections with your family life.

• What are you and your child looking forward to on your journey of faith this year?

LET'S PRAY >>>

 Encourages family prayer connected to the example of our People of Faith.

Holy men and women, you model faith, hope, and love. Pray for us as we journey through this year. Amen.

 For a multimedia glossary of Catholic Faith Words, Sunday readings, seasonal and Saint resources, and chapter activities go to **aliveinchrist.osv.com**.

Queen of the Holy Rosary

 Let Us Pray

Leader: God, our Father,
We give you thanks for the life and example of the
Blessed Virgin Mary. We ask you to bless us with faith
and hope as strong as hers that we may follow her
example and always be open to your call.
We pray in Jesus' name.

"Blessed be the name of the LORD
both now and forever." **Psalm 113:2**

All: Amen.

 Scripture

The angel said to her in reply, "The holy Spirit will come
upon you, and the power of the Most High will overshadow
you. Therefore the child to be born will be called holy, the
Son of God. And behold, Elizabeth, your relative, has also
conceived a son in her old age, and this is the sixth month for
her who was called barren; for nothing will be impossible for
God." Mary said, "Behold, I am the handmaid of the
Lord. May it be done to me according to
your word." Then the angel departed
from her. Luke 1:35–38

? What Do You Wonder?

- Did Mary have any doubts?

- Why do we call Mary Queen of the
Holy Rosary?

The Rosary

Throughout the liturgical year, the Church honors Mary with many feasts and celebrations. The entire month of October is dedicated to Mary as Our Lady of the Rosary. Many parishes have special Rosary prayer times or services during the month.

Saying "Yes" to God

Catholics have been praying the Rosary for hundreds of years. One reason the Rosary is associated with the month of October is that Christian forces won an important battle on October 7, 1571. They believed that praying the Rosary helped them attain victory. The Church celebrates the Feast of Our Lady of the Rosary on October 7.

In 1917, three young children who lived in Fátima, Portugal, had a special experience of Our Lady. The Blessed Virgin Mary appeared to them several times from May through October. On her last visit in October, she told them to pray the Rosary each day so that there would be peace in the world. She also told them to encourage others to pray the Rosary often.

The message the children of Fátima received asked them to make others aware of the world's need for prayer. Like Mary, these children said "yes" to God. Few people will have apparitions of Mary, but God speaks to those who are open to hearing his voice.

Mary appeared to Blessed Jacinta Marto, Lúcia dos Santos, and Blessed Francisco Marto in their town of Fátima, Portugal.

Pray to Say "Yes"

Mary is honored above all other Saints, as the Mother of God. When the Angel Gabriel told Mary that she would be the Mother of Jesus, Mary believed and accepted God's plan. Her "yes" sets the example for all believers. Praying the Rosary and meditating on the mysteries can help you say "yes" to God.

The mysteries of the Rosary take us through Mary's life with Jesus. They begin with the Joyful Mysteries, which tell the story of Mary agreeing to be Jesus' Mother, his birth, and his childhood. The Sorrowful Mysteries center on Jesus' Death. The Glorious Mysteries tell about Jesus' Resurrection and Ascension and the happy events after that. These include Pentecost, Mary's Assumption, and her Coronation in Heaven. The Luminous Mysteries center on special events in Jesus' life, including his baptism, his first miracle at the wedding at Cana, his Proclamation of the Kingdom, the Transfiguration, and the Institution of the Eucharist. Pray the Rosary often, and continue to listen for God's voice.

→ **In what ways is God calling you to believe and trust?**

Activity

Day by Day What are some ways you are like Mary by saying "yes" to God each day? With a partner, make a list of ways to say "yes" to God at home, at school, and with friends.

_____

_____

_____

_____

_____

_____

People of Faith

Chapter	Person	Feast Day
1	Saint Hildegard of Bingen	September 17
2	Saint Augustine	August 28
3	Saint Benedict	July 11
4	Saint Athanasius	May 2
5	Saint Cecilia	November 22
6	Saint Thomas More	June 22
7	Blessed María Vicenta Rosal Vásquez	August 24
8	Saint Catherine of Siena	April 29
9	Saint Paul Miki	February 6
10	Saint Robert Bellarmine	September 17
11	Pope Saint John Paul II	October 22
12	Queenship of Mary	August 22
13	Saint Gemma Galgani	April 11
14	Saint Cyril of Jerusalem	March 18
15	Saint John Vianney	August 4
16	Saint Louis de Montfort	April 28
17	Saint Jerome	September 30
18	Saint Clare of Assisi	August 11
19	Saint Francis Xavier	December 3
20	Saint Stephen	December 26
21	Saint Vincent de Paul	September 27

Celebrate Mary

The prayer you will pray today is an act of faith. You say in words and actions that you believe in God and his call to you.

🤍 Let Us Pray

Gather and pray the Sign of the Cross together.

Leader: Blessed be God.

All: Blessed be God forever.

Leader: Let us pray.
Bow your heads as the leader prays.

All: Amen.

Leader: As Mary and the children in Fátima said "yes," so you, too, can say "yes" to God.
Bow to the cross and say "I say yes, my Lord."

 All: Sing "God Keeps His Promises"

Prayer of the Faithful

Leader: Let us pray. God our Father, we ask your blessing and Mary's intercession for the needs we put before you.

Respond to each prayer with these words.

All: Hear us, O Lord.

Leader: Let us pray in the words Jesus taught us.

All: Our Father…

Go Forth!

Leader: Go forth with God's blessing.

All: Amen.

FAMILY+FAITH
LIVING AND LEARNING TOGETHER

TALKING ABOUT ORDINARY TIME >>>

Feasts of Mary and the Saints occur all during the Church year. Ordinary Time is the longest of all the Church seasons. It has thirty-three or thirty-four Sundays. It is called Ordinary Time because all the Sundays are numbered in order. Ordinary Time is divided into two parts. The first is from the end of the Christmas season until Ash Wednesday. The second is from the end of the Easter season until the first Sunday of Advent of the next cycle. Following the Feast of the Holy Cross, the Church celebrates the Feast of Our Lady of the Rosary on October 7. This feast affirms the important role of the Rosary in Catholic life.

Scripture

 Read **Luke 1:26–38**. It describes the appearance of the angel to Mary and her positive response to God's call to be the Mother of his Son. It is one of the optional Gospels read on feasts of Mary. When in your life have you realized that "nothing is impossible with God"?

HELPING YOUR CHILD UNDERSTAND >>>

Mary

- Children this age are usually open to different types of prayer, such as meditation on the Mysteries of the Rosary and seeing the Rosary as a prayer.

- Because many fifth-grade children have already taken on secular role models, they will be able to see Mary and talk about her as a role model for their own spiritual life.

- Ordinarily, children at this age love participating in rituals, such as the family Rosary and creating a special altar or shrine for Mary. Create a place of reverence with a candle, an image of Mary, and a tablecloth to represent the season.

CATHOLIC FAMILY CUSTOMS >>>

Praying the Rosary

Set aside a time to gather in a peaceful part of your home. Together, pray at least one decade of the Rosary. Allow your child to choose the Mystery on which you will reflect. In the traditional family Rosary, a parent prays the first part of each Hail Mary (through "blessed is the fruit of thy womb, Jesus"), and other family members respond with the conclusion of the prayer (from "Holy Mary, Mother of God" to the end).

FAMILY PRAYER >>>

Say this prayer at bedtime or before a family meal during the month of October:

Mary, Queen of the Rosary, pray for us and our world that peace will reign in our hearts and in the hearts of all nations who are at war.

Amen.

For a multimedia glossary of Catholic Faith Words, Sunday readings, seasonal and Saint resources, and chapter activities go to **aliveinchrist.osv.com**.

Get Ready!

 ## Let Us Pray

Leader: God our Father,
Send your Holy Spirit on us during this season of
being ready that we may see you more clearly and
walk in your ways. Through Christ our Lord.

"O God, restore us;
light up your face and we shall be saved." **Psalm 80:4**

All: Amen.

1 Scripture

I give thanks to my God always on your account for the grace of God bestowed on you in Christ Jesus, that in him you were enriched in every way, with all discourse and all knowledge, as the testimony to Christ was confirmed among you, so that you are not lacking in any spiritual gift as you wait for the revelation of our Lord Jesus Christ. He will keep you firm to the end, irreproachable on the day of our Lord Jesus [Christ]. God is faithful, and by him you were called to fellowship with his Son, Jesus Christ our Lord. **1 Corinthians 1:4–9**

? What Do You Wonder?

- How might others give thanks for you?
- What are the best gifts you have ever been given?

The O Antiphons

During Advent, the Church calls us to ask for forgiveness of our sins, and invites us to reach out to those in need as Jesus did. The color purple is used to remind us to repent. Advent wreaths and calendars are some of the signs of this season. The Church also uses special prayers and devotions throughout Advent to help you prepare for Jesus' Second Coming.

One of the special prayers the Church often uses is an ancient Advent prayer called the *O Antiphons*. An antiphon is a verse, usually taken from the Bible, which is recited or sung at a liturgy. The Advent antiphons are called the O Antiphons because each one begins with the word "O"; for example, "O sacred Lord of ancient Israel." These ancient preparation prayers called on the Messiah to save the people as God had promised. Each antiphon uses a name of the promised Messiah found in the Old Testament. Christians believe that Jesus is the promised Messiah. The commonly used Advent song, "O Come, O Come, Emmanuel," is a sung version of the O Antiphons.

➤ **What are some other titles for Jesus that remind you of his saving love?**

Advent

The Season of Advent is a four-week period of preparation for the Feast of Christmas. During Advent, we:

- hear the biblical accounts of those who prepared the way for the Messiah

- prepare our own hearts for the coming of Christ

- pray with the Scriptures

- prepare our hearts for the Second Coming of Christ

Jesus is often called a flower of the root of the tree of Jesse (see Isaiah 11:1). This artwork shows Jesse, the father of the biblical King David, and his "family tree," including Jesus' ancestors and the baby Jesus himself in Mary's arms.

Celebrate Emmanuel

 Let Us Pray

Gather and pray the Sign of the Cross together.

Leader: Our help is in the name of the Lord.

All: Who made Heaven and Earth.

Leader: Let us pray.
Bow your heads as the leader prays.

All: Amen.

Listen to God's Word

Reader: A reading from the holy Gospel according to Mark.
Read Mark 13:33–37.

The Gospel of the Lord.

All: Praise to you, Lord Jesus Christ.

Leader: Let us pray. God our Father, hear our prayers.
Respond to each prayer with these words.

All: Hear our prayer, O Lord.

Sing "O Come, O Come, Emmanuel"

Leader: Let us pray words of praise to God. Glory be to the
Father and to the Son and to the Holy Spirit,

All: as it was in the beginning is now, and ever shall be
world without end. Amen.

Go Forth!

Leader: Let us go forth to welcome Christ into our lives.

All: Thanks be to God.

FAMILY + FAITH
LIVING AND LEARNING TOGETHER

TALKING ABOUT ADVENT >>>

Advent, the first four weeks of the Church year, is an opportunity to prayerfully prepare our hearts for the coming of Jesus. During the season of Advent, the color purple reminds us of the call to change our hearts and repent. The Advent Wreath, Jesse Tree, and O Antiphons introduce a spirit of waiting, with joyful expectation.

Scripture

Read **1 Corinthians1:4–9**. Paul is encouraging the Church community at Corinth to have hope and courage. In what areas of your life do you need God's strength?

HELPING YOUR CHILD UNDERSTAND >>>

Advent

- At this age, many children are beginning to develop an interest in history and historical persons. Encourage them to research some of the Old Testament people who waited for the Messiah (e.g., Daniel, Isaiah).

- It is common for children of this age to enjoy being a part of meaningful rituals. Provide opportunities for leading family prayer and participating in parish Advent rituals.

CATHOLIC FAMILY CUSTOMS >>>

Feast of Saint Barbara (December 4)

There is a custom observed in Saint Barbara's honor that ties into the meaning of the Advent season. A Barbara branch is the name given to a twig that is broken from a fruit tree (especially cherry), placed in a bowl of water, and kept in a warm, well-lit part of the house. Barbara branches call to mind the image of Christ as a flower from the root of Jesse (Isaiah 11:1). You might use a Christmas cactus or an amaryllis and adapt. The custom can help children grasp the meaning of Advent and Christmas. The branches can also be placed around the Nativity Scene when they have blossomed.

FAMILY PRAYER >>>

At a family meal on each of the four Sundays of Advent, light the appropriate number of candles on the Advent wreath or candelabra and pray this blessing:

Blessed are you, Lord, God of all creation: in this food and in our sharing. Blessed are you as we await the blessed hope and the coming of our Savior, Jesus Christ. For the kingdom, the power, and the glory are yours, now and forever.

Come, Lord Jesus! Come quickly! Amen.

For a multimedia glossary of Catholic Faith Words, Sunday readings, seasonal and Saint resources, and chapter activities go to **aliveinchrist.osv.com**.

Season of Love

 ## Let Us Pray

Leader: God, you are our generous Creator,
You made us to be one with you and one another.
Deepen in us your spirit of love.
Through your Son Jesus who lives with us forever.

"You, yes you, O LORD, my God,
have done many wondrous deeds!" **Psalm 40:6**

All: Amen.

📖 Scripture

Put on then, as God's chosen ones, holy and beloved, heartfelt compassion, kindness, humility, gentleness, and patience, bearing with one another and forgiving one another, if one has a grievance against another; as the Lord has forgiven you, so must you also do. And over all these put on love, that is, the bond of perfection. **Colossians 3:12–14**

? What Do You Wonder?

- When have you heard about someone being kind or having compassion toward someone else?

- Who is the most forgiving person you know?

Feasts of the Season

Christmas, or the Feast of the Nativity, is a major feast in the Church's liturgical year. This feast is too important to be celebrated for only one day. Instead, the Church celebrates an entire Christmas Season, marked by the celebration of several feasts. With each celebration, we learn more about the events in Jesus' early life. The entire season is filled with joy. You will notice that the priest wears white or gold vestments and the Church is decorated to rejoice!

- The Christmas Season begins with the celebration of Jesus' birth, starting with the Christmas Eve Vigil, December 24.
- After Christmas Day, the Church celebrates the Feast of the Holy Family.
- Catholics honor Mary, the Mother of God, on January 1.
- On the Solemnity of the Epiphany, the Church tells the story of how the Magi search for God's manifestation through the Christ Child and that they bear gifts to honor and worship him.
- Finally, the Church celebrates Jesus' baptism in the Jordan River, where he is declared the beloved Son of God.

The Holy Family

On the Feast of the Holy Family, the Church celebrates in a special way the love and unity of Jesus, Mary, and Joseph. Mary and Joseph were devout Jews who followed Jewish law. They accepted Mary's special role as Mother of the Son of God. When Jesus was born, they brought him to the Temple to present him to the Lord. As Jesus grew, he prayed and celebrated the great Jewish feasts with his family. The Holy Family is a model of respect and peace for all families.

Families of Love

Mary and Joseph did not always understand Jesus, but they continued to trust in God and love their son. Trust in God and respect for one another are very important in families. You can honor your parents and guardians in many ways. You can obey them, do kind things for them, and appreciate the sacrifices they make. Sharing what we have with other family members is another way to show love for God and one another.

➜ How can your family follow the example of the Holy Family?

Make a Banner In groups, talk about ways families can grow closer and stronger. Come up with specific things you can do to be more respectful at home. Make a list of things younger children can do, too. Design a "Respect Banner" for your parish.

Celebrate the Holy Family

A celebration of the Word is a moment of prayer with the Church using the Scriptures.

Let Us Pray

Gather and pray the Sign of the Cross together.

Leader: Blessed be the name of the Lord.

All: Now and for ever.

Leader: Let us pray.

Bow your heads as the leader prays.

All: Amen.

Listen to God's Word

Leader: Lord, open our minds so that we may understand your Word.

All: Lord, open our hearts so that we may live by your Word.

Stand silently as the Bible is carried to the prayer table. Take turns respectfully bowing in front of it.

Reader: A reading from the holy Gospel according to Luke. Read Luke 2:22, 29–40.

The Gospel of the Lord.

All: Praise to you, Lord Jesus Christ.

Dialogue

In what way did Simeon and Anna surprise Mary and Joseph? In what ways can you give thanks to God the Father for the gift of his Son, Jesus, who saved us?

Prayer of the Faithful

Leader: Let us pray.
God our Father, we ask you to listen to our prayers, which we offer now as gifts to you.

Respond to each prayer with these words.

All: Lord, accept our prayer.

Leader: Glory be to the Father and to the Son and to the Holy Spirit,

All: as it was in the beginning is now, and ever shall be world without end. Amen.

Go Forth!

Leader: Let us go forth to show respect and love for our families.

All: Thanks be to God.

 Sing "Jesus, the Light of the World"

FAMILY+FAITH
LIVING AND LEARNING TOGETHER

TALKING ABOUT CHRISTMAS >>>

Christmas is not merely a day. It's an entire season to celebrate. This Christmas, resolve to make the liturgical rhythms and commemorations of the Christmas Season a more significant part of your family's celebration. By participating as fully as possible in these feasts, which extend from the Christmas Eve Vigil through the Feast of the Baptism of the Lord in early January, your family can focus on the greatest gift—Jesus.

Scripture

Read **Colossians 3:12–21**. Paul is addressing the Colossians on how they are to live their Christian life in the world. Reflect on how you live your Christian life in today's world.

HELPING YOUR CHILD UNDERSTAND >>>
Christmas

- At this age, children may be less self-centered and more open to seeing Christmas as a season of giving and sharing.

- Some children at this age will be interested in the geography and history surrounding the Christmas events.

- Fifth-graders can be taught reverence. Remind them to be reverent during the reading of the Word, during prayer, and while in church.

CATHOLIC FAMILY CUSTOMS >>>
Feast of the Holy Family

The Feast of the Holy Family is celebrated on the Sunday after Christmas unless Christmas falls on a Sunday. Then it is celebrated on December 30. The Christmas Season is, in a very real way, a celebration of the Holy Family—and of your family—because you are called to be holy, too. Holiness is not an abstract idea. It includes times of kindness and compassion as well as times of forgiving and asking forgiveness within your own family.

Make the feast a family celebration by having family members share in preparing a meal or inviting another family over for a pot luck dinner. Follow the meal with games and or a sing-along of Christmas music.

FAMILY PRAYER >>>

Gather around your Nativity Scene on the Sundays of the Christmas season and pray:

God of Mary and Joseph, of shepherds and animals, bless us through all the days of Christmas.

Fill our house with hospitality, joy, gentleness, and thanksgiving, and guide our steps in the way of peace.

Grant this through Christ our Lord. Amen.

 For a multimedia glossary of Catholic Faith Words, Sunday readings, seasonal and Saint resources, and chapter activities go to **aliveinchrist.osv.com**.

Time for Change

 ## Let Us Pray

Leader: Lord, God, send your Holy Spirit to dwell in us,
and teach us how to pray and how to reverence God
in our thoughts and actions.
Through Christ, our Lord.

"A clean heart create for me, God;
renew within me a steadfast spirit." **Psalm 51:12**

All: Amen.

Scripture

Son though he was, he learned obedience
from what he suffered; and when he was
made perfect, he became the source of eternal
salvation for all who obey him…
Hebrews 5:8–9

What Do You Wonder?

• Why do you think Jesus prayed?

• What do we learn from suffering?

The Forty Days

For six weeks before Easter, the Church observes the Season of Lent. This season offers the Church community an opportunity to repent or turn away from selfish ways of living and turn toward God. The liturgical color of Lent is purple. Purple reminds us of repentance. Lent prepares you to celebrate Easter with joy!

Turn Back to God

During Lent, the Church asks her members to pray, to fast, and to give alms. Through prayer, you can ask God to show you how to make your relationships with him and others stronger. Fasting leaves you with a sense of hunger and an emptiness.

This helps you see that God alone can satisfy all your needs. Giving alms means to give some of what you have to those who are in need. As a work of mercy, almsgiving may consist of feeding those who are hungry, clothing those who do not have proper clothing, and giving drink to those who are thirsty. Sometimes you might give money or time.

Whatever form of love and charity you choose, there should be some kind of sacrifice involved. This is a reminder that during Lent, you are showing your dependence on God and that all things come from God and are meant to be shared with others.

➡ **How can you rely on God during the season of Lent?**

Celebrate Lent

This prayer form is a Penitential Act, in which you ask God's mercy for your sins and the sins of the world. This Act, which we pray at Mass, is called the *Confiteor*, or "I Confess."

Let Us Pray

Gather and pray the Sign of the Cross together.

Leader: O Lord, open my lips.

All: That my mouth shall proclaim your praise.

Leader: Let us pray.

Bow your heads as the leader prays.

All: Amen.

Penitential Act

Leader: Let us now ask God and one another to forgive us.

All: I confess to almighty God ...

See page 323 in the Our Catholic Tradition of your book for the Confiteor.

Move into a circle and kneel in silent reflection.

Go Forth!

Leader: Let us go forth to live in God's grace.

All: Thanks be to God.

 Sing "Through My Fault"

FAMILY+FAITH
LIVING AND LEARNING TOGETHER

TALKING ABOUT LENT >>>

Purple is the color of Lent, and it is a reminder that we are called to repentance during this season. Lent is a forty-day journey that begins on Ash Wednesday. The receiving of ashes on one's forehead marks one's promise to repent or change to grow closer to God and the Church. Lent is a call for inner change. The three Lenten practices of prayer, fasting, and almsgiving help families repent and change.

Scripture

 Read **Hebrews 5:5–9** and reflect on Jesus' trust in and obedience to his Father. Why is obedience important in a family?

HELPING YOUR CHILD UNDERSTAND >>>
Lent

- An interest in money is common for children of this age; therefore, the Lenten practice of almsgiving will have greater meaning.

- Most children this age are already feeling pressure to conform to the behavior of others. Lent is a good time to help them reflect on how Christians are called to follow Jesus; sometimes this means we are "set apart" from those around us.

- Rituals and symbols are significant at this age. Many fifth-graders will be open to engaging in Lenten rituals. The rituals will effect more change if celebrated in the community of their family or friends.

CATHOLIC FAMILY CUSTOMS >>>
Lent

Lent is a time to renew ourselves spiritually. Show your child that you value opportunities to grow in grace.

- As a family, attend a parish Reconciliation service.

- During family prayer times in Lent, read Psalm 130. This short psalm is about trust in God's mercy, a major Lenten theme.

FAMILY PRAYER >>>

 Pray the following during your prayer times through the season of Lent.

Leader: Blessed are you, Lord, God of all creation.

All: You make us hunger and thirst for holiness. You call us to true fasting, to set free the oppressed, to share our bread with the hungry, to shelter the homeless and to clothe the naked. Amen.
Based on a prayer from Catholic Household Blessings and Prayers

For a multimedia glossary of Catholic Faith Words, Sunday readings, seasonal and Saint resources, and chapter activities go to **aliveinchrist.osv.com**.

Triduum

 Let Us Pray

Leader: Lord, God, we want to be your obedient servants. Teach us your ways and show us your will for us. Through Christ, our Lord.

"How can I repay the Lord
for all the great good done for me?" **Psalm 116:12**

All: Amen.

 Scripture

[Jesus], fully aware that the Father had put everything into his power and that he had come from God and was returning to God, he rose from supper and took off his outer garments. He took a towel and tied it around his waist. Then he poured water into a basin and began to wash the disciples' feet and dry them with the towel around his waist....

So when he had washed their feet [and] put his garments back on and reclined at table again, he said to them, "Do you realize what I have done for you? You call me 'teacher' and 'master,' and rightly so, for indeed I am. If I, therefore, the master and teacher, have washed your feet, you ought to wash one another's feet. I have given you a model to follow, so that as I have done for you, you should also do.

John 13:3–4, 12–15

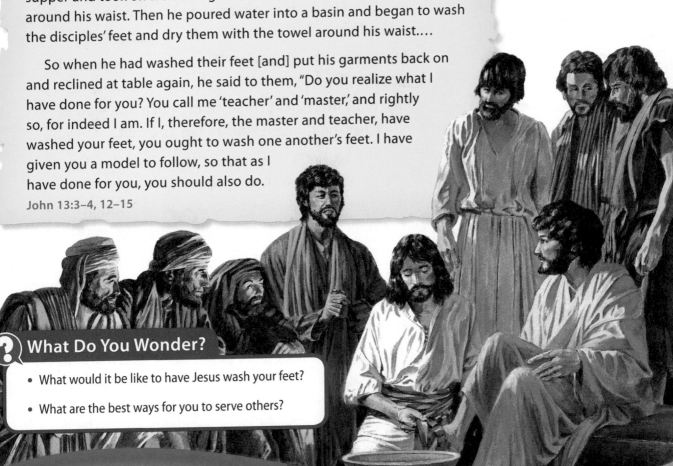

? What Do You Wonder?

- What would it be like to have Jesus wash your feet?

- What are the best ways for you to serve others?

Three Holy Days

The three days of Triduum begin with the Mass of the Lord's Supper on Holy Thursday evening and end with evening prayer on Easter Sunday.

The Mass of the Lord's Supper on Holy Thursday is the first plunge into the mystery of salvation. The first Eucharist was a sign of the events that would come. In the Eucharist, we are brought back to God through Christ's sacrifice on the Cross.

With the gift of the Holy Eucharist, Jesus showed us how to love. When Jesus washed the feet of his Apostles at the Last Supper, he showed his followers how to serve one another. The Church remembers these actions and their meanings in the ritual of foot washing on Holy Thursday.

As the Triduum continues, we recall Jesus' suffering and Death on the Cross. Good Friday is the most solemn day in the Church year. During the liturgy, we thank Jesus for his sacrifice.

Holy Saturday is a day of silent prayer as the Church waits for the joy of Resurrection. At the Easter Vigil, the third sacred day begins. This day begins the special celebration of Jesus' Resurrection. It is our celebration of new life.

➜ How does your parish celebrate Triduum?

Celebrate Love

This celebration marks your commitment to be of service as Jesus was when he washed the disciples' feet on Holy Thursday.

♥ Let Us Pray

Gather and pray the Sign of the Cross together.

Leader: God, come to my assistance.

All: Lord, make haste to help me.

Leader: Glory be to the Father and to the Son and to the Holy Spirit,

All: as it was in the beginning is now, and ever shall be world without end. Amen.

Leader: Let us pray.
Bow your heads as the leader prays.

All: Amen.

Leader: I give you a new commandment: love one another. As I have loved you, so you also should love one another.   John 13:34

Let us pray. God, our Father, hear our prayers.
Respond to each prayer with these words.

All: Lord, hear our prayer.

Leader: Let us pray together the prayer that Jesus gave us.

All: Our Father …

Leader: Let us go forth to glorify the Lord by our lives.

All: Thanks be to God.

 Sing "Pange Lingua Gloriosi/Sing, My Tongue, the Savior's Glory"

FAMILY+FAITH
LIVING AND LEARNING TOGETHER

TALKING ABOUT TRIDUUM >>>

Holy Week is the holiest week of the Church year. It begins on Palm Sunday and continues until Evening Prayer on Easter Sunday. The Triduum or "three days" mark the most sacred time of Holy Week. It begins at sundown on Holy Thursday and ends at sundown on Easter Sunday. During these three days, the whole Church fasts and prays with anticipation and hope. On Good Friday, the Church commemorates the Crucifixion. No Mass is said on this day; the service consists of reading the Passion, praying for the Church and the entire world, veneration of the Cross, and Communion. To reflect the solemnity of the occasion, the sanctuary is bare and the organ is usually silent.

Scripture

 Read **John 13:1–15**. It is the story of the Washing of the Feet. How do we as a family serve others?

HELPING YOUR CHILD UNDERSTAND >>>

Holy Week and Triduum

- At this age, children are beginning to sense the depth of meaning behind the events of Holy Week.

- Children at this age may find it helpful to identify with some of the major characters in the Passion story, such as Peter, Simon of Cyrene, or the Good Thief.

- Often, fifth-graders will be more aware of and interested in participating in the Holy Week rituals.

CATHOLIC FAMILY CUSTOMS >>>

Holy Week and Triduum

Many families choose to observe Good Friday by participating in the Stations of the Cross. Some parishes set aside a time for this, or families can visit the church for private devotions.

- Consider getting a booklet that explains the devotion from a parish library or conduct Internet research with your child to find resources.

- Walk through your parish church; stopping at each station, quietly discuss its meaning with your child.

FAMILY PRAYER >>>

Your family can celebrate the washing of the feet as a prayer on Holy Thursday. Ask your child to read aloud John 13:1–15. Then take turns washing one another's feet with care, while you play reflective music in the background. Ask family members to think of this gesture as a symbol of all the ways in which you love and serve one another—and those in need—every day.

 For a multimedia glossary of Catholic Faith Words, Sunday readings, seasonal and Saint resources, and chapter activities go to **aliveinchrist.osv.com**.

He Lives

 Let Us Pray

Leader: Lord, God, through your Resurrection,
you continue to be present among us.
We are grateful.
Help us to come to know you better.
Through Christ, our Lord.

"You will show me the path to life,
abounding joy in your presence,
the delights at your right hand forever." **Psalm 16:11**

All: Amen.

Scripture

Children, let us love not in word or speech but in deed and truth. [Now] this is how we shall know that we belong to the truth and reassure our hearts before him in whatever our hearts condemn, for God is greater than our hearts and knows everything.... Those who keep his commandments remain in him, and he in them, and the way we know that he remains in us is from the Spirit that he gave us. **1 John 3:18–20, 24**

What Do You Wonder?

• What is God really like?

• How do you know God's Spirit is in you?

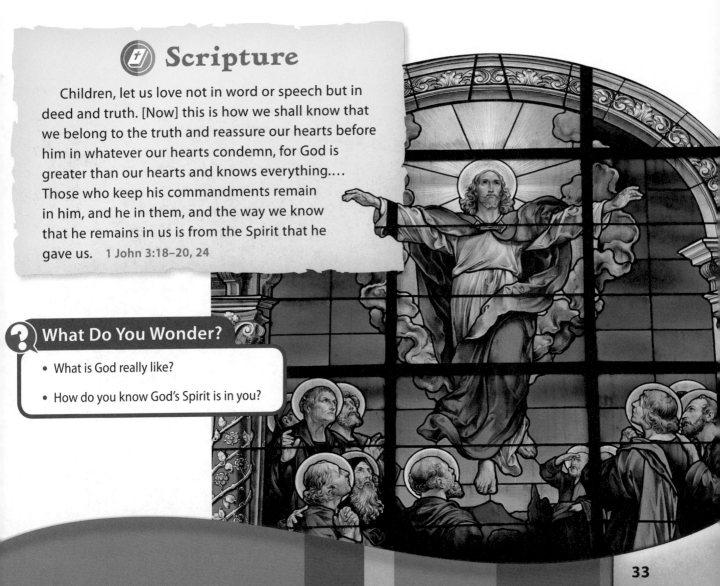

In the Breaking of the Bread

Jesus' disciples were very downcast and frightened. How could they go on? They thought Jesus was dead forever.

As we read in the Gospel according to Luke (See Luke 24:13–35) two of Jesus' disciples were walking home from Jerusalem, and a stranger joined them on the road. He explained the Scriptures to them as they walked along. Although the disciples did not recognize the man, they invited him to stay with them for the night in the town of Emmaus. The stranger agreed. As they shared a meal together, the two disciples recognized the stranger when he blessed and broke the bread. It was Jesus!

Jesus walks along the road with you, too. Jesus is present in the midst of the assembly gathered for Mass. He speaks God's Word to you through the Scripture readings, and he shares himself with you in the Eucharist. Your eyes are opened to see that it is Jesus, the Risen Lord, who is sharing this special meal with you.

➨ **What can you do to help others recognize Jesus' presence in their lives?**

Easter

On Easter, the Church celebrates Jesus' Resurrection from the dead.

- The joyful celebration of Easter lasts for fifty days.

- During the Easter Season, the priest wears white vestments.

- We sing Alleluias and renew our baptismal promises.

Jesus Is Present

In the Easter Season, you come to a deeper realization that Jesus is alive and present. You can recognize Jesus just as the disciples recognized him at Emmaus. Jesus is present in the Scriptures and the Seven Sacraments, and most especially in the Eucharist. Jesus comes to you every day in people and in prayer.

➔ Where will you look for Jesus this week?

Activity

Act It Out Imagine that the story of the disciples on the road to Emmaus took place today. What would keep the disciples from recognizing Jesus? What distractions might they have today? Where would they be going? How would they travel? In a small group, plan a modern-day Emmaus skit and act it out for the whole group.

Celebrate Easter

The prayer you are about to pray is a celebration of the Word. You listen and reflect on God's Word and conclude with the Lord's Prayer and the ritual prayer of the sign of peace.

Let Us Pray

Gather

 All: Sing "Pan de Vida"
Pan de Vida, Cuerpo del Señor,
cup of blessing, Blood of Christ the Lord.
At this table the last shall be first.
Poder es servir, porque Dios es amor.

Pray the Sign of the Cross together.

Leader: Light and peace in Jesus Christ, our Lord, Alleluia.

All: Thanks be to God, Alleluia.

Leader: Let us pray.

Bow your heads as the leader prays.

All: Amen.

Listen to God's Word

Reader: A reading from the holy Gospel according to Luke.
Read Luke 24:13–35.

The Gospel of the Lord.

All: Praise to you, Lord Jesus Christ.

Dialogue

Why do you think the disciples didn't recognize Jesus on the road? What is one way you recognize Jesus in your life?

The Lord's Prayer and Sign of Peace

Leader: At the Savior's command
and formed by divine teaching,
we dare to say:

All: Our Father …

Leader: May the God of life and hope fill our hearts and lives.

Offer one another a sign of the peace of Christ.

Go Forth!

Leader: May we see God's kindness to us.

All: Amen.

Leader: May we go out to serve him with joy.

All: Amen.

Leader: Let us leave this place strengthened to recognize Jesus' presence, Alleluia, Alleluia.

All: Thanks be to God, Alleluia, Alleluia.

FAMILY+FAITH
LIVING AND LEARNING TOGETHER

TALKING ABOUT EASTER >>>

The celebration of the Easter Season includes the fifty days following the Triduum. The Easter liturgies reflect the joy of salvation. The *Alleluia* is sung once again. The people of God renew their baptismal commitment in the sprinkling rite. The Gospels unpack the meaning of the Easter event and help the assembly to celebrate God's saving power. The people of God are sent out from the Easter celebrations to spread the Good News.

Scripture

 Read **1 John 3:18–24**. In it, John points out the ways we know that God is with us. What are the signs in our family life that God abides in us?

HELPING YOUR CHILD UNDERSTAND >>>

Easter

- Usually, children this age have no problem seeing Easter as a day of celebration. Including them in preparations for family or cultural rituals helps them to understand the meaning of the celebration.

- Most children this age enjoy family group activities and will benefit by being involved together in Easter acts of charity.

- Ordinarily, fifth-graders can understand the presence of the Risen Christ when it is compared to the way they experience presence in their family and friendships.

FEASTS OF THE SEASON >>>

Easter and Mary

Depending on when Easter occurs, some part of the season will occur during the month of May. The month of May is often celebrated as the month dedicated to Mary, the Virgin Mother of God. You may wish to honor Mary as a family during the month by reciting a decade of the Rosary whenever you are together in the car.

FAMILY PRAYER >>>

 Pray this blessing together at your Easter meal:

God of glory, the eyes of all turn to you
as we celebrate Christ's victory over
 sin and death.
Bless us and this food of our Easter meal.
May we who gather at the Lord's table
continue to celebrate the joy of his
 Resurrection
and be admitted finally to his heavenly
 banquet.
We ask this through Christ our Lord. Amen.

For a multimedia glossary of Catholic Faith Words, Sunday readings, seasonal and Saint resources, and chapter activities go to **aliveinchrist.osv.com**.

Ascension

 Let Us Pray

Leader: Come, Holy Spirit, show us how to spread the Good
News in the world today. Guide us to be witnesses of
the coming of God's Kingdom.
Through Christ, our Lord.

"Bless the LORD, my soul!
LORD, my God, you are great indeed!"   **Psalm 104:1**

All: Amen.

 Scripture

The eleven disciples went to Galilee, to the mountain to which
Jesus had ordered them. When they saw him, they worshipped,
but they doubted. Then Jesus approached and said to them, "All
power in heaven and on earth has been given to me. Go,
therefore, and make disciples of all nations, baptizing
them in the name of the Father, and of the Son,
and of the holy Spirit, teaching them to observe
all that I have commanded you. And behold,
I am with you always, until the end of the
age."   **Matthew 28:16–20**

? What Do You Wonder?

• What does it mean to be someone's
disciple?

• How do people know Jesus is with them?

The Commission

When Jesus was about to return to his Father, he gave his disciples the commission to make disciples, and to baptize and teach them to love God and others. The disciples followed Jesus' direction and their followers did, too.

The Church grew and grew. Today, the Church can be found all over the world because for almost two thousand years people have been following Jesus' command.

Evangelization

Bringing the Good News to others is called evangelization. It is your responsibility to evangelize, too. In order to evangelize, you must first have a good relationship with Jesus. When you have this, you will want to share it with others. You evangelize when you:

- talk to others about Jesus and how important your faith is
- share how your faith helps you make choices every day
- use your gifts and talents to help others
- share with those who are in need

➤ **In what ways can you evangelize this week?**

Ascension

The Feast of the Ascension celebrates Jesus going to join his Father in Heaven.

- The Ascension is celebrated forty days after Easter.

- For this feast, the priest wears white vestments. White is always worn on feasts of Jesus except during Holy Week.

Disciples

Disciples are followers of Jesus who believe in him. We become true disciples as we grow in our relationship with Jesus. The mission of the disciple is to evangelize. If you are going to spread the Good News, you have to come to know Jesus better. You do this by:

- meditating on the Scriptures
- spending time in prayer
- attending Mass every week
- receiving the Sacraments
- being around other believers
- performing acts of justice and charity

Activity

Good Qualities List three reasons why you qualify to be one of Jesus' disciples.

1. _____

2. _____

3. _____

Celebrate the Ascension

Today you will pray a celebration of the Word and a commissioning. Listen to God's Word and think about God's message to you.

Let Us Pray

Gather and pray the Sign of the Cross together.

Leader: Blessed be the name of the Lord, Alleluia.

All: Now and forever, Alleluia.

Leader: Let us pray.

Bow your head as the leader prays.

Lord, open our hearts to preach the Good News in our words and actions.

All: Amen.

Listen to God's Word

Leader: A reading from the Letter to the Ephesians.
Read Ephesians 1:17–23.
The word of the Lord.

All: Thanks be to God.

Dialogue

When do you have opportunities to be a disciple of Jesus? What gives you strength to do this?

Prayer of the Faithful and Lord's Prayer

Come forward and gather around the prayer table.

Leader: Let us pray for ourselves, the Church, and the world, that God's Kingdom will come.

Bow your head as the leader prays.

Rejoice in the Good News. Go forth and share it with others.

All: Thanks be to God.

Join hands and pray the Lord's Prayer.

Leader: At the Savior's command
and formed by divine teaching,
we dare to say:

All: Our Father …

Go Forth!

 Sing "Come to Us, Holy Spirit"
Come to us Holy Spirit
So we can know God's love
Come to us Holy Spirit
So we can know God's love

FAMILY + FAITH
LIVING AND LEARNING TOGETHER

TALKING ABOUT ASCENSION >>>

Catholics celebrate the Feast of Ascension Thursday forty days after Easter. In some dioceses and parishes, the feast is moved from Thursday to the seventh Sunday of Easter. The Feast of the Ascension celebrates the Risen Jesus returning to his Father in Heaven. In the United States, Ascension Thursday is a Holy Day of Obligation.

Scripture

 Read **Matthew 28:16–20**. It describes the conversation Jesus had with his disciples before his Ascension. How does our family share the Good News with others?

HELPING YOUR CHILD UNDERSTAND >>>

Ascension

- Most children this age are curious about how the Ascension happened.

- Typically, children this age like activity. They are likely to be easily motivated to engage in evangelizing activities with others.

- Fifth-graders tend to do better if they are shown real-life models of how others evangelize.

FEASTS OF THE SEASON >>>
Visitation of Mary

May 31 is the Feast of the Visitation of the Virgin Mary to her cousin Elizabeth. Both Mary and Elizabeth shared with each other the Good News of God's presence in their lives.

FAMILY PRAYER >>>

 Say this prayer for your family meals from Ascension Thursday to Pentecost.

Come Holy Spirit, make us ready to receive the gifts we need to share the Good News of Jesus with those around us. Grant this through Christ our Lord. Amen.

For a multimedia glossary of Catholic Faith Words, Sunday readings, seasonal and Saint resources, and chapter activities go to **aliveinchrist.osv.com**.

Pentecost

 Let Us Pray

Leader: Come Holy Spirit,
anoint us with your power and strength
that we will share in Jesus' mission
now and forever.
Through Christ our Lord.

"May the glory of the LORD endure forever;
may the LORD be glad in his works!" **Psalm 104:31**

All: Amen.

Scripture

The spirit of the Lord GOD is upon me,
because the LORD has anointed me;
He has sent me to bring good news to the afflicted,
to bind up the brokenhearted,
To proclaim liberty to the captives,
release to the prisoners... Isaiah 61:1

What Do You Wonder?

- How does God anoint people?

- Who has brought you the
Good News?

The Holy Spirit Strengthens God's People

On the first Pentecost, the early Church community received the gift of the Holy Spirit. The first Christians were strengthened to live as followers of Jesus. With the Holy Spirit's help, they were able to serve people in need.

The Holy Spirit gives you the strength to serve others, too. God the Holy Spirit empowers you to live a good Christian life. The Holy Spirit helps the Church community remember the teachings of Jesus, especially his command to serve one another. At Baptism and Confirmation, you are anointed with holy oil. Anointing with oil is an ancient custom. In the time of Jesus, anointing someone with oil was a sign that he or she had been given a very important mission. It was also a sign of healing.

When you are anointed with oil in the Sacraments of Baptism and Confirmation, you are entrusted with a share in Jesus' mission. Jesus asks you to continue to be a sign of the Kingdom of God that he came to establish. An important part of Jesus' mission is loving service to others.

➜ **When have you called on the Holy Spirit for strength and guidance?**

Courage to Serve

The Holy Spirit gives you the gifts of strength and courage so that you can be a faithful follower of Jesus. Through your service, others will come to know God. Without the Spirit's presence in your life, you could not share the Good News with others.

➜ What other Gifts of the Holy Spirit would strengthen you as a follower of Jesus?

Share Your Time Together, with your family or a group of friends, decide this week how you will serve others through a special project. You might decide to volunteer at a soup kitchen or food pantry or to work with others to clean up a neighborhood park or lot.

Celebrate Pentecost

Today you will participate in a celebration of the Word. Listen and reflect on God's Word. You will have your hands signed with the Sign of the Cross as a ritual prayer of service.

Let Us Pray

Gather and pray the Sign of the Cross together.

Leader: Come, Holy Spirit, fill the hearts of your faithful;

All: And kindle in them the fire of your love.

Leader: Send forth your Spirit and they shall be created.

All: And you will renew the face of the earth.

Leader: Let us pray.

Bow your head as the leader prays.

All: Amen.

Listen to God's Word

Reader: A reading from the Acts of the Apostles.
Read Acts 2:1–11.

The word of the Lord.

All: Thanks be to God.

Take a moment of silence to let the Word of God speak to your heart and mind.

Dialogue

Why do you think the images of wind and flames are used to describe the coming of the Holy Spirit? How might a young person like you experience God's Spirit?

Signing of Hands

Take a few quiet moments to pray to the Holy Spirit. Ask the Spirit of God to give you the strength you need to be a faithful follower of Jesus. One by one the leader will mark your hands with the Sign of the Cross.

Leader: (Name), may your hands willingly serve those in need.

All: Amen.

Leader: Let us offer a prayer of praise to God—Father, Son, and Holy Spirit.

All: Glory be to the Father …

Go Forth!

Leader: Let us go forth to serve others through the power of the Holy Spirit.

All: Thanks be to God.

 Sing "Spirit, Come Down"

FAMILY+FAITH
LIVING AND LEARNING TOGETHER

TALKING ABOUT PENTECOST >>>

The Feast of Pentecost, which happens fifty days after Easter, commemorates the coming of the Holy Spirit to the Apostles and Mary and the beginning of the Church. It also marks the end of the Easter season. On Pentecost, the Apostles—and, by extension, all of us as their spiritual descendants—were anointed in the Holy Spirit and sent forth to love and serve all members of the human family in Jesus' name. Pentecost is a time of recommitment to the evangelizing mission of Church.

Scripture

 Read **Isaiah 61:1**. In this Scripture, the prophet Isaiah proclaims that he has been anointed by the Lord to bring Good News to the broken-hearted and release to the captives. How does Jesus give you freedom?

HELPING YOUR CHILD UNDERSTAND >>>

Pentecost

- Often, children this age picture only the miraculous events at Pentecost and may need assistance in relating to and making the feast appropriate to their own lives.

- Fifth-grade children can begin to understand the meaning of anointing as being set apart for a special purpose.

- Children this age typically need concrete examples of spirit-filled people to make connections with their own life.

FEASTS OF THE SEASON >>>

Pentecost

Because Pentecost commemorates the coming of the Holy Spirit to the Apostles and Mary, Pentecost symbols often include a dove, which represents the Spirit. Some altar cloths may have doves woven into their design, and wooden or paper doves may be lowered over the assembly during the Mass.

FAMILY PRAYER >>>

 Pray this traditional prayer to the Holy Spirit at dinner or bedtime.

Leader: Come, Holy Spirit, fill the hearts of your faithful.

All: And kindle in them the fire of your love.

Leader: Send forth your Spirit and they shall be created.

All: And you will renew the face of the earth. Lord, by the light of the Holy Spirit you have taught the hearts of your faithful. In the same Spirit, help us to relish what is right and always rejoice in your consolation.

Leader: We ask this through Christ our Lord.

All: Amen.

For a multimedia glossary of Catholic Faith Words, Sunday readings, seasonal and Saint resources, and chapter activities go to **aliveinchrist.osv.com**.

Units at a Glance

Revelation

Our Catholic Tradition

- Divine Revelation is the way God makes himself and his plan known. God reveals himself through Sacred Scripture and Sacred Tradition. (CCC, 82)

- We can discover God by reflecting on the gifts of his creation. We use his gifts in the Seven Sacraments. (CCC, 1692)

- God puts longings in our hearts for him, and our response is faith. (CCC, 27)

- One way we respond to God's invitation to know him and be in his presence is by our worship and participation in the Seven Sacraments. (CCC, 356)

How does God communicate with us?

God's Plan for All Creation

♥ Let Us Pray

Leader: Wonderful God of all, you have made us and all things. You have blessed us with life and love. Accept our song of praise.

"I will sing to the LORD all my life;
I will sing praise to my God while I live."
Psalm 104:33

All: Blessed be the Lord our God! He is worthy of all glory, honor, and praise! Amen.

📖 Scripture

Come, let us sing joyfully to the LORD;
cry out to the rock of our salvation.
Let us come before him with a song of praise,
joyfully sing out our psalms.
Enter, let us bow down in worship;
let us kneel before the LORD who made us.
For he is our God,
we are the people he shepherds,
the sheep in his hands.
Psalm 95:1–2, 6–7

? What Do You Wonder?

- Why do we worship God, giving him glory, honor, and praise?
- Why has God given humans a unique role in creation?

God Reveals Himself

In what ways does God reveal himself to us?

We know that God is all-good, that he loves all of us, and that he wants us to be saved. He is eternal, just, merciful, and all-powerful. We know these things because God told us about himself through a process called **Divine Revelation**.

Learning about God

We can learn about God in many ways, including through all that he has created. However, God has revealed himself to us in a unique way through **Sacred Scripture** and **Sacred Tradition**.

Sacred Scripture is the collection of inspired writings also known as the Bible. God, the Bible's author, inspired its human writers, giving them the gift of the Holy Spirit to write about his saving truth. Scripture tells the story of God and his People in the two parts of the Bible, the Old and New Testaments.

Sacred Tradition is God's Word to the Church, beginning with what was passed down from the Apostles. Guided by the Holy Spirit, popes, bishops, members of councils, and scholars have safeguarded these teachings about God and what he has made known for future generations.

→ **What are some things you have learned about God from Sacred Scripture and Sacred Tradition?**

Catholic Faith Words

Divine Revelation the way God makes himself, and his plan for humans, known to us

Sacred Scripture another name for the Bible; Sacred Scripture is the inspired Word of God written by humans

Sacred Tradition God's Word to the Church, safeguarded by the Apostles and their successors, the bishops, and handed down verbally—in her Creeds, Sacraments, and other teachings—to future generations

In God's Image

We also learn about God through his creation. The beauty of the desert, the majesty of mountains, and the complexity of animals all tell us something about God and his ways. The vastness of space gives us a glimpse of eternity.

People are God's most magnificent creation. God created us in his own image and likeness. The marvels within our bodies show us how much he cares about us.

Human beings, unlike the rest of creation, can think and choose. God created us with free will, or the ability to choose between good and evil. We are able to recognize and respond to God's goodness. We were also created with the desire to be in relationship with other people. As we relate to one another, we are revealing God to others.

Underline what makes humans different from the rest of God's creation.

God has given humans a unique role in creation. We are to respect and care for one another and for all of the rest of creation. Part of God's plan is for humans to live in communities that show that respect and care.

Share Your Faith

Reflect Think about the ways that we use our unique human abilities to learn about God. Write your thoughts below.

_____

_____

_____

_____

_____

Share With a partner, discuss how humans can fulfill our unique roles in creation.

Praise God's Work

How are stewardship and God's providence connected?

Creation is all things that exist, made by God from nothing and held together by his love. The world was made for the glory of God, and the wonders of creation never cease to praise their Creator. In return, God in his **providence** cares for all he has created. This is one of many psalms that praise God, the Creator.

 Scripture

The Coming of God

Shout with joy to the LORD, all the earth;
  break into song; sing praise.
Sing praise to the LORD with the lyre,
  with the lyre and melodious song.
With trumpets and the sound of the horn
  shout with joy to the King, the LORD.
Let the sea and what fills it resound,
  the world and those who dwell there.
Let the rivers clap their hands,
  the mountains shout with them for joy,
Before the LORD who comes,
  who comes to govern the earth,
To govern the world with justice
  and the peoples with fairness.   Psalm 98:4–9

➜ **What are some ways in which God in his providence cares for humans?**

Creation and the Sacraments

When Jesus wanted to create ways for humans to celebrate his presence after he returned to his Father, he thought of the works of his Father's creation. Jesus used gifts from God, such as water, oil, wheat, and grapes, to perform his saving works. When these created things are used in the Seven Sacraments, they remind you of God's creative power and make God's power present to you now. Strengthened by the Sacraments, you can continue Jesus' work in the world. Work and worship become one.

When you choose to care for creation, you help the world achieve its purpose: to praise God and show God's goodness. Caring for creation is a way to praise God through your actions.

In God's plan, the goodness of creation unfolds through time. All humans have a choice to help or harm the world during

their lives. You are the crown of God's creation, created in his image and likeness. The divine likeness of all human beings is the result of being created by God. Jesus invites you and all other people to reflect God's image by practicing **stewardship** of all God's gifts—time, talent, treasure, and the resources of creation.

➜ **What are some practical examples of stewardship?**

Connect Your Faith

See Signs of God's Love How are each of these gifts of creation used in the Sacraments as signs of God's presence?

_____

_____

_____

Our Catholic Life

What is your role in the stewardship of God's creation?

When you care for any part of God's creation, you are sharing in his plan. What you do will echo his glory. Here are some ways to make sure that your stewardship of God's creation will be successful.

1. Circle any of these steps that you have followed in the past for a project.

2. Draw a star next to a step you want to try in the future.

10 Steps to Successful Stewardship of Creation

1. Choose a small project that will improve the environment. Find something you can do in your neighborhood, so that you can see results.

2. Work for changes that will last. If you can discover the cause of a problem, work on solving it.

3. Work with others who have experience. Often you can volunteer your time to groups. They will teach you what needs to be done.

4. Respect the feelings, rights, and property of others. Another person may not agree with your opinions.

5. Be aware of how your actions will affect others. Remember that you are helping solve a problem, not blaming anyone.

6. Create feelings of cooperation and goodwill. Always ask for permission and thank those who help you.

7. Ask yourself: How does my plan help? Who or what might my plan hurt?

8. Finish what you start. You will gain respect and more cooperation from others in the future.

9. Follow up and evaluate. Plan a way to learn whether your action accomplished its purpose.

10. Ask God to bless what you have done.

People of Faith

Saint Hildegard of Bingen, 1098–1179

Saint Hildegard was an abbess, the head of a group of nuns, in Bingen, Germany. At a time when few women could read or write, Hildegard could do both. Her curiosity and love for God's creation led her to study nature. She wrote and illustrated books on gardening and herbal medicine. Hildegard knew that when you care for God's creation, you share in his plan for the entire world. She also composed music and painted pictures inspired by her love of nature.

Discuss: What part of creation leaves you most amazed at God's love?

Learn more about Saint Hildegard at **aliveinchrist.osv.com**

Live Your Faith

Write your own psalm of praise to God. Follow these steps:

- Ask others to praise God.
- Tell God two reasons why you are praising him.
- Close by asking again that others praise God.

_____

_____

_____

_____

_____

_____

_____

_____

_____

_____

_____

Let Us Pray

Psalm of Praise

Gather and begin with the Sign of the Cross.

Leader: Sisters and brothers, let us give thanks to God who made the universe.

Reader 1: We see your glory in the heavens above.

All: Praise to you, Creator God!

Reader 2: The moon and stars you have put in place.

All: Praise to you, Creator God!

Reader 3: You made the birds in the sky and all the ocean creatures.

All: Praise to you, Creator God!

Reader 4: You have made humans little less than a god.

All: Praise to you, Creator God!

Leader: God, you have given us every good thing. Teach us your tender care for creation!

All: Amen. **Based on Psalm 8**

 Sing "Jubiláte Deo"
Jubiláte! Jubiláte Deo!
Jubiláte Deo! Jubiláte Deo!
Omnis terra, jubiláte Deo!

FAMILY+FAITH
LIVING AND LEARNING TOGETHER

YOUR CHILD LEARNED >>>

This chapter examines Divine Revelation, God's providence, and the role humans play in stewardship of God's creation.

Scripture

 Read **Psalm 95:1–2, 6–7** to find out why we give glory, honor, and praise to God.

Catholics Believe

- Divine Revelation is the process by which God makes himself, and his plan for humans, known to us.
- Humans share in the Creator's loving plan by caring for creation.

To learn more, go to the *Catechism of the Catholic Church #302, 303, 307, 339, 2415* at **usccb.org**.

People of Faith

This week, your child learned about Saint Hildegard of Bingen. Saint Hildegard was known for her love for God's creation.

CHILDREN AT THIS AGE >>>

How They Understand Stewardship of God's Creation Fifth-graders often learn a great deal about science and nature in their classes at school. Many become quite concerned when they hear about endangered species and other crises in the environment. Their sense of purpose and autonomy increases when they know small, practical things they can do to make things better. And there is no better time than when we are young to get into good habits of environmental stewardship.

CONSIDER THIS >>>

Do you think global warming is fact or fiction?

Regardless of your opinion on the matter or the science that supports the theory, as Catholic disciples, we are called to care for all creation. As Catholics, "we show our respect for the Creator by our stewardship of creation. Care for the earth ... is a requirement of our faith. We are called to protect people and the planet, living our faith in relationship with all of God's creation" (*USCCB, Excerpts from Sharing Catholic Social Teaching: Challenges and Directions [Washington, DC: USCCB, 1998]*).

LET'S TALK >>>

- Ask your child to explain providence as God's loving care for all things.
- Share how your family lives as good stewards of God's creation.

LET'S PRAY >>>

 God, help us to always see your love for us in the world around us as Saint Hildegard did. May we always do our part to help take care of your world. Amen.

For a multimedia glossary of Catholic Faith Words, Sunday readings, seasonal and Saint resources, and chapter activities go to **aliveinchrist.osv.com**.

Chapter 1 Review

A **Check Understanding** Fill in the circle next to the correct response.

1. You share in God's _____ by caring for creation.
   - ○ power to create
   - ○ plan
   - ○ Sacraments
   - ○ knowledge

2. When you care for creation, you are _____.
   - ○ praising God
   - ○ being selfish
   - ○ committing a sin
   - ○ earning money

3. You should care for yourself and others because you are made _____.
   - ○ in God's image
   - ○ with one purpose only
   - ○ of flesh and blood
   - ○ humble by it

4. God's loving care and will for creation is called _____.
   - ○ grace
   - ○ providence
   - ○ stewardship
   - ○ divine blueprint

5. The way we appreciate and use God's gifts is _____.
   - ○ a Sacrament
   - ○ providence
   - ○ loyalty
   - ○ stewardship

6. _____ is the inspired Word of God written by humans.
   - ○ Sacred Scripture
   - ○ Sacrament
   - ○ Sacristy
   - ○ Stewardship

7. God makes himself and his plan known to us through _____.
   - ○ the Sacraments
   - ○ stewardship
   - ○ Divine Revelation
   - ○ providence

8. The _____ begins with the creation of the world.
   - ○ Old Testament
   - ○ New Testament
   - ○ Psalms
   - ○ Creed

9. God makes his power present in the Sacraments through _____.
   - ○ our work
   - ○ stewardship
   - ○ created things
   - ○ his mercy

10. _____ are God's most magnificent creation.
    - ○ Birds
    - ○ Mountains
    - ○ People
    - ○ Oceans

 Go to aliveinchrist.osv.com for an interactive review.

Made to Be with God

 Let Us Pray

Leader: Gracious God, Saint Augustine said, "You have made us for yourself, and our hearts are restless until they rest in you." Hear, then, our restless call:

"'Come,' says my heart, 'seek his face';
　　your face, LORD, do I seek!" **Psalm 27:8**

All: O God, you are our heart's desire. Fill us with the longing, the hope, and the promise of your love forever. Amen.

Scripture

O God, you are my God—
　　it is you I seek!
For you my body yearns;
　　for you my soul thirsts...
For your love is better than life;
　　my lips shall ever praise you!
I will bless you as long as I live;
　　I will lift up my hands, calling on your name. **Psalm 63:2, 4–5**

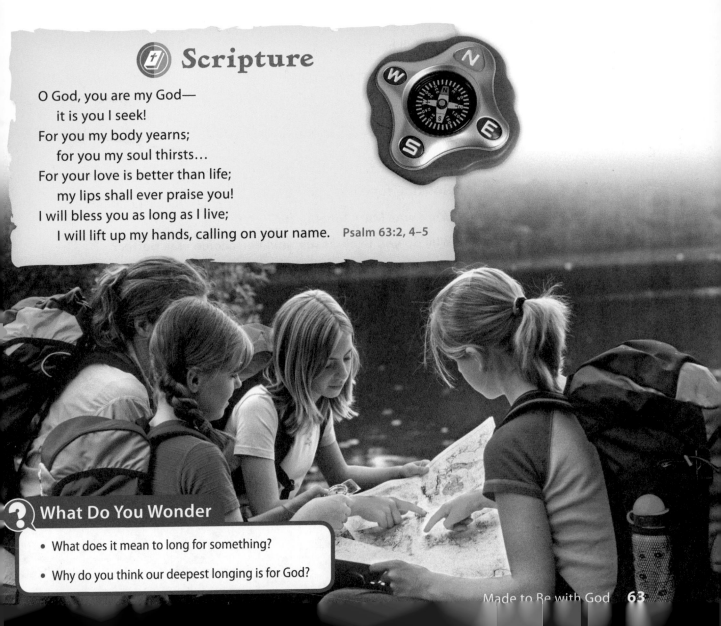

? What Do You Wonder

• What does it mean to long for something?

• Why do you think our deepest longing is for God?

What We Want

Why are longings important?

Some people long for things that others take for granted. Some long for things they really don't need. Still others long for friends, or family, or a closeness in relationships. Read this passage to discover what is more important to Jesus.

 Scripture

Martha and Mary

[Jesus] entered a village where a woman whose name was Martha welcomed him. She had a sister named Mary [who] sat beside the Lord at his feet listening to him speak.

Martha, burdened with so much serving, came to him and said, "Lord, do you not care that my sister has left me by myself to do the serving? Tell her to help me."

The Lord said to her…"Martha…you are anxious and worried about many things. There is need of only one thing. Mary has chosen the better part and it will not be taken from her." Luke 10:38–42

Both Martha and Mary welcomed Jesus, but Mary showed she was looking for something more.

➤ What was Mary longing for?

➤ Why do you think Jesus said her choice was better?

The Gift of Longing

People long for—hope for, desire, really want—all kinds of things. Some of these things are important, and some are not. Both Martha and Mary welcomed Jesus into their home. Martha provided hospitality and served her guest. Mary, however, longed for something more. She wanted to connect with Jesus. What a wonderful gift she received as she listened to Jesus' teaching.

There are many layers of longing in the world. You may long for things, or for the right words to say. You may long to be loved and accepted by others. You may long for good health, or to win a game, or to be chosen for a special honor. All of your longings are part of your desire to be truly happy.

Longing is actually a gift in itself. It is planted inside you by God. God wants you to find your way home to him at the end of your life on Earth. **Religion** is the way you express your longing for God. Religion gives you a language to express your thoughts and feelings about God.

➜ What are the most important things that you would like to have?

Share Your Faith

Reflect Fill in the first column below with some of the ways you express your thoughts and feelings about God. In the second column, explain what those actions mean to you.

Action	What it Means for Me
_____	_____
_____	_____
_____	_____

Share Discuss your chart with a partner.

What God Gives

Who alone can satisfy your longing?

Jesus knows our longings and offers us all we need, as we learn in this account from the Gospel according to John.

Underline the message Jesus wanted to give the woman.

Scripture

The Samaritan Woman

A woman of Samaria, tired and hot, trudged along with her water jars. At the well, she noticed a Jewish stranger. Contrary to custom, the man spoke directly to her, asking for a drink. He then said, "If you knew the gift of God and who is saying to you, 'Give me a drink,' you would have asked him and he would have given you living water."

She asked where she could get this "living water." The stranger, who was Jesus, said he did not mean ordinary water. The water he spoke of was God, who wants everyone to worship him in the Spirit and in truth. The woman said, "I know that the Messiah is coming, the one called the Anointed; when he comes, he will tell us everything." Jesus answered, "I am he, the one who is speaking with you."

At that, the woman forgot about the water she had come for. This news of "living water" was more important. She ran to tell everyone, asking, "Could he possibly be the Messiah?"   Based on John 4:7–29

➜ Why do you think Jesus chose the image of water in his teaching?

God Satisfies You

When you long for God, only the living water of his **grace** will satisfy you. Jesus knows that deep in the human heart is a longing that only God can fill. The desire for God is more powerful than your thirst for water on a hot day. The Samaritan woman's response to Jesus shows the beginning of her **faith** in him as the **Messiah**.

Faith is a gift from God that enables you to believe and trust in God and the things he has revealed to us, even though you cannot see him. Faith is also a human action by which you choose to respond to God's presence in your life. You received this gift in the Sacrament of Baptism. In the waters of Baptism, you became a child of God and a member of the Body of Christ.

Helping Faith Grow

Baptism is the beginning of your faith journey. Your faith continues to grow and develop. In this life, you come to know God through creation, through the Bible, and, most of all, through Jesus. You are helped by your parents and the Church community. Your faith grows through praying, reading Scripture, and being active in your parish. Like the Samaritan woman, you are called to share your growing faith and joy with others.

Catholic Faith Words

grace God's free, loving gift of his own life and help to do what he calls us to do. It is participation in the life of the Holy Trinity.

faith the Theological Virtue that makes it possible for us to believe in God and the things that he has revealed to us. Faith leads us to obey God. It is both a gift from him and something we choose.

Messiah the promised one who would lead his People. The word *Messiah* means "God's anointed," or "God's chosen one." Jesus is the Messiah.

Connect Your Faith

Write a Poem Create an acrostic poem using the word *faith*. For each letter, write a word or phrase that helps you grow in faith. The letter *a* is done for you.

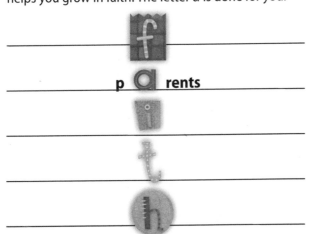

f _____

p a rents

i _____

t _____

h _____

Our Catholic Life

How do you seek God?

We help satisfy our longing for God by searching for him in prayer and Scripture. If we are willing to listen, God will speak to us and help us follow him.

No matter where or when you decide to pray or read the Bible, your effort will bring you closer to God. However, some places help you be a better listener.

Church

The parish church is the house of God. Even when the community is not worshipping there, Christ is present. Go there and tell him everything in your heart. Then be still and listen for his answer.

Outdoors

Jesus often prayed outdoors. There, he felt close to his Father, the Creator of all. Being out in the natural world can lead you to a spirit of grateful praise.

Home

Sometimes it is best to go to a separate room and close the door when you want to talk to God. Any quiet room will work.

In the space provided, draw or write about a place you go to seek God.

People of Faith

Saint Augustine, 354–430

Augustine had a Christian mother and a pagan father. His mother wanted him to be baptized, but he studied many other ideas before he became a Christian. He became a monk and a priest and later was the bishop of Hippo, a city near his hometown in North Africa. Saint Augustine was a great teacher and writer. He tells us that everyone longs to love God, and we will never be happy until we know God. One of his prayers to God begins, "You have made us for yourself, and our hearts are restless until they rest in you."

Discuss: How is having a restless heart like being homesick when you are away?

 Learn more about Saint Augustine at **aliveinchrist.osv.com**

Live Your Faith

Solve the rebus puzzle to learn one thing you can do to help satisfy your longing for God. Fill in the blanks below each picture with a word that describes what the picture represents. Then, fill in the Answer box with the sentence you create.

_____   _____   _____

2   **God**

Answer:

_____

_____

_____   _____

Explain to a partner how you would do this.

Let Us Pray

A Prayer for Beginnings and Renewals

As we begin this new year together, we renew our never-ending journey of faith. We live each day as disciples of Jesus.

Gather and begin with the Sign of the Cross.

Leader: Blessed are you, Lord God,
Creator of body and mind and heart;
you have sent the Spirit of wisdom and knowledge
to guide your people in all their ways.

Side 1: At the beginning of this new school year, we pray for your mercy: bless us that together we may grow in faith, hope, and love as we learn from you and each other how to follow your Son Jesus.

Side 2: Expand the limits of our minds that we may grow in wisdom, understanding, and knowledge; deepen our commitment to seek the truth of your ways; and enliven our faith to reach out to those in need.

All: Glory and praise to you, Lord God, in the Church and in Christ Jesus forever and ever. Amen.
Based on Prayers for School [Source: Book of Blessings, page 300]

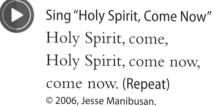 Sing "Holy Spirit, Come Now"
Holy Spirit, come,
Holy Spirit, come now,
come now. (Repeat)
© 2006, Jesse Manibusan.
Published by spiritandsong.com ®,
a division of OCP. All rights reserved.

FAMILY+FAITH
LIVING AND LEARNING TOGETHER

YOUR CHILD LEARNED >>>

This chapter explores our deepest longings, explains grace as participation in the life of the Holy Trinity, and examines faith as the free, loving gift of God's own life and help.

Scripture

 Read **Psalm 63:2, 4–5** to find out about our longing for God.

Catholics Believe

• True happiness can come only through communion with God.

• Religion expresses our relationship with God through beliefs, prayers, and practices.

To learn more, go to the *Catechism of the Catholic Church #27–28* at **usccb.org**.

People of Faith

This week, your child learned about Saint Augustine, one of the great theologians of early Christianity. He says that our hearts are restless until they rest in God.

CHILDREN AT THIS AGE >>>

How They Understand Communion with God Fifth-graders are just beginning to think about what sort of man or woman they will be someday. As they approach middle school, they will become more and more concerned with their own identity. It's important that from the very beginning of this process, they hear that we are all made to be in relationship with God, and that we cultivate this relationship by talking with God and listening to him in the variety of ways he speaks to us.

CONSIDER THIS >>>

How many people do you know who say they are spiritual but not religious?

In our culture today, some people have negative feelings about institutions, including organized religion. Some argue that the time, money, and effort it takes to maintain the institution can minimize the mission of the institution. As Catholics, we know that "there is no doubt that the Church is called to be a community of love in the Father, the Son, and the Holy Spirit. The risen Jesus himself presented a model of Church leadership based in love when he solicited three affirmations of love from Peter (cf. Jn 21:15–17). At the same time, though, the Church has many structures that are needed to build up the bond of love" *(USCCA p. 121)*.

LET'S TALK >>>

• Ask your child to explain faith as a journey.

• Share how you help your child grow in faith.

LET'S PRAY >>>

 Saint Augustine, you know we long to know what God wants us to do. Help us to find God, as you did, so that we may rest in his love. Amen.

For a multimedia glossary of Catholic Faith Words, Sunday readings, seasonal and Saint resources, and chapter activities go to **aliveinchrist.osv.com**.

Chapter 2 Review

A **Work with Words** Complete each sentence with the correct word from the Word Bank.

1. _____ is the Theological Virtue that makes it possible for us to believe in God and the things that he has revealed to us.

2. "God's anointed," the promised one who leads God's People, refers to Jesus, the _____.

3. God's free, loving gift of his own life and help to do what he calls us to do is _____.

4. You became a member of the Church through _____.

5. _____ is a group of beliefs, prayers, and practices that help people to express their longing for God.

Word Bank

Messiah

faith

religion

grace

Baptism

B **Check Understanding** Match each description in Column 1 with the correct term in Column 2.

Column 1	Column 2
6. helps you on your faith journey	creation
7. a gift planted inside us by God	Mary
8. can improve your prayer	parish community
9. longed to listen to Jesus	a quiet place
10. one of the ways in which we come to know God in this life	longing

Go to **aliveinchrist.osv.com** for an interactive review.

Signs of God's Presence

💟 Let Us Pray

Leader: Here, there, and everywhere, we see your face, O God.

"The heavens declare the glory of God;
the firmament proclaims the works of his
hands." **Psalm 19:2**

All: Loving God, thank you for not being the God of far
away but for being close by. Thank you for the many
signs of your loving presence. Open our eyes and
hearts to see them all. Amen.

📖 Scripture

"For we are the temple of the living God;
as God said:

I will live with them and move among them,
and I will be their God
and they shall be my people. ...

and I will be a father to you,
and you shall be sons and
daughters to me,
says the Lord Almighty."
2 Corinthians 6:16, 18

❓ What Do You Wonder?

• Since God lives and moves with us, what are
some signs of his presence?

• What is the greatest sign of God's presence?

The artwork at right shows Moses' reaction to the burning bush. Explain to a partner how you would have felt if you were in Moses' position.

Powerful Signs

What are some signs of God's presence?

Some signs help you remember someone or something you have seen at an earlier time. But certain signs can remind you of things you cannot see. The most powerful signs remind you of God's presence. God is a mystery. He is pure spirit and cannot be seen or heard directly. So God uses signs to help you understand what he wants you to know. This is how God spoke to Moses.

 **Scripture**

The Burning Bush

Moses had a lot on his mind. His people, the Hebrews, were enslaved by the Egyptians and were being treated unjustly. Moses himself was hiding because he had killed an Egyptian who was mistreating one of the Hebrews. As Moses arrived at Horeb, the mountain of God, he heard a voice.

Suddenly, Moses noticed that a nearby bush was in flames—but it wasn't burning up. As Moses moved closer, the voice called to him, "Remove your sandals from your feet, for the place where you stand is holy ground." God was speaking to Moses from the burning bush!

Moses and God talked. God had heard the cries of the Hebrew people, and he intended to free them. Moses asked God what he should tell people when they asked who had told him all this. God replied, "This is what you shall tell the Israelites: I AM has sent me to you." Moses knew that by revealing his name, God was promising to be with his people. **Based on Exodus 3:1–15**

➡ **What did God want Moses to understand?**

Signs Point the Way

The burning bush was a sign. A sign is something you can see, hear, smell, touch, or taste. A sign points beyond itself to something more. Thunder is a sign of possible rain. A stop sign is only letters on red-painted metal, but everyone knows that there could be danger if you do not obey the sign. Sign language gives people who cannot hear well a way to communicate.

God uses signs to communicate with people. The wonders of creation and the events of human life contain signs of God's awesome power and nearness. They tell of his eternal goodness, strong justice, and gentle mercy. When Moses first saw the burning bush, he was puzzled and surprised. But this sign of the presence of God was not the end of Moses' encounter. The experience opened the way for Moses to know God better.

At first Moses did not realize that God was with his People in their hardship and distress. But when Moses saw the sign of the burning bush, he began to understand that God was present and wanted to help the Israelites. You may not see, hear, smell, taste, or touch God, but signs can show you that God is with you.

Underline what some signs of God's presence tell us about him.

Share Your Faith

Reflect Think about a place, other than church, where you experience signs of God's presence. Describe this place in two sentences.

_____

_____

_____

_____

Share Trade descriptions with a partner, and discuss what your descriptions have in common.

Covenant Signs

What are signs of God's promise to his People?

Throughout history God has communicated his presence and shown his love for people through signs. He commanded the Hebrew people, later known as the Israelites, to eat a special meal the night before Moses led them out of slavery. It was called the Passover meal, and it became a sign of the **covenant**, a sacred promise or agreement between God and the people he saved.

The Hebrews understood that the meal was a sign of the agreement God had made with them. Because of the meal's importance as a sign, the Hebrews made it a part of their faith and tradition. Today, Passover is still a Jewish holy day that celebrates God's leading the Israelites out of slavery in Egypt.

The New Covenant

Jesus' Death and Resurrection became the basis for a new covenant. You hear about this covenant when you attend Mass. The bread and wine come from wheat and grapes, signs of God's goodness in creation. At the Last Supper, Jesus gave new, life-giving meaning to the bread and wine by changing them into his Body and Blood. He said they were to be shared in a meal with those who believe that Jesus fulfilled God's saving promise.

➤ **What is the relationship between the Mass and the Jewish Passover meal?**

Catholic Faith Words

covenant a sacred promise or agreement between God and humans

Seven Sacraments effective signs of God's life, instituted by Christ and given to the Church. In the celebration of each Sacrament, there are visible signs and Divine actions that give grace and allow us to share in God's work.

Effective Signs

Sacrament	Outward Sign—	God's Action
Baptism	water and words (I baptize you …)	new life in Christ
Confirmation	Sacred Chrism and laying on of hands by bishop	strengthening by the Holy Spirit
Eucharist	bread and wine that become Jesus' Body and Blood, the priest's words of consecration, receiving Holy Communion	nourishment by the Body and Blood of Christ
Reconciliation	words of absolution and extension of hand by priest	conversion and forgiveness
Anointing of the Sick	the priest's anointing the sick with the oil	healing and strengthening
Matrimony	mutual consent and total giving of the man and woman to each other in married love	loving union and commitment
Holy Orders	the bishop's laying on of hands and the Prayer of Consecration prayed over the man	ordained ministry for God's people

The **Seven Sacraments** are signs of the new covenant made through the life and sacrifice of Jesus. They point to God and to his love. Christ himself acts in the Sacraments. In the celebration of each Sacrament, there are visible signs and Divine actions that give grace and allow us to share in God's work. Sacraments are celebrations of God's presence in and with his People.

Jesus himself is truly the Sacrament—the one great universal sign of God's love—because he is the Son of God who became human. In this chart, you can see how Jesus chose powerful signs to show how God is present in important moments of life.

Connect Your Faith

Make a Contract Brainstorm ideas for a group contract. Include in your agreement what you will do for others over the coming year. Choose a group sign as a way to remind one another to keep the agreement.

Our Catholic Life

How do you see the signs God sends to you?

God speaks to us in his Word and through the Church. In personal prayer, we open our minds and hearts to his way. Through practice, you can become more attentive to signs of God's will and presence.

Answer the questions with what you discovered this week.

Become More Aware

1. Over the next week, pay close attention to what is happening around you. Take a second to step back and look at things a little differently.

2. Ask yourself, "What is God trying to tell me today?" Look for clues about this in the things that have happened today or over the past few days. Answer these questions:

   • What have you seen and heard?

   _____

   • What have people been saying to you?

   _____

3. At Mass, listen well to the readings, the music, and the homily.

4. At the end of the day or week, sit quietly. Ask the Holy Spirit to open your heart and mind. Answer these questions:

   • What did God say to you?

   _____

   • How can you respond?

   _____

   • How did you respond?

   _____

People of Faith

July 11

Saint Benedict, 480–550

As a young man, Benedict wanted to live alone in silence and prayer. But people moved near him so he could teach them about how to become holy. Benedict knew that if people were to live in a group, they had to have an agreement on how to live. So he made a plan to help people live together in a way that would please God. His plan, called the Rule of Saint Benedict, balances prayer, study, work, and rest. Even today, people use his Rule to live a happy and holy life.

Discuss: What kind of rules do you have at school or at home that help everyone get along?

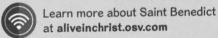

Learn more about Saint Benedict at **aliveinchrist.osv.com**

Live Your Faith

Name or draw one thing you can do to listen more actively for God speaking to you in your everyday life.

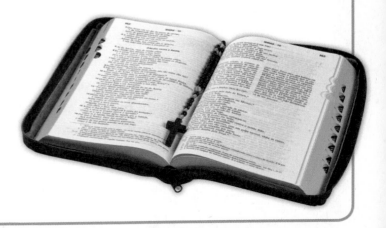

 Let Us Pray

Litany of Praise

In this litany, we give praise and thanks for the many ways God is continually and constantly present with us.

Gather and begin with the Sign of the Cross.

Leader: Our God is closer to us than we are to ourselves. We can see signs of God in all of the things he has created. What a gift God continually gives us!

Reader 1: God is with us in the majesty and simplicity of creation.

All: Wondrous God, thank you for your everywhere-presence!

Reader 2: God is with us in people who care for us and people we haven't yet met.

All: Wondrous God, thank you for your everywhere-presence!

Reader 3: God is with us in the life-giving grace of the Sacraments.

All: Wondrous God, thank you for your everywhere-presence!

Leader: How else is God with us in our everyday lives?

All: Wondrous God, thank you for your everywhere-presence!

Leader: Let us pray.

Bow your heads as the leader continues to pray.

All: Amen. **Based on Psalms 65, 66**

 Sing "Glory and Praise to Our God"
Glory and praise to our God,
who alone gives light to our days.
Many are the blessings he bears
to those who trust in his ways.
Dan Schutte © 1976, OCP. All rights reserved.

FAMILY+FAITH
LIVING AND LEARNING TOGETHER

YOUR CHILD LEARNED >>>

This chapter describes how God uses signs to communicate with us, and explains the Seven Sacraments as effective signs of God's life, given by Christ to the Church.

Scripture

 Read **2 Corinthians 6:16** to find out about God's presence among us.

Catholics Believe

- One way God communicates his love is through signs.
- Through the visible signs and Divine actions in each Sacrament, we receive grace and are helped to share in God's work.

To learn more, go to the *Catechism of the Catholic Church #774, 1084, 1147, 1152* at **usccb.org**.

People of Faith

This week, your child learned about Saint Benedict, the founder of Western Christian monasticism. Benedict's Rule of Life emphasized both work and prayer.

CHILDREN AT THIS AGE >>>

How They Understand the Sacraments Fifth-graders are approaching the age when children become more able to understand signs, symbols, and other abstract content. Some children this age are still very concrete in their thinking, yet others are more capable of imagining hypothetical situations and understanding analogies. The Sacraments are both concrete and abstract, sensory and mystical. Because of this, it's important that fifth-graders have a clear sense that there is "something more" to the Sacraments than what we experience with our senses, even if that understanding will still need to unfold over time.

CONSIDER THIS >>>

If you were separated from someone you love, how important would it be to communicate with them?

Most have us have missed someone enough to count down the days until we would see them again. We may have written letters or emails as a way to communicate while they were away. Until we are with God in Heaven, God communicates with us through the Sacraments. As Catholics, we know that "as we come to understand the Sacraments, it is important to recognize that the Sacraments have a visible and invisible reality, a reality open to all the human senses but grasped in its God-given depths with the eyes of faith… The invisible reality we cannot 'see' is God's grace" (*USCCA p. 168*).

LET'S TALK >>>

- Ask your child to explain how God communicates through signs.
- Have each family member share how he or she recognizes God's presence.

LET'S PRAY >>>

 Saint Benedict, pray for us that we may always find time for work and prayer, as well as rest and play. Amen.

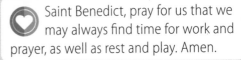 For a multimedia glossary of Catholic Faith Words, Sunday readings, seasonal and Saint resources, and chapter activities go to **aliveinchrist.osv.com**.

Chapter 3 Review

A **Work with Words** **Complete the following statements.**

1. Signs point to something you cannot know through your

   _____.

2. God appeared to Moses in the _____.

3. The one great universal sign of God's love is _____.

4. The Passover meal is a sign of the _____ between God and the Israelites.

5. _____ become the Body and Blood of Christ.

B **Check Understanding** **In complete sentences, explain the following:**

6. Creation

   _____

   _____

7. Seven Sacraments

   _____

   _____

8. Signs of Confirmation

   _____

   _____

9. God's presence in the Sacrament of Anointing of the Sick

   _____

   _____

10. A way to improve or strengthen your prayer life

    _____

    _____

    _____

Go to **aliveinchrist.osv.com** for an interactive review.

A Work with Words Complete each sentence with the correct
term from the Word Bank.

> ### Word Bank
>
> water   Sacred Scripture   faith
>
> works   trees   grace
>
> Prayer   signs   appreciate
>
> stewardship

1. The Seven Sacraments, and _____, and creation
   are all signs of God's free, loving gift of his own life and help, also
   called _____.

2. _____, reading or listening to _____,
   and the guidance of your parish community help you build up your faith.

3. People show good _____ by the way they
   _____ and use God's gifts and the resources of creation.

4. Using _____ sparingly rather than wasting it and planting
   _____ rather than cutting them down are ways to show
   respect for God's gift of our environment.

5. Living water and the burning bush are _____ of God's
   presence because God _____ through them.

B Check Understanding Write answers to the question on spaces 6 through 9. Find and circle these answers in the word search. The remaining letters form a message. Write the message on the spaces for number 10.

```
J   E   S   U   S   U   S   E
O   I   L   D   T   H   E   S
S   G   I   F   T   S   F   W
R   O   M   C   R   E   A   A
T   I   O   N   T   T   O   P
E   R   F   O   E   R   M   H
I   S   G   R   A   P   E   S
S   A   V   I   N   G   W   O
W   H   E   A   T   R   K   S
```

What gifts of creation did Jesus use for signs of his Sacraments?

6. _____

7. _____

8. _____

9. _____

10. ☐☐☐☐☐ ☐☐☐☐
☐☐☐☐☐ ☐☐☐☐☐
☐☐☐☐ ☐☐☐☐☐☐☐☐
☐☐ ☐☐☐☐☐☐☐ ☐☐☐
☐☐☐☐☐☐ ☐☐☐☐☐.

Match each description in Column 1 with the correct term in Column 2.

Column 1

Column 2

11. God's Word to the Church, safeguarded by the Apostles and their successors, the bishops, and handed down verbally

Providence

12. enables us to trust in God and the things that he has revealed to us

Sacred Tradition

13. the way God makes himself, and his plan for humans, known to us

Seven Sacraments

14. God's loving care for all things, God's will and plan for creation

faith

15. effective signs of God's life, instituted by Christ

Divine Revelation

C **Make Connections** Write a response to each question or statement.

16. "Remove your sandals from your feet, for the place where you stand is holy ground." How do you imagine this place affected Moses' attitude toward God?

_____

17. Give an example of how you practice stewardship.

_____

18. What are signs of a loving union and commitment between married people?

_____

19. Describe an example of how longing for something caused you to try harder or work longer than you might have otherwise.

_____

_____

20. What did Jesus mean by "living water" for the soul?

_____

Trinity

Our Catholic Tradition

- The mystery of the Holy Trinity is the central mystery of the Christian faith and life. It is revealed to us and celebrated in many ways. (CCC, 234, 259)

- When we follow the First Commandment, we live in faith, hope, and charity. (CCC, 2086)

- We respond to God's love with prayer, with worship, and by practicing virtues in our everyday life. (CCC, 143)

How does our belief in the Holy Trinity affect the way we worship and the way we live?

The Mystery of the Trinity

💛 Let Us Pray

Leader: Almighty God, we can scarcely imagine the wonder that is you.

"Who has gone up to heaven and come down again—
who has cupped the wind in the hollow of the hand?
Who has bound up the waters in a cloak—
who has established all the ends of the earth?"

Proverbs 30:4

All: God of signs and wonders, help us to adore the wonder that is you. Amen.

📖 Scripture

"…Jesus came from Nazareth of Galilee and was baptized in the Jordan by John. On coming up out of the water he saw the heavens being torn open and the Spirit, like a dove, descending upon him. And a voice came from the heavens, 'You are my beloved Son; with you I am well pleased.'" **Mark 1:9–11**

❓ What Do You Wonder?

- Why did Jesus go to be baptized if he knew that he was God?

- What does this passage reveal about the mystery of God?

More Than Can Be Known

What gift did Saint Patrick bring to the Irish people?

We can't always see God's plan for us. Blessings often come in the form of hardships. The story of Saint Patrick is a good example of finding blessing in hardship.

Saint Patrick

Patrick, the son of a Roman official, lived on the western coast of Britain. While working on his father's farm one day, he was seized by a group of raiders and sold as a slave.

Patrick was taken to Ireland, a place completely new to him. Again he worked on a farm, but now he had no warm clothing to wear and almost nothing to eat. He had no family and no friends. Angry with God, Patrick thought only of his misery. Why had God allowed this terrible thing to happen?

➜ **What is a word or symbol that describes what you would think or feel if you were Patrick?**

The Mystery Unfolds

As time went by, Patrick began to realize that despite his harsh life, the lives of his Irish masters were even harder because they did not know Jesus. They did not know the Christian faith, which is full of hope and love. Patrick prayed with all his heart, turning his life and his future over to God. After six years, he escaped and made the long, hard journey home. His parents were overjoyed. They hoped that he would never leave them again.

But Patrick kept thinking about the Irish people he had left. He never stopped wondering about the mystery of his life and what good might come from his time among those people. One night he dreamed that they were calling him. All at once it became clear to him that because he knew their language, he could bring them the Christian faith. Although the studies were hard for him, Patrick prepared to become a priest. In time, he became a bishop and returned to Ireland. When the Irish people heard Patrick speak, great numbers of them asked to be baptized. Because of his great holiness and love for God, the Church made Patrick a Saint.

Experience taught Saint Patrick that the mysteries in human life draw people toward the **mystery** of God, who is so much more than they can ever grasp.

One God in Three Divine Persons

Who is the Holy Trinity?

Like Saint Patrick, people today wonder about the mystery of God and the way God works in their lives. God wants to be known, yet he is greater than anyone can tell or understand. From earliest Old Testament times, the Israelites learned through revelation that God is one, unfailing in truth and love.

Jesus revealed a deeper level of this mystery, showing that the one God is three Divine Persons: Father, Son, and Holy Spirit—the **Holy Trinity**. Patrick emphasized and honored the Trinity in all his teaching. Jesus and his followers invite you into a deeper understanding of the mystery of the God you cannot see.

Catholic Faith Words

Holy Trinity the mystery of one God in three Divine Persons: Father, Son, and Holy Spirit

virtues good spiritual habits that strengthen you and enable you to do what is right and good. They develop over time with our practice and openness to God's grace.

Underline how God the Father made himself known during Jesus' baptism.

 Scripture

John the Baptist's Testimony to Jesus

John the Baptist testified that Jesus was the Son of God, sent by the Father and filled with the Holy Spirit:

"I saw the Spirit come down like a dove from the sky and remain upon him. I did not know him, but the one who sent me to baptize with water told me, 'On whomever you see the Spirit come down and remain, he is the one who will baptize with the holy Spirit.' Now I have seen and testified that he is the Son of God." John 1:32–34

Whenever the Church baptizes, she does so using the names of the three Divine Persons of the Holy Trinity. Those who are baptized enter into the very life of God, who is love. Every time we make the Sign of the Cross, we are reminded of our Baptism and our participation in the life of the Holy Trinity.

All of the Sacraments offer a share in God's life and into the divine mystery that is God—Father, Son, and Holy Spirit. In the Sacraments and personal prayer, we profess our belief in the Trinity when we pray the Apostles' and Nicene Creeds.

Living Your Faith

The Sign of the Cross helps you recall that the Trinity is with you, protecting and guiding you to live as Jesus did. When you renew your baptismal promises, you are reminded that the Trinity gives you new life that never ends.

The First Commandment is this: I am the Lord your God; you shall not have other gods before me. This Commandment calls you to believe in God, to hope in him, and to love him above everything else. In obeying this Commandment, you live in relationship with the Trinity.

A **virtue** is a good spiritual habit that strengthens you and enables you to do what is right and good. The virtues of faith, hope, and charity (love) are called Theological Virtues because they are gifts from God.

All people are made in the image of God because they are created by God.

The Theological Virtues

Faith	The virtue that makes it possible for us to believe in God and the things that he has revealed
Hope	The virtue that helps us trust in the true happiness God wants us to have and in Jesus' promise of eternal life, and to rely on the help of the Holy Spirit
Charity (Love)	The virtue that directs us to love God above all things and our neighbor as ourselves, for the love of God

If you try, you can see traces of the Trinity reflected in every person. When people love one another, they reflect the communion of the three Divine Persons in one God.

➡ **How do some of the people you know reflect the image of God?**

Connect Your Faith

Symbols of the Trinity Legend says that Saint Patrick used the shamrock as an image for the Trinity. How could the shamrock be useful in explaining the Trinity? What other images would help explain the Trinity? Draw one or more of them in this space.

Our Catholic Life

How do you respond to the love God shows you?

The Theological Virtues of faith, hope, and charity are actions that people do and see others doing every day. Here are some everyday examples.

In the space below each virtue, explain how you have responded to God in faith, hope, and charity.

Virtues in Action

Faith

- Peter goes through the process of becoming a Catholic.
- Amanda makes the Sign of the Cross each day when she wakes up.
- Carlos attends a Bible study.
- _____
- _____
- _____

Hope

- Elena goes to Mass with her family on the anniversary of her grandfather's death.
- Tony gathers with other people of his parish to pray for peace.
- Shannon asks God to show her how to deal with her temper.
- _____
- _____
- _____

Charity

- Meg helps the teacher of a first-grade religion class every Saturday.
- Andrew helps serve dinner at a homeless shelter.
- José volunteers at a nursing home after school.
- _____
- _____
- _____

People of Faith

May 2

Saint Athanasius, c. 295–373

Saint Athanasius was a bishop in Egypt. He lived at a time when some people said that Jesus was not really the Son of God. Athanasius taught that Jesus was both God and man. He also defended the doctrine of the Trinity. He helped people understand that there are three Divine Persons in one God. He suffered many hardships because of his faith. He was even sent far away from his home—not once, but five times! When he was alone, he spent his time writing, praying, and encouraging other Christians.

Discuss: How do you show your faith in the Holy Trinity?

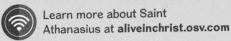

Learn more about Saint Athanasius at **aliveinchrist.osv.com**

Live Your Faith

Name one way you can live each of the Theological Virtues: faith, hope, and charity.

Faith

_____
_____
_____
_____
_____

Hope

_____
_____
_____
_____
_____

Charity

_____
_____
_____
_____
_____

Role-play a short scene that shows one of these virtues in action.

 **Let Us Pray**

The Apostles' Creed

Gather and begin with the Sign of the Cross.

Leader: Let us affirm what we believe.
After each reader, say: I do believe!

Reader 1: I believe in God,
the Father almighty,
Creator of heaven and earth,
and in Jesus Christ, his only Son, our Lord,

At the words that follow, up to and including *the Virgin Mary,* all bow.

Reader 2: who was conceived by the Holy Spirit,
born of the Virgin Mary,
suffered under Pontius Pilate,
was crucified, died and was buried;
he descended into hell;
on the third day he rose again from the dead;

Reader 3: he ascended into heaven,
and is seated at the right hand of God the Father almighty;
from there he will come to judge the living and the dead.

Reader 4: I believe in the Holy Spirit,
the holy catholic Church,
the communion of saints,
the forgiveness of sins,
the resurrection of the body,
and life everlasting. Amen.

 Sing "Holy, Holy, Holy"

FAMILY+FAITH

LIVING AND LEARNING TOGETHER

YOUR CHILD LEARNED >>>

This chapter addresses the mystery of the Holy Trinity—God the Father, God the Son, and God the Holy Spirit—and defines faith, hope, and charity as the Theological Virtues.

Scripture

 Read **Mark 1:9–11** to find out about the baptism of Jesus.

Catholics Believe

• The Trinity is the central mystery of Christian faith and life.

• Virtue is the habit of doing good. The Theological Virtues of faith, hope, and charity are gifts from God.

To learn more, go to the *Catechism of the Catholic Church #234, 1812, 1813* at **usccb.org**.

People of Faith

In this chapter, your child learned about Saint Athanasius. He is known for his courage to speak out about the Holy Trinity and his defense of Jesus as the true Son of God.

CHILDREN AT THIS AGE >>>

How They Understand God as Trinity The central mystery of our faith is also the most mysterious—how can God be Three and also One? Some theologians explain this mystery in terms of relationship. God, in his very nature, is a communion of Divine Persons, and he wants to be in communion with us. Relationships, especially "best friend"-ships, are increasingly important to children this age, and consequently they can identify with this relational nature of God in a way they could not when they were younger.

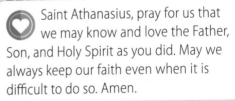

CONSIDER THIS >>>

Has someone ever taught you how to stretch before participating in physical activities?

We need to warm up and stretch our muscles before we begin physical activity. Then our muscles perform better and we decrease risk of injury. God gives us the Theological Virtues to help strengthen our lives. As Catholics, we understand that "the Theological Virtues of faith, hope, and charity (love)... are not acquired through human effort but, beginning with Baptism, they are infused within us as gifts from God. They dispose us to live in relationship with the Holy Trinity. Faith, hope, and charity influence human virtues by increasing their stability and strength for our lives" (*USCCA, p. 317*).

LET'S TALK >>>

• Ask your child to explain virtue as the habit of doing God's will.

• Share how your family lives the Theological Virtues of faith, hope, and charity (or love).

LET'S PRAY >>>

 Saint Athanasius, pray for us that we may know and love the Father, Son, and Holy Spirit as you did. May we always keep our faith even when it is difficult to do so. Amen.

For a multimedia glossary of Catholic Faith Words, Sunday readings, seasonal and Saint resources, and chapter activities go to **aliveinchrist.osv.com**.

Chapter 4 Review

A **Work with Words** Fill in the circle next to the choice that best completes the sentence.

1. A virtue is a _____.
   - ○ prayer prayed during Mass
   - ○ spiritual habit
   - ○ symbol

2. The Theological Virtue that expresses your expectation that God will grant you eternal life is _____.
   - ○ patience
   - ○ charity
   - ○ hope

3. A truth of faith that God has shown in Sacred Scripture, in the life of Jesus, or in the teaching of the Church is called a _____.
   - ○ stewardship
   - ○ covenant
   - ○ mystery

4. The divine likeness in each person, the result of being created by God, is known as _____.
   - ○ the image of God
   - ○ virtue
   - ○ faith

5. The mystery beyond words is _____.
   - ○ the Trinity
   - ○ virtue
   - ○ creation

B **Check Understanding** Circle True if a statement is true, and circle False if a statement is false. Correct any false statements.

6. Faith in God means that God is not a mystery. **True/False**

   _____

   _____

7. The mystery of one God in three Divine Persons is called the image of God. **True/False**

   _____

   _____

8. Jesus reveals to people the God they cannot see. **True/False**

   _____

   _____

9. Those who are baptized are baptized into the very life of God. **True/False**

   _____

   _____

10. The Theological Virtues are feelings that give us comfort. **True/False**

    _____

    _____

Go to **aliveinchrist.osv.com** for an interactive review.

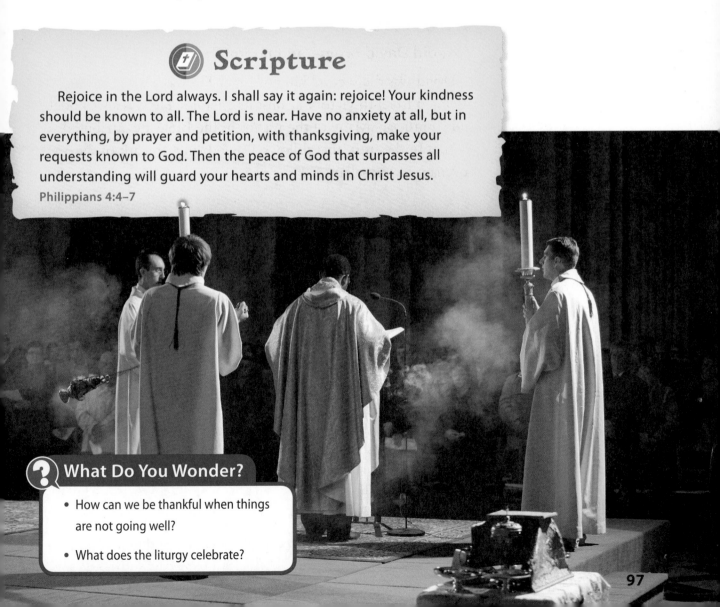

Prayer and Worship

Let Us Pray

Leader: The wonder and mystery of your presence, O Lord, calls us to respond in prayer.

"LORD, I call to you; hasten to me;
   listen to my plea when I call.
Let my prayer be incense before you;
   my uplifted hands an evening offering."

Psalm 141:1–2

All: We lift hands and hearts to you, O Lord. Hear us when we pray. Amen.

Scripture

Rejoice in the Lord always. I shall say it again: rejoice! Your kindness should be known to all. The Lord is near. Have no anxiety at all, but in everything, by prayer and petition, with thanksgiving, make your requests known to God. Then the peace of God that surpasses all understanding will guard your hearts and minds in Christ Jesus.

Philippians 4:4–7

? What Do You Wonder?

- How can we be thankful when things are not going well?

- What does the liturgy celebrate?

97

God with Us

How did David praise and honor God?

David was the second king of Israel. He was a soldier who often led Israel to victory against its enemies. He was also a poet and a musician. Many of the psalms in the Bible are attributed to him. In the story that follows, David brings the ark of the covenant to Jerusalem.

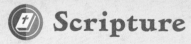 **Scripture**

The Ark Brought to Jerusalem

David's armies had carried the ark of the covenant—a box containing the tablets of the Law—into battle as a sign of God's presence. Now David brought the ark to Jerusalem, where it would signal God's presence to all the people.

To celebrate the ark's arrival, David organized a great procession and invited musicians and singers to take part. Singing with joy, the people followed the ark through the streets. David led the procession, dressed not as a soldier or a king, but in the simple clothes of a priest of the Lord—and he danced with abandon before the Lord!

Based on 2 Samuel 6:1–15

➜ **What do you think was in David's heart as he danced?**

Responding to God's Love

From the earliest days of the Christian community, the followers of the Risen Christ gathered for prayer and worship. Like David, they praised God with great faith and joy.

 Scripture

The Early Church Gathers

"Every day they devoted themselves to meeting together in the temple area and to breaking bread in their homes. They ate their meals with exultation and sincerity of heart, praising God and enjoying favor with all the people." **Acts 2:46–47a**

Prayer and worship are ways to show **reverence** for God and respond to God's love as King David did. The Bible is filled with stories of Jesus at prayer.

Today, you can lift your mind and heart to God through prayer. You also honor God through worship, by offering words and actions of praise and adoration. The Mass is the Church's greatest act of worship. It unites the whole People of God gathered around the table of the Lord Jesus. In the Mass, the Church reads from both the Old and New Testaments, most especially the Gospels, to recall those saving events of God in the Old Testament that found their fulfillment in the mystery of Jesus, the Christ.

Share Your Faith

Reflect What other words and actions during the Mass show reverence for God?

Share Compare your thoughts with a partner.

The Work of God and His People

What is liturgy?

The Third Commandment is this: Remember to keep holy the Lord's Day. This means that faithful people have a duty to pray and to offer **worship** to God on the Lord's Day. But that duty is also a joy and a gift. Spending time with someone who loves you, someone whom you love very much, is not a chore.

Worship is a natural response to God's loving goodness. There are times and places for individual acts of prayer, but worship is centered in the community of faith.

The Church's formal practices of communal worship are known as the **liturgy**. In the liturgy, you are participating along with the whole Body of Christ in the saving work accomplished through Jesus' life, Death, Resurrection, and Ascension.

Catholic Faith Words

worship to adore and praise God, especially in the liturgy and in prayer

liturgy the public prayer of the Church. It includes the Sacraments and forms of daily prayer.

Underline what it means to say that the liturgy is a form of work.

The Catholic Church's Liturgy	
The Eucharist	the heart of the Church, from which all other Sacraments flow and the central act of her worship
The Other Sacraments	Baptism, Confirmation, Penance and Reconciliation, Anointing of the Sick, Matrimony, and Holy Orders
The Liturgy of the Hours	the Church's cycle of daily prayer; morning and evening prayer are most commonly prayed

Members of the Church participate in the Sacraments of Eucharist and the Anointing of the Sick.

The Role of the Trinity

The presence of the Trinity is at the core of the Church's liturgy.

- Prayers are offered to the Father in Jesus' name.
- Christ is the one true Priest who offers himself through the actions of the priest, the deacon, and the assembly.
- The Holy Spirit guides and sustains the Church in the way of prayer and worship.

Through the liturgy, Heaven and Earth are joined in one hymn of praise.

The work of the Father, Son, and Holy Spirit is acknowledged in many prayers at Mass. From the Sign of the Cross at the beginning of Mass until the final blessing, the entire liturgy is a celebration of the saving love of the Holy Trinity poured out to all the world. In the Glory to God, the readings, the Creed, the Eucharistic Prayer, and the Great Amen, the Holy Trinity is called upon. And over and over, the people respond: Amen!

Connect Your Faith

Explore the Church's Liturgy Explain how each of the three Divine Persons of the Holy Trinity are at the core of the Church's liturgy.

God the Father

_____

_____

Jesus Christ, the Son

_____

_____

The Holy Spirit

_____

_____

Our Catholic Life

How do you pray with your whole self?

God wants you to worship him not only with your mind, but also with your body. Some postures and gestures are used frequently in prayer and worship.

1. Circle the positions in which you feel most comfortable praying.
2. In the space provided, write when these actions are performed during the Mass.

Body Language for Prayer

Hands clasped shows:	• concentration in prayer • sincerity • _____	
Standing shows:	• your complete attention and commitment • respect at Mass for the Gospel • _____	
Sitting shows:	• willingness to rest • willingness to reflect • _____	
Kneeling shows:	• humility • the need for God • repentance • _____	
Hands raised, palms upward shows:	• openness to receiving a gift from God • praise	
Hands extended shows:	• blessing • giving of the Spirit	

People of Faith

November 22

Saint Cecilia, second or third century

Saint Cecilia lived in Rome. Because of her faith, she was killed by the Emperor. A story says that her husband, Valerian, was a martyr, too. The legend also says that Cecilia sang to God on her wedding day as well as when she was dying. Cecilia used her beautiful voice to pray to God in song. That is why she is the patron Saint of music and musicians. On her feast day, many people remember her by singing songs and playing instruments. We can be like Saint Cecilia when we use our musical talents to honor God.

Discuss: How do you praise God with music or song?

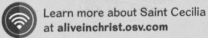 Learn more about Saint Cecilia at **aliveinchrist.osv.com**

Live Your Faith

Write a song chorus about one way you praise and honor God. If you know how to play an instrument or use a music program on a computer, set your chorus to music.

_____

_____

_____

_____

_____

_____

_____

_____

_____

_____

Let Us Pray

Prayer of Thanks and Petition

Gather and begin with the Sign of the Cross.

Leader: Loving God, every breath we take—every good thing we are, have, and do—comes from you. Speak to us in your Word.

Reader 1: A reading from the Letter to the Philippians.

Read Philippians 4:4–7.

The word of the Lord.

All: Thanks be to God.

Leader: Let us offer our thanks and praise to God.

Respond to each petition: Thank you for your blessings, Lord.

Reader 2: For creating us in your image, we pray:

Reader 3: For revealing yourself to us that we might praise you, Father, Son, and Holy Spirit, we pray:

Reader 4: For all those who love and care for us, we pray:

Leader: Lord, we now offer you our prayers of thanksgiving.

Add your individual prayers of thanks.

Leader: Let us pray.

Bow your heads as the leader prays.

All: Amen.

 Sing "Praise the Lord"
Praise, praise the Lord.
Praise, praise the Lord.
Praise the name of the Lord God most high.
© 2011, Banner Kidd. Published by Our Sunday Visitor, Inc

FAMILY+FAITH
LIVING AND LEARNING TOGETHER

YOUR CHILD LEARNED >>>

This chapter defines liturgy, examines worship as a natural response to God's loving goodness, and identifies the ways in which the Holy Trinity is at work in the Mass.

Scripture

 Read **Philippians 4:4–7** to find out what Saint Paul writes about prayer.

Catholics Believe

- Prayer and worship are ways to show love for God and to thank him for his blessings.
- When we pray and worship, God fills us with joy, strength, and hope.

To learn more, go to the *Catechism of the Catholic Church #1077–1083, 2637, 2638, 2648* at **usccb.org**.

People of Faith

This week, your child learned about Saint Cecilia, who is the patron Saint of music and musicians.

CHILDREN AT THIS AGE >>>

How They Understand Prayer Children in fifth grade might think of prayer as memorized pages they recite to God. However, their increasing ability to communicate what is on their minds makes this an ideal time to encourage them to pray to God in their own words as well. In this way, they can begin to understand prayer as conversation with a friend.

CONSIDER THIS >>>

What would you most want for your child—to be joyful, to be strong, or to be hopeful?

Most parents want all three! The good news is that our children can have all three. As Catholics, we know that when people pray and worship, God fills them with joy, strength, and hope (see *CCC 1082*). That is why helping your child become a good pray-er and choosing to celebrate Mass on Sunday in your parish community will not only give God his due, but it will also shape your child's heart with the joy, strength, and hope they will need to walk the path of life.

LET'S TALK >>>

- Ask your child to explain worship as a natural response to God's loving goodness.
- Discuss the importance of worship being centered in a community of faith.

LET'S PRAY >>>

 Dear God, help us be like Saint Cecilia and sing your praises in both the happy and sad times of our lives. Amen.

 For a multimedia glossary of Catholic Faith Words, Sunday readings, seasonal and Saint resources, and chapter activities go to **aliveinchrist.osv.com**.

Chapter 5 Review

A **Work with Words** Complete each sentence with the correct term from the Word Bank.

> ### Word Bank
> ● ● ● ● ● ● ● ● ● ● ● ● ● ● ● ● ● ● ●
>
> Holy Spirit   Third
>
> priest   public
>
> prayer

1. The _____ prayer of the Church, such as the celebration of the Seven Sacraments, is called the liturgy.

2. The _____ Commandment tells you to offer prayer and worship to God.

3. _____ can be silent or spoken, formal or spontaneous.

4. Christ is the one true

   _____ who offers himself in the liturgy.

5. The _____ guides and sustains the Church in the way of prayer.

B **Check Understanding** Fill in the circle next to the correct response.

6. Worship is praise and adoration shown to God, especially in _____.
   - ○ Church
   - ○ the open
   - ○ prayer
   - ○ song

7. Dancing, King David led the procession that brought the _____ into Jerusalem.
   - ○ army
   - ○ harvest
   - ○ ark
   - ○ Scriptures

8. The Church's greatest act of worship is _____.
   - ○ the Mass
   - ○ Baptism
   - ○ the Rosary
   - ○ Christmas

9. The Church's cycle of daily prayer is the _____.
   - ○ Mass
   - ○ Liturgy of the Hours
   - ○ Scripture
   - ○ benediction

10. The Sign of the Cross acknowledges the work of _____.
    - ○ the priest
    - ○ grace
    - ○ Jesus
    - ○ the Trinity

Go to aliveinchrist.osv.com for an interactive review.

A Life of Virtue

 Let Us Pray

Leader: God, show us the way to follow your will.

"Let us choose what is right;
let us determine among ourselves what is
good." **Job 34:4**

All: God of goodness and love, help us do good things
as you are good. Amen.

📖 Scripture

"You have been told, O mortal, what is good,
and what the LORD requires of you:
Only to do justice and to love goodness,
and to walk humbly with your God."

Micah 6:8

❓ What Do You Wonder?

- What virtues can help us "walk humbly" with God?
- How can following the Great Commandment help us "love goodness"?

The Way to Goodness

What does Jesus teach about following God's Commandments?

Knowing how to be your best self and how to do good is not always easy. Often you need to ask for advice or learn from the examples of others. In Jesus' time, a special group of people called scribes studied the Law of God and helped others understand what God wanted them to do. It was not unusual for Jesus to meet with scribes and join in their debate about points of God's Law. Scribes concerned themselves with minor as well as major matters. We learn from the following story about one particular scribe who asked Jesus a very important question.

Catholic Faith Words

Cardinal Virtues the four principal moral virtues—prudence, temperance, justice, and fortitude—that help us live as children of God and from which the other moral virtues flow. We strengthen these good habits through God's grace and our own efforts.

 Scripture

The Greatest Commandment

One of the scribes, when he came forward and heard them disputing and saw how well [Jesus] had answered them, asked him, "Which is the first of all the commandments?" Jesus replied, "The first is this: 'Hear, O Israel! The Lord our God is Lord alone! You shall love the Lord your God with all your heart, with all your soul, with all your mind, and with all your strength.' The second is this: 'You shall love your neighbor as yourself.' There is no other commandment greater than these."

The scribe said to him, "Well said, teacher. You are right in saying, 'He is One and there is no other than he.' And 'to love him with all your heart, with all your understanding, with all your strength, and to love your neighbor as yourself' is worth more than all burnt offerings and sacrifices." And when Jesus saw that [he] answered with understanding, he said to him, "You are not far from the kingdom of God." Mark 12:28–34

➤ How do you keep these two Commandments in your own life?

Worship That Pleases God

In Jesus' time, religious people thought that it was important to worship God with burnt offerings and sacrifices. But Jesus praised the scribe, who understood that a person who shows love for God and neighbor by doing good makes an even greater act of worship.

The first step is understanding that God wants you to love him and love your neighbor. The next step is putting that understanding to work in everyday life. Learning to do this is a lifelong process. You will need to practice. Just as physical exercise builds the strength of your body, so the exercise of doing good builds virtue.

The four **Cardinal Virtues** are central to becoming a good person. They provide a foundation for moral living.

1. Write a P next to each virtue you practice.
2. Write an R next to a virtue you need to work on, and ask God's help in practicing it.

The Cardinal Virtues

Prudence is knowing what is right and good and choosing it. Prudence helps you be practical and make correct decisions on what is morally good, with the help of the Holy Spirit and a well-formed conscience.

Temperance is keeping a balance in life. Temperance helps you use moderation, be disciplined, and have self-control.

Justice is giving to God and to each person their due. Justice helps you build up the community by respecting rights and promoting the common good.

Fortitude is showing courage, especially in the face of evil. Fortitude gives you strength to get through difficult times and helps you not give up when doing good.

Share Your Faith

Reflect Illustrate one way in which the people in your group or family practice a Cardinal Virtue.

Share Explain your illustration to a partner.

Living the Cardinal Virtues

How does living the Cardinal Virtues show love for God and others?

Virtues are habits that help you live according to your conscience; they strengthen your ability to know right from wrong. All of the virtues help you act for good. When you do good, you become the person God wants you to be.

Practicing virtue, or living a morally good life, is a way to praise God—but it is also a challenge. We often see ways to be and act that are not the Christian way. Consider the challenges to virtuous living that these young people face. Imagine what you would do in these situations.

With Justice for All

"See the new kid over there?" one of his school friends asked Miguel. "Well, he isn't like us—he sounds funny when he talks. Let's get the other guys and gang up on him. He deserves it." Miguel paused before responding.

➤ **What response would show that Miguel knows about the virtue of justice?**

A Prudent Choice?

Jill and Kenzie were in the mall. Kenzie wanted a new bracelet, but she didn't have the money for it. "So just take it," Jill said. "No one will see you."

"But that's stealing," Kenzie replied.

"Not really," returned Jill. "They overcharge for this stuff, anyway."

➤ **How could the virtue of prudence help Kenzie decide to do the right thing?**

It Takes Courage

"Move your arm, Phan," Ty whispered. "I can't see your answers." During recess, Ty had pressured Phan to let him cheat during the test. Phan had not wanted to refuse in front of the other fifth-grade boys who were listening. They would all call him chicken if he did not go along with Ty.

➤ **If you were Phan, what would you do to show the virtue of courage?**

Out of Balance

Marisol loved her new computer. She spent hours emailing her friends and playing games online. One day her little sister asked, "Why don't you ever play with me anymore?" Then their mother gently reminded Marisol of some unfinished projects and chores.

➤ **If you were Marisol, how could you practice temperance?**

Connect Your Faith

Write Your Own Story Think of a short problem story in which someone has an opportunity to practice one of the four Cardinal Virtues. Outline your story in the space below. Then read it aloud and pose a question to the group.

_____

_____

_____

_____

Our Catholic Life

How do you decide what is right and wrong?

Every day you make choices about how to behave. People of faith can turn to the teachings of Jesus and the Church for help in making choices between what is morally right and wrong.

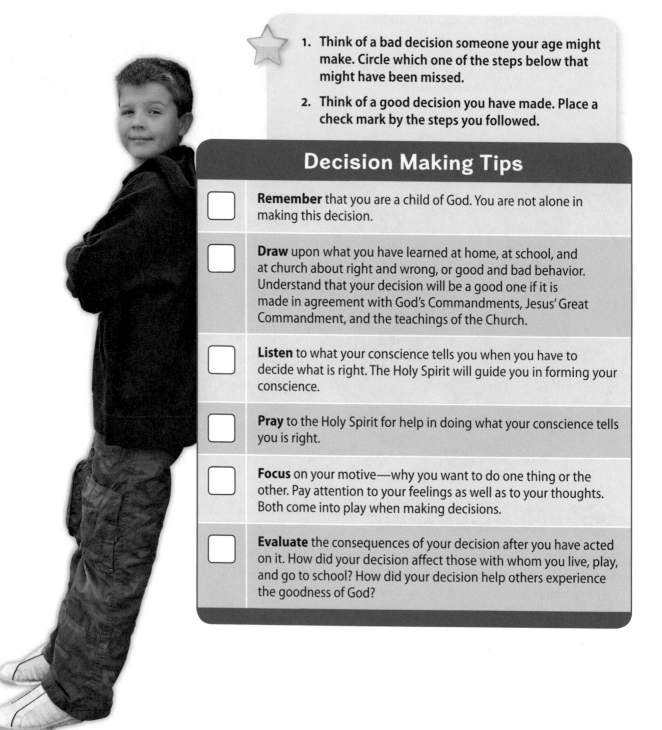

1. Think of a bad decision someone your age might make. Circle which one of the steps below that might have been missed.

2. Think of a good decision you have made. Place a check mark by the steps you followed.

Decision Making Tips

☐ **Remember** that you are a child of God. You are not alone in making this decision.

☐ **Draw** upon what you have learned at home, at school, and at church about right and wrong, or good and bad behavior. Understand that your decision will be a good one if it is made in agreement with God's Commandments, Jesus' Great Commandment, and the teachings of the Church.

☐ **Listen** to what your conscience tells you when you have to decide what is right. The Holy Spirit will guide you in forming your conscience.

☐ **Pray** to the Holy Spirit for help in doing what your conscience tells you is right.

☐ **Focus** on your motive—why you want to do one thing or the other. Pay attention to your feelings as well as to your thoughts. Both come into play when making decisions.

☐ **Evaluate** the consequences of your decision after you have acted on it. How did your decision affect those with whom you live, play, and go to school? How did your decision help others experience the goodness of God?

People of Faith

June 22

Saint Thomas More, c. 1477–1535

Sir Thomas More was a lawyer in England with an important job—Lord Chancellor. He was also a special advisor and friend to King Henry VIII. Henry wanted Thomas to say that the king was the head of the Church in England, not the Pope. Thomas couldn't do that. King Henry got so angry at Thomas that he had him beheaded. Thomas knew the meaning of fortitude. He loved God so much he was willing to do the right thing even though he would be killed. He became a Saint and a martyr because he obeyed his conscience.

Discuss: Tell about a time when you followed your conscience even though it was difficult to do.

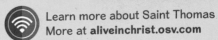

Learn more about Saint Thomas More at **aliveinchrist.osv.com**

Live Your Faith

Choose one of the Cardinal Virtues and try to practice it for a week. Fill in the chart with how you can follow your chosen virtue.

My Chosen Virtue: _____

Step	How To Follow It
Remember that you are a child of God.	_____
Draw upon what you have learned.	_____
Listen to what your conscience tells you.	_____
Pray to the Holy Spirit.	_____
Focus on your motive.	_____
Evaluate the consequences of your decision.	_____

Let Us Pray

Psalm of Praise

Gather and begin with the Sign of the Cross.

Leader: God, come to my assistance.

All: Lord, make haste to help me.

Side 1: Happy those whose way is blameless, who walk by the teaching of the Lord.

Side 2: Happy those who observe God's decrees, who seek the Lord with all their heart.

Side 1: May my ways be firm in the observance of your laws!

Side 2: Then I will not be ashamed to ponder all your commands.

All: I will praise you with a sincere heart.
Based on Psalm 119:1–2, 5–7

Reader: A reading from the Letter to the Philippians.

Read Philippians 1:3–6.

The word of the Lord.

All: Thanks be to God.

Leader: Let us pray.

Bow your heads as the leader prays.

All: Amen.

▶ Sing "May God Bless and Keep You"
May God bless and keep you.
May God's face shine on you.
May God be kind to you and give you peace.

Text: Based on Numbers 6:22–27. Text and music © 1988 Christopher Walker.
Published by OCP. All rights reserved.

FAMILY+FAITH
LIVING AND LEARNING TOGETHER

YOUR CHILD LEARNED >>>

This chapter explains the Great Commandment and Cardinal Virtues and their role in a person's decision-making process.

Scripture

 Read **Micah 6:8** to find out what the Lord requires of you.

Catholics Believe

- The Great Commandment states that you should love the Lord, your God, with all your heart, soul, and mind.
- The Cardinal Virtues —prudence, temperance, justice, and fortitude— play a central role in helping people lead morally good lives.

To learn more, go to the *Catechism of the Catholic Church* *#1805–1809, 2055* at **usccb.org**.

People of Faith

This week, your child learned about Saint Thomas More, who refused to accept King Henry VIII as the head of the Church. Because he followed his conscience, the king had him beheaded.

CHILDREN AT THIS AGE >>>

How They Understand Moral Behavior Children in fifth grade often understand moral behavior in terms of rules and norms that are agreed upon by a group. For this reason, it is important that they are identifying strongly with the Catholic community, forming friendships with other Catholic children, and cultivating an understanding of how Catholics define "doing good." The Great Commandment and the Cardinal Virtues are great starting points because they help children identify key values from which other guidelines for behavior may be derived.

CONSIDER THIS >>>

Have you ever seen the damage caused by a tree with weak roots?

In a strong wind or storm, trees with weak root systems can be blown over, roots and all. Like a tree, we need a strong root system, or foundation, to live a spiritually healthy life. The Cardinal Virtues can help us do just that. As Catholics, we understand that "compassion, responsibility, a sense of duty, self-discipline and restraint, honesty, loyalty, friendship, courage, and persistence are examples of desirable virtues for sustaining a moral life" (USCCA, p. 316).

LET'S TALK >>>

- Ask your child to explain the Great Commandment.
- Share one way your family lives the Great Commandment.

LET'S PRAY >>>

 Saint Thomas More, pray for us that we may follow our conscience and always obey God's laws. Amen.

For a multimedia glossary of Catholic Faith Words, Sunday readings, seasonal and Saint resources, and chapter activities go to **aliveinchrist.osv.com**.

Chapter 6 Review

A **Check Understanding** Fill in the circle next to the choice that best completes each sentence.

1. By doing good, you _____.
   - ○ learn to be a scribe
   - ○ become your best self
   - ○ avoid having to listen to your conscience

2. Loving your neighbor means that you _____.
   - ○ remind people to be good to you
   - ○ get people to do whatever you want
   - ○ care for others and live virtuously

3. Practicing virtue is _____.
   - ○ a way to praise God
   - ○ a sign that you can't make up your mind
   - ○ a Sacrament

4. Avoiding situations that could influence you to make wrong choices is one way you can practice the Cardinal Virtue of _____.
   - ○ temperance
   - ○ justice
   - ○ prudence

5. Virtues are acquired through _____.
   - ○ human effort and God's grace
   - ○ human effort alone
   - ○ God's grace alone

B **Make Connections** Write a brief response to each statement or question.

6. Give an example of how a student might show temperance on the playing field.

   _____

   _____

   _____

7. How have you been prudent at home or in school?

   _____

   _____

   _____

8. What is the benefit of the Cardinal Virtues?

   _____

   _____

9. How might justice be part of making a moral decision?

   _____

   _____

   _____

   _____

   _____

10. Explain the "listen" step in decision making.

   _____

   _____

Go to **aliveinchrist.osv.com** for an interactive review.

A **Work with Words** Solve the puzzle, using the clues provided.

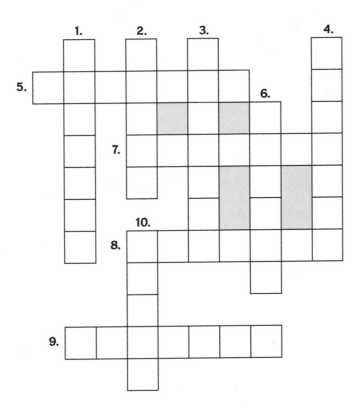

Across

5. Prayer and _____ are ways to respond to God's love as King David did.

7. We worship the Holy Trinity in the Church's _____.

8. God is called a _____ because humans never completely know and understand him.

9. The "Glory to God," or doxology, praises the _____.

Down

1. Fortitude is showing _____, especially in the face of evil.

2. King David wrote a particular prayer of praise called a _____.

3. _____ are spiritual habits of doing good that help humans grow in love of God.

4. The _____ to worship God on the Lord's Day is also a gift.

6. _____ is talking and listening to God.

10. Humans can pray by playing _____.

B Check Understanding Match each description in Column 1 with the correct term in Column 2.

Column 1

11. a box containing the tablets of the law

12. means "work of the people"

13. says that faithful people have a duty to pray and to offer worship to God on the Lord's Day

14. Divine likeness in each person

15. "Hear O Israel! The Lord our God is Lord alone! You shall love the Lord your God with all your heart, with all your soul, with all your mind, and with all your strength."

Column 2

image of God

ark of the covenant

the First Commandment

liturgy

the Third Commandment

C Make Connections Write a response to each statement.

Choose the Theological Virtue you understand most clearly, and in a few sentences explain:

16. What it means:

_____

_____

_____

17. How you practice it:

_____

_____

_____

Describe a moral decision you have made. Be sure to cover these steps:

18. Listen

_____

_____

_____

_____

_____

19. Focus

_____

_____

_____

_____

_____

20. Evaluate

_____

_____

_____

_____

_____

Jesus Christ

Our Catholic Tradition

- Jesus is the perfect image of God because he is God. In Jesus we are given the greatest sign of God's presence. (CCC, 381, 479)

- Jesus teaches about the Kingdom of God through parables and shows us the Kingdom in his miracles. (CCC, 546–547)

- We continue to know God's presence, and to experience the Paschal Mystery of Jesus, through the Seven Sacraments. (CCC, 1115)

Why do we call Jesus Divine, Redeemer, King?

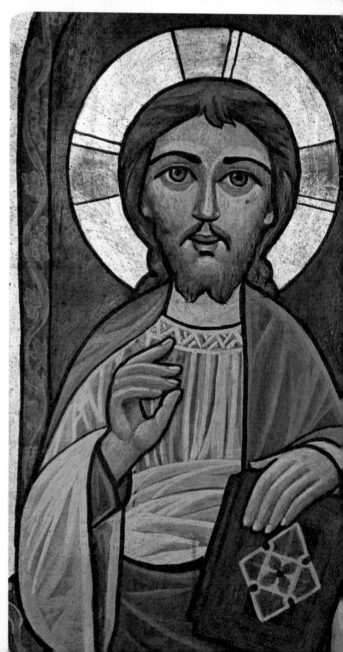

Living Image of Christ

 Let Us Pray

Leader: Creator God, teach us to mirror your amazing love.

"You formed my inmost being;
  you knit me in my mother's womb.
I praise you, because I am wonderfully made;
  wonderful are your works!" **Psalm 139:13–14**

All: Creator God, teach us to see your amazing love not only in ourselves, but in everyone we meet.

Scripture

Then God said: Let us make human beings in our image, after our likeness. Let them have dominion over the fish of the sea, the birds of the air, the tame animals, all the wild animals, and all the creatures that crawl on the earth.

God created mankind in his image;
  in the image of God he created them;
  male and female he created them. **Genesis 1:26–27**

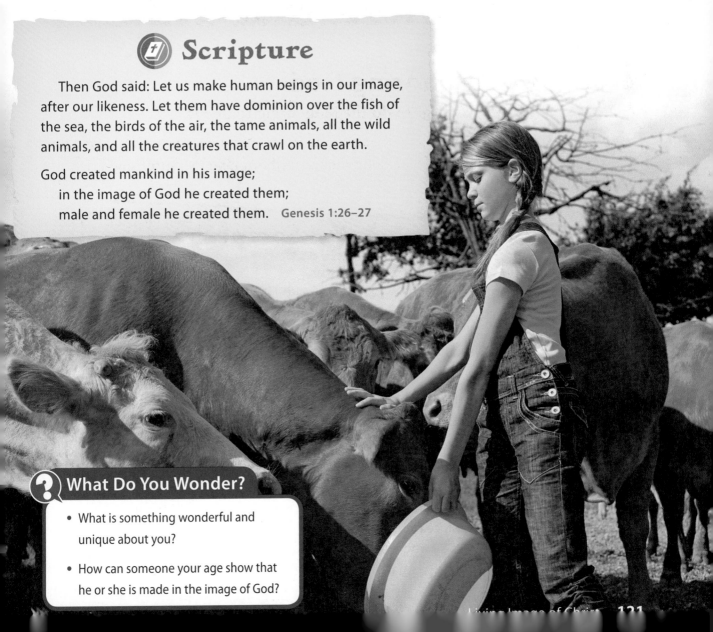

What Do You Wonder?

• What is something wonderful and unique about you?

• How can someone your age show that he or she is made in the image of God?

Honoring God

What gifts do the Magi bring to Jesus?

This is a Scripture passage about wise leaders who looked for signs of God and found a newborn king in a surprising place.

 **Scripture**

The Visit of the Magi

When Jesus was born in Bethlehem of Judea, in the days of King Herod, behold, magi from the east arrived in Jerusalem, saying, "Where is the newborn king of the Jews? We saw his star at its rising and have come to do him homage."

When King Herod heard this, he was greatly troubled, and all Jerusalem with him. Assembling all the chief priests and the scribes of the people, he inquired of them where the Messiah was to be born. They said to him, "In Bethlehem of Judea, for thus it has been written through the prophet:

'And you, Bethlehem, land of Judah,
　　are by no means least among the rulers of Judah;
since from you shall come a ruler,
　　who is to shepherd my people Israel.'"

Then Herod called the magi secretly and ascertained from them the time of the star's appearance. He sent them to Bethlehem and said, "Go and search diligently for the child. When you have found him, bring me word, that I too may go and do him homage."

After their audience with the king they set out. And behold, the star that they had seen at its rising preceded them, until it came and stopped over the place where the child was. They were overjoyed at seeing the star, and on entering the house they saw the child with Mary his mother.

They prostrated themselves and did him homage. Then they opened their treasures and offered him gifts of gold, frankincense, and myrrh. And having been warned in a dream not to return to Herod, they departed for their country by another way.   Matthew 2:1–12

Gold

Frankincense

➔ How did the magi honor Jesus? How can you honor Jesus today?

➔ There is a saying: "Wise people still seek him." When or how do you seek God?

Myrrh

Share Your Faith

Reflect Your good works are your gifts for Jesus. Think about some of the good things you have done in your life. Write some examples below.

_____

_____

_____

_____

Share with a partner two of the good things you have done.

1. _____

2. _____

In His Image and Likeness

What does it mean to reflect the image of God?

Catholic Faith Words

Incarnation the mystery that the Son of God took on human nature in order to save all people

Savior a title for Jesus, who came into the world to save all people who were lost through sin and to lead them back to God his Father

free will the God-given freedom and ability to make choices. God created us with free will so we can have the freedom to choose good.

soul the spiritual part of a human that lives forever

The Magi saw a human baby whom they thought would be the king of the Jews. But Jesus is even greater than the wise men could have known. He is both God and man, and he came to Earth not only for the Jewish people, but for all people.

The mystery of how the Son of God, the Second Divine Person of the Trinity, took on a human nature is called the **Incarnation**. The word *Incarnation* means "coming into flesh."

The Church calls the Incarnation a mystery because it can only be understood through faith. In faith, Catholics believe that Jesus is both fully Divine and fully human at the same time. Jesus is both true God and true man. Jesus is the perfect image of God because he is God. Sometimes he is called the Sacrament of God because he makes God truly present among us. To meet Jesus is to meet God.

The name Jesus means "God saves." Jesus saved all people from the power of sin and everlasting death, and so he is rightly called the **Savior** of the world.

➜ **What are some things you have learned about God through the teachings of Jesus?**

Pilgrims entering the Birth Grotto, the traditional birthplace of Jesus, in the Church of the Nativity, Bethlehem.

God's Image in You

Because he is God, Jesus reveals God fully. In his ministry, Jesus set out to love, heal, and forgive—to show that God is with his People. All people are made in the image of God because they are created by God. When people love one another, they reflect the communion of three Divine Persons in one God. When people respect and protect the life of others—including the unborn, the ill, and the elderly—they respect God's image in each person.

→ **How do people you know show they are made in God's image?**

Signs of God's Love

God created all people in his image and likeness, with the ability to love, **free will** (freedom to choose), and a **soul** that will live on after death. You are given God's very life and the grace to be a living image of Christ every day.

Every time you offer help, every time you are a good listener, every time you

forgive, every time you pray before making a decision, and every time you look for the good in others, you follow Jesus' example and are a sign of God's love. Your human dignity as a child of God becomes clearer the more you become like Jesus. The more you cooperate with God's grace and care for others, the more you reflect God's image. Jesus is the image of God. When you follow him, you are a sign of God also.

 Underline one thing you have done this week to be a sign of God's love.

Connect Your Faith

Show the Face of God Explain to a partner how the people in the photos above are living as signs of God's love.

Write one thing you do that shows you are following Jesus and living as a sign of God's love.

_____

Our Catholic Life

Who is Jesus?

When you call Jesus Savior, you affirm the Good News that Jesus came to save all people and give them eternal life. Jesus has been given many titles, and each one teaches us something about who he is. You may have heard Jesus referred to as the Lamb of God, the Good Shepherd, or the Son of Man.

Read the following Scripture passages to learn some of the titles given to Jesus. Reflect on them, and see how they expand your understanding of who Jesus is. Remember some titles from the Old Testament are applied to Jesus.

1. Write the title of Jesus on the line beside the Scripture reference.

2. Tell which qualities of Jesus are suggested in each passage.

The Many Faces of Christ

Scripture	Title	Qualities
Matthew 1:23		
Mark 1:1		
Luke 2:11		
Isaiah 9:5		

People of Faith

August 24

Blessed María Vicenta Rosal Vásquez, 1820–1886

Blessed María Vicenta grew up in Guatemala. She wanted to always show God's love to the world, so she took a new name when she became a nun. She became María de la Encarnación del Corazón de Jesús (Mary of the Incarnation of the Heart of Jesus). With her new name, she would always remind people that Jesus loves us with his whole heart. When the Guatemalan government began arresting Catholics, she moved to Costa Rica. There she built schools and homes for orphans. She even founded the first college for women in the country.

Discuss: How do you reflect the image of God in your life?

Learn more about Blessed María Vicenta at **aliveinchrist.osv.com**

Live Your Faith

Work in small groups to talk about the ways each group member will live as a sign to others of God's love in school, at home, and with friends next week.

Design a wristband to wear as a reminder of your plans.

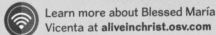

❤ Let Us Pray

Prayer of Thanksgiving

This litany prayer helps us to reflect on some of the many titles of Jesus. We are grateful for the many gifts that Jesus gives us. He shows that God is life, he restores our relationship to the Father, and he calls us to be disciples.

Gather and begin with the Sign of the Cross.

Leader: We gather to show our thanks for all that Jesus is and does.

Reader 1: Jesus, the Good Shepherd,

All: we always feel your care for us.

Reader 2: Jesus, the Light of the World,

All: we can see our way because of you. We are grateful.

Reader 3: Jesus, the Vine,

All: we are your branches, alive because we are connected to your love. Thank you.

Reader 4: Jesus, the Bread of Life,

All: we are nourished and fed to be your Body in our world. We give thanks.

Leader: What other titles and names might there be for Jesus, our brother and Savior, image and sign of God?

All: We are grateful that you are our brother and Savior, Jesus, Son of God.

 Sing "You Are God"
Jesus, you are God. There is none like you.
Jesus, you are God, and we worship you.
© 2011, Banner Kidd. Published by Our Sunday Visitor, Inc.

FAMILY+FAITH

LIVING AND LEARNING TOGETHER

YOUR CHILD LEARNED >>>

This chapter recognizes Jesus as the fullness of God's Revelation and explores ways in which humans reflect the image of God.

Scripture

 Read **Genesis 1:26–27** to find out about God creating people in his image.

Catholics Believe

- The Incarnation is the mystery that the Son of God became man in order to save all people.

- God created all people in his image and likeness, with the ability to love, free will (freedom to choose), and a soul that will live on after death.

To learn more, go to the *Catechism of the Catholic Church #461–464, 470, 483* at **usccb.org**.

People of Faith

This week, your child learned about Blessed María Vicenta Rosal Vásquez, the first person from Guatemala to be beatified. As a nun, her name was María de la Encarnación del Corazón de Jesús (Mary of the Incarnation of the Heart of Jesus).

CHILDREN AT THIS AGE >>>

How They Understand Jesus and Themselves as Images of God As they begin to grow to look more like young men and women and less like small children, fifth-graders have likely heard people comment on how much they look like their mother or father, or perhaps someone else in the family. While it's still an abstract concept for them, fifth-graders are ready to be challenged to think more figuratively about how they are also made in the image of God. Jesus serves as a perfect model of God's image in human form, because he is God himself.

CONSIDER THIS >>>

Do you ever wonder why God chose to become human?

Unlike those in other religious traditions, Christians believe that God knew that human beings needed to experience the fullness of his love in order that we might believe in him. God's love for us is made visible in Jesus—God fully human in the Incarnation. As Catholics, we remember that "God so loved the world that he gave his only Son, so that everyone who believes in him might not perish but might have eternal life" **(John 3:16)**.

LET'S TALK >>>

- Ask your child to explain how Jesus is both human and Divine.

- Share how family members reflect the image of God.

LET'S PRAY >>>

 Blessed María, pray for us that we may be an image of Jesus to the whole world in all we do and say. Amen.

 For a multimedia glossary of Catholic Faith Words, Sunday readings, seasonal and Saint resources, and chapter activities go to **aliveinchrist.osv.com**.

Chapter 7 Review

A **Work with Words** Match each description in Column 1 with the correct term in Column 2.

Column 1	Column 2
1. A title for Jesus, who came into the world to save all people who were lost through sin, and to lead them back to God his Father.	Incarnation
2. This is the mystery by which the second Divine Person of the Holy Trinity took on human nature.	Magi
3. This means God, like God, or of God.	free will
4. Their story indicates that Jesus' message of salvation is for all people.	Divine
5. The God-given freedom and ability to make choices.	Savior

B **Make Connections** Write a brief response to each question or statement.

6. Explain the meaning of the gifts that the Magi brought.

_____

_____

7. Why is Jesus the "perfect image of God"?

_____

_____

8. What is the connection between the Holy Trinity and Jesus' command to love?

_____

_____

9. How do you become a sign of God's love to the world?

_____

10. Name the title of Jesus that is most meaningful to you, and explain why.

_____

_____

Go to aliveinchrist.osv.com for an interactive review.

Proclaim the Kingdom

 ## Let Us Pray

Leader: God of justice, love, and peace, may your
Kingdom come.

"Your kingdom, O Lord, is a kingdom for all ages;
your reign is for every generation."
Based on Psalm 145:13

All: God of signs and wonders, may your Kingdom come.
Amen.

 ## Scripture

[Jesus] went around all of Galilee, teaching in their synagogues,
proclaiming the gospel of the kingdom, and curing every disease and
illness among the people.   Matthew 4:23

What Do You Wonder?

- What signs of the presence of God's Kingdom
did you hear in today's Scripture?

- What prayer do you know that asks for the
coming of God's Kingdom?

The Power of Stories

How did Jesus teach about the Kingdom of God?

When Jesus told his followers stories of the **Kingdom of God**, wonderful things happened. As they listened to Jesus, people understood better what they had to do to enter God's Kingdom. Many decided to change the way they lived. Then, as they shared Jesus' stories with others, their faith became stronger.

Jesus was a great teacher. He understood that people remember ideas better when they are expressed in an interesting way. That's why Jesus used stories to spread his message and to invite people into God's Reign of justice, love, and peace.

➔ How can retelling Jesus' stories help your faith grow stronger?

Catholic Faith Words

Kingdom of God God's rule of peace, justice, and love that exists in Heaven, but has not yet come in its fullness on Earth

Parables as Examples

Jesus told many stories that are known as parables. A **parable** is a story that makes a comparison by using examples from everyday life to bring to light something that is hidden. Here is one example that Jesus used to show what it means to be open to the Word of God so that you can enter his Kingdom.

Scripture

The Parable of the Sower

A sower went out to sow. As he sowed, some seed fell on the path, and birds came and ate it. Some seed fell on rocky ground, where it had little soil. It sprang up at once because the soil was not deep; but when the sun rose, the seed was scorched, and it withered for lack of roots. Some seed fell among thorns, and the thorns grew up and choked it. But other seed fell on rich soil, and produced fruit, as much as a hundredfold. Whoever has ears ought to hear. **Based on Luke 8:5–8**

➤ In this parable, who is the sower?

➤ What do the seeds represent?

Share Your Faith

Reflect Read about other images for the Kingdom of God in Matthew 13:44–50. Sketch the image you like best.

Share Discuss with a partner why you like the image you chose.

Signs and Wonders

How do we cooperate with God's grace?

Jesus proclaimed the Kingdom of God in many ways. He preached the Good News. He told stories and parables about the Kingdom. He also performed signs and wonders, or **miracles**, as ways of showing that God's Kingdom was being established. These miracles included casting out demons and curing people who were sick.

Jesus himself was a proclamation of the Kingdom. He welcomed and ate with sinners, showing that forgiveness is part of the Kingdom. He paid attention to children, women, lepers, those from other lands, and others who were often ignored. He showed that everyone is invited into God's Kingdom, which will come in fullness at the end of time when Christ returns in glory.

Jesus announced that the Kingdom of God in this world began in him. Jesus established the seeds of God's Kingdom on Earth, and invites us all to become parts of the Kingdom by following him. However, not everyone lives in the way that God intends. Whenever you cooperate with God's grace by loving, acting justly, or making peace, you cooperate with God as he builds his Kingdom.

Underline some of the ways that Jesus proclaimed the Kingdom of God.

The Grace to Change

Jesus Christ is still present in the world today. The Church and her Sacraments keep the words and actions of Jesus present in our lives. The Sacraments give us grace and can change the way in which we relate to God and others.

You can be changed as you gather with the Church community to hear the Word of God and experience the power of the Holy Spirit through the words and actions of the Sacraments. The Scripture readings you hear and the prayers you pray invite you to become a part of God's Kingdom.

You can be changed at Eucharist when, by the power of the Holy Spirit and through the actions of the priest, you are offered the Body and Blood of Christ and a grow closer to him as you receive Holy Communion. When the priest says at the end of Mass, "Go in peace, glorifying the Lord by your life," he is sending you in the name of Jesus to be a sign of Jesus to the world.

When you have sinned, God calls you to experience **conversion**. With his help, you can change your heart and place your sin before him. In the Sacrament of Reconciliation, you receive God's grace and forgiveness through the ministry of the Church. You are renewed and strengthened to live a moral life that draws you closer to God and into service for his Kingdom.

Catholic Faith Words

miracle an event that cannot be explained by science because it happened by the power of God

conversion the continual process of becoming the people God intends us to be through change and growth. It is a response to God's love and forgiveness.

Connect Your Faith

Keep an Open Heart
Inside the heart, write a few words that tell which story of Jesus has helped you understand his message most clearly.

Our Catholic Life

How can you understand parables?

To understand the message of the parables Jesus told, you need to consider how parables work. Below are some points to look for.

A parable answers a question. A parable may give an answer to a question, such as "Who is my neighbor?" or "How often must I forgive?" The answer to the question is what the parable is intended to teach.

1. Review your favorite parable in the Bible.
2. Answer the questions in the spaces provided.

My Chosen Parable:

_____

- **What question does your chosen parable answer?**

_____

- A parable **compares two things**. Jesus' parables often begin with the words "The kingdom of heaven is like . . ." Parables like this compare two things. **What does your favorite parable compare?**

_____

- A parable **uses examples from everyday life**. The places and people in a parable were familiar to the people listening to Jesus. For example, many parables are about people who work in fields or on farms. Many people in Jesus' time did such work, and those references are understood by people today, too. **What examples from everyday life can you see in your parable?**

_____

- A parable reveals a hidden truth. Often, a parable has a surprise ending. It reveals a hidden truth. This is the surprise. **What does the parable you selected reveal?**

_____

- A parable **prompts a decision** or action. A parable challenges its listeners to decide or act. "What will you do now?" is the question the parable leaves you to answer. The question is understood rather than stated. **What action or decision is your parable asking you to make?**

_____

People of Faith

April 29

Saint Catherine of Siena, 1347–1380

Saint Catherine of Siena was one of twenty-five children. From the time she was very young, she wanted to serve God by helping to take care of her brothers and sisters. She was so wise about spiritual matters that she became an adviser to many people, including two Popes. Throughout her life, Saint Catherine found strength to face hard things through Holy Communion. She said that each time we receive the Eucharist, it helps to make our faith in Jesus' love grow stronger and allows us to help build God's Kingdom as we love our family and friends more.

Discuss: How can receiving Holy Communion help you love your family and friends?

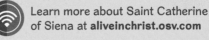

Learn more about Saint Catherine of Siena at **aliveinchrist.osv.com**

Live Your Faith

Describe what is happening in the picture. How does the rich soil fortify a growing plant?

_____

_____

_____

_____

_____

Write the name of someone you know who has grown from rich soil. Then tell how this person has been a model of faith for you.

_____

_____

_____

_____

_____

_____

Let Us Pray

Prayer of Intercession

This prayer of intercession is in the form of the Prayer of the Faithful, the prayer we pray in the liturgy, knowing we are dependent upon God for our needs.

Gather and begin with the Sign of the Cross.

Leader: We gather as creatures of our Loving God, dependent upon God for our needs, knowing that God always hears us.

Reader 1: For our Church, that we may share the love, peace, and justice that are signs of God's Kingdom. Let us pray to the Lord.

All: Lord, hear our prayer.

Reader 2: For leaders in our world, that the peace, love, and justice of God's Kingdom be in their decisions. Let us pray to the Lord.

All: Lord, hear our prayer.

Reader 3: For those in need, especially the poor, that they may be signs to us of the Kingdom of God. Let us pray to the Lord.

All: Lord, hear our prayer.

Reader 4: For our parish and our neighborhood, that the compassion of God's Kingdom grows each day. Let us pray to the Lord.

All: Lord, hear our prayer.

Leader: For what else shall we pray?

All: Lord, hear our prayer.

Leader: God, we know you are with us as we continue Jesus' work, helping others to see the love, peace, and justice that are signs of your Kingdom.

All: Amen.

 Sing "I Will Sing"

FAMILY+FAITH
LIVING AND LEARNING TOGETHER

YOUR CHILD LEARNED >>>

This chapter identifies the Kingdom of God as present now and yet to come and describes Jesus' proclamation in his teaching, signs, and wonders.

Scripture

 Read **Matthew 4:23** to find out about Jesus proclaiming the Kingdom of God.

Catholics Believe

• God's Kingdom is present and grows in the Church and her Sacraments until God's Reign comes in fullness at the end of time.

• Jesus proclaimed the Kingdom of God through his actions and parables.

To learn more, go to the *Catechism of the Catholic Church* *#546–547, 567, 763–769* at **usccb.org**.

People of Faith

This week, your child learned about Saint Catherine of Siena, a spiritual counselor to two Popes.

CHILDREN AT THIS AGE >>>

How They Understand the Kingdom of God The Kingdom of God is an abstract concept that may be difficult for fifth-graders, who are just beginning to have the capacity to think more figuratively. This is particularly true of the paradoxes we traditionally hold by faith about the Kingdom—that the Kingdom is now and is also yet to be, that it is on Earth and also in Heaven. The parables of the Kingdom are useful for children this age in that they can continue to draw new meanings from these stories over time as they are ready.

CONSIDER THIS >>>

Did your parents ever say to you, "Do as I say, not as I do"?

For Jesus, there was no difference between what he said and what he did. His words and actions were one, and both made God's Kingdom present. As Catholics, we understand that "the proclamation of the Kingdom of God was fundamental to Jesus' preaching. The Kingdom of God is his presence among human beings calling them to a new way of life as individuals and as a community. It is the Good News that results in love, justice, and mercy for the whole world. The Kingdom is realized partially on earth and permanently in heaven" (*USCCA, p. 79*).

LET'S TALK >>>

• Ask your child to explain how Jesus made God's Kingdom present.

• Read together a favorite parable about the Kingdom of God.

LET'S PRAY >>>

 Saint Catherine, may we find our strength in Jesus like you did. Amen.

 For a multimedia glossary of Catholic Faith Words, Sunday readings, seasonal and Saint resources, and chapter activities go to **aliveinchrist.osv.com**.

Chapter 8 Review

A **Work with Words** Complete each sentence with the correct term from the Word Bank.

> ### Word Bank
>
> conversion   miracles
>
> Kingdom of   parables
> God
>
>   proclamation

1. Jesus worked

   _____ to

   help us see the presence of the Kingdom of God.

2. _____ are stories that make comparisons in order to teach something.

3. _____ is the continual process of change and growth and becoming the people God intends us to be.

4. Jesus himself was a

   _____ of the Kingdom.

5. The _____ is God's reign of justice, love, and peace.

B **Check Understanding** Fill in the circle next to the correct response.

6. Events that have no scientific explanation because they happened by God's power are called _____.
   - ○ parables
   - ○ miracles
   - ○ Sacraments

7. Through his stories and actions, Jesus invited people into the _____.
   - ○ Temple
   - ○ Kingdom of God
   - ○ desert

8. The _____ of the Church pass on the words and actions of Jesus and point to the Kingdom of God.
   - ○ prophets
   - ○ Sacraments
   - ○ rulers

9. Telling a story is one way to _____.
   - ○ love God
   - ○ make friends
   - ○ teach

10. Jesus did all of these to tell about the Reign of God except _____.
    - ○ tell parables
    - ○ work miracles
    - ○ fast

Go to **aliveinchrist.osv.com** for an interactive review.

Celebrating the Paschal Mystery

 Let Us Pray

Leader: God of life, you who break the bonds of death, lead us to life in you.

"You will show me the path to life,
abounding joy in your presence,
the delights at your right hand forever." **Psalm 16:11**

All: Lead us, O God, from death into life. Amen.

📖 Scripture

I heard a loud voice from the throne saying, "Behold, God's dwelling is with the human race. He will dwell with them and they will be his people and God himself will always be with them [as their God]. He will wipe every tear from their eyes, and there shall be no more death or mourning, wailing or pain, [for] the old order has passed away."

The one who sat on the throne said, "Behold, I make all things new." Then he said, "Write these words down, for they are trustworthy and true." He said to me, "They are accomplished. I [am] the Alpha and the Omega, the beginning and the end."
Revelation 21:3–6

❓ What Do You Wonder?

- How can all things be made new?
- What is the Paschal Mystery?

141

A Witness to God's Love

How did Mother Teresa witness to Jesus' love for all?

In the slums of Calcutta, India, a small figure dressed in white ministered to the needs of the poor and sick. She was a teacher, a nurse, and a champion of the powerless. She was Mother Teresa, and her influence has spread throughout the world.

Blessed Mother Teresa

Blessed Mother Teresa was born to Albanian parents in what is now Macedonia in 1910. When she was eighteen, she followed her vocation to Ireland, where she joined the Sisters of Loreto. After training, she went to the sisters' mission in Calcutta.

While teaching high school there, she saw poor people suffering all around her. In 1946, Mother Teresa experienced her "call within a call." She knew God wanted her to begin a missionary order that served the poor.

In December 1948, after months of prayer and preparation, Mother Teresa began her new work. She dressed simply, in a white sari with blue trim. She spent long days in Calcutta's slums, caring for those dying in the streets. Then she recruited others to help her feed the hungry, tend the sick, and teach children.

Mother Teresa began her work with nothing, counting on God's providence. In her first school, she taught by writing in the dirt. As word of her work spread, volunteers joined her. People gave her money, food, clothing, supplies, and buildings.

Mother Teresa founded the Missionaries of Charity in Calcutta. This order now assists poor people all over the world.

Mother Teresa holds a baby during a Right to Life convention in Washington, D.C. in 1985.

The Mission Expands

Mother Teresa and her workers set up health clinics for the sick and open-air schools for children. They worked with blind people, elderly people, and disabled people. They established a leper colony and a hospice. All of these organizations showed the dignity God has given to each person. They also reflected the joy of a love-filled life.

Mother Teresa with mothers and children at her mission in Calcutta, India.

Mother Teresa traveled to many places of extreme suffering, pain, and death, all effects of **Original Sin**. In Ethiopia, she helped famine victims. In Armenia, she assisted earthquake victims. She was called to help radiation victims near Chernobyl and war victims in Beirut.

Mother Teresa was beatified in 2003 by Pope Saint John Paul II. She also received many honors, including the John XXIII Peace Prize in 1971 and the Nobel Peace Prize in 1979. She accepted these awards "for the glory of God and in the name of the poor."

At the time of her death in 1998, Mother Teresa's order had over 4,500 sisters and brothers working in more than 100 countries. The little woman in the white sari had shared her "call within a call," and thousands of people had answered.

Catholic Faith Words

Original Sin the sin of our first parents, Adam and Eve, which led to the sinful condition of the human race from its beginning

Share Your Faith

Reflect Think about the way that Mother Teresa inspired others to share her mission. Write how you think the story of Mother Teresa reflects Jesus' teachings.

_____

_____

_____

_____

Share With a partner, talk about the qualities Mother Teresa must have had to be so faithful.

Work of Redemption

What is the Paschal Mystery, and how is it celebrated?

Because of Original Sin, life on Earth includes suffering and death. The good news is that Jesus broke the power of evil through his **sacrifice**—choosing to suffer and die on the Cross. He is the Redeemer of the human race, bringing it back from the slavery of sin and everlasting death. The Gospel according to Luke tells us that the Resurrection was first discovered and announced by several women who were followers of Jesus.

Catholic Faith Words

sacrifice giving up something out of love for someone else or for the common good (the good of everyone). Jesus sacrificed his life for all people.

Paschal Mystery Christ's work of redemption through his suffering, Death, Resurrection, and Ascension

liturgical year the feasts and seasons of the Church calendar that celebrate the Paschal Mystery of Christ

 Scripture

The Resurrection of Jesus

They [the angels] said to [the women], "Why do you seek the living one among the dead? He is not here, but he has been raised. Remember what he said to you while he was still in Galilee, that the Son of Man must be handed over to sinners and be crucified, and rise on the third day." And they remembered his words. Then they returned from the tomb and announced all these things to the eleven and to all the others.   Luke 24:5b–9

The Three Maries at the Tomb, by Fra Angelico.

The Resurrection, Jesus being raised from death to new life by God the Father through the power of the Holy Spirit, is the cornerstone of the Paschal Mystery. The **Paschal Mystery** refers to the suffering, Death, Resurrection, and Ascension of Jesus. Because of it, Christians live in hope.

You participate in the Paschal Mystery throughout the **liturgical year**. You are united to this mystery through the grace of the Holy Spirit that you first received in the Sacrament of Baptism and that you celebrate in the Sacrament of Eucharist.

Participating in the Paschal Mystery

	Baptism	You die with Christ in the waters of Baptism, and then you are raised to the new life of grace.
	Confirmation	You die to selfishness and live in compassion as the Holy Spirit moves you to acts of charity and service.
	Eucharist	This sacrificial meal is the greatest celebration of the Paschal Mystery. You enter into Jesus' saving Death and Resurrection. You are raised and sent forth to serve God as Jesus did.
	Holy Orders	You die to selfishness in your own will and needs and are raised to a new life of ordained ministry to God's people.
	Matrimony	You die to yourself and rise to new life in a family as you become one with another.
	Penance and Reconciliation	You die to sin and are raised to new life in forgiveness and community.
	Anointing of the Sick	You become one with Jesus' suffering and Death and rise to renewed health or pass over to eternal life.

The Celebration of the Mystery

Death is not the end but the beginning of life forever with God. Every Sunday is a day of joy as the Church remembers the Resurrection of Jesus. Because of the Resurrection, we believe that Jesus will one day return in glory.

Each of the Seven Sacraments celebrates, in some way, the Paschal Mystery of Jesus' dying and rising to new life. Each offers a new way of looking at the mystery of your life. Jesus, who died and was raised, is at work in and through the Sacraments.

Connect Your Faith

Role-Play the Resurrection Story
With your group, act out the story of the discovery of Jesus' Resurrection as recorded in Luke 24:1–12. When you have finished, imagine that you are one of the first disciples and write a message to a friend, telling what you have seen and what it means.

Our Catholic Life

What images remind you of Jesus' Death and Resurrection?

The Paschal Mystery is central to the Catholic faith. The Church uses art and design to illustrate this truth of the mystery of Jesus's dying and rising to new life, and to help us understand it.

Complete the descriptions of the symbols with words from the Word List.

Symbols of Victory

Cross and Shroud	In the empty tomb, the disciples found only a burial cloth. A white cloth hanging over the Cross is a symbol of Christ's Death and Resurrection.
Baptismal Font	The vessel of _____ for Baptism is a symbol of the Paschal Mystery. Through Baptism, you share in the Paschal Mystery and receive new _____. (See Romans 6:4.)
Risen Christ on the Cross	A crucifix displays the risen Savior. His _____ extend to embrace the world he has redeemed.
Victorious Lamb	Christ is compared to the Passover lamb, whose blood saved the people. A victory pennant, held high by the _____, symbolizes the Resurrection.
Paschal Candle	This large candle is a symbol of _____ and the new life of the Resurrection. The five grains of incense in the candle recall his _____ wounds.

Word List
. . . .

arms

life

Christ

water

lamb

five

People of Faith

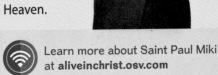

Saint Paul Miki, c. 1564–1597

February 6

Saint Paul Miki came from a wealthy Japanese family. He wanted to become a priest. While he was studying to be ordained, he convinced many people to become Christian. The ruler of Japan was afraid that Christians would take over, so he had Paul and twenty-five others tied to crosses and then stabbed. Through his suffering, Saint Paul shared in the Paschal Mystery of Christ. As he hung on the cross, he talked about Jesus. He wasn't afraid to die, because he knew that death was not the end, but the beginning of life forever with God in Heaven.

Discuss: How does offering up something you don't like to do help you share in the Paschal Mystery?

Learn more about Saint Paul Miki at **aliveinchrist.osv.com**

Live Your Faith

Create a banner that explains one way you show your belief in the Resurrection, the cornerstone of the Paschal Mystery.

Let Us Pray

Prayer of Praise

Gather and begin with the Sign of the Cross.

Leader: Jesus, you are risen from the dead and call us to walk in newness of life. We trust in you. We shall not fear.

Reader 1: We shall not fear the lightning or thunder, the roar of the sea, or the trembling of the Earth.

All: Alleluia.

Reader 2: We shall not fear the dark of night, the emptiness of silence, or the times of being alone.

All: Alleluia.

Reader 3: We shall not fear the jeers of our enemies or the smallness and meanness of those who wish us harm.

All: Alleluia.

Leader: Yes, Lord, by embracing death for our sake, you have shown us that death cannot overcome the power of life. By your glorious Resurrection, you have conquered sin and death, and you give us the courage to sing:

 Sing "Alle, Alle, Alleluia"
Alle, alle, alleluia,
alle, alle, alleluia.
Alle, alle, alleluia.
Alle, alle, alle, alleluia.
© 1996, Fr. Richard Ho Lung, M.O.P., and Missionaries of the Poor.

FAMILY+FAITH
LIVING AND LEARNING TOGETHER

YOUR CHILD LEARNED >>>

This chapter describes the Paschal Mystery and explains how each of the Seven Sacraments celebrates Christ's work of redemption and new life.

Scripture

 Read **Revelation 21:3–6** to find out about the hope of eternal life.

Catholics Believe

- Through his sacrifice, Jesus Christ is the Redeemer of the human race.
- Through the Sacraments, Christ unites his followers to his Paschal Mystery—Passion, Death, Resurrection, and Ascension.

To learn more, go to the *Catechism of the Catholic Church #515, 571, 618, 628, 654, 655, 1010, 1067, 1076* at **usccb.org**.

People of Faith

This week, your child learned about Saint Paul Miki, a sixteenth-century Japanese convert and martyr who was crucified for his faith.

CHILDREN AT THIS AGE >>>

How They Understand New Life As Catholics, we are intimately connected with the Paschal Mystery. Baptized into Jesus' Death and reborn as sons and daughters of God, we are often able to see our own lives as a series of endings and new beginnings. Children in fifth grade will be less able to make this abstract connection between the Paschal Mystery and their own lives, partly due to their limited life experience and partly due to their concrete style of thinking. However, spending some time in reflection on this mystery helps to lay the foundations for finding greater meaning in the endings and beginnings of life.

CONSIDER THIS >>>

Have you ever looked into a newborn child's eyes and wondered at the possibilities?

It is the wonder of possibility that makes everyone want to gaze at the face of an infant. Yet, nothing in our life offers more possibility of new life than Jesus' suffering, Death, and Resurrection. We call this the Paschal Mystery. Death is not the end but the beginning of life forever with God. As Catholics, we know that "above all it is in the Paschal Mystery… that we participate most profoundly in the mystery of Christ…. In Christ we die to self and sin. We rise to participate in his divine life through the Resurrection" (*USCCA*, p. 80).

LET'S TALK >>>

- Ask your child to explain how Blessed Mother Teresa joined her life to Christ's in the Paschal Mystery.
- Read together Luke's account of the Resurrection, in Luke 24:1–12.

LET'S PRAY >>>

 Saint Paul Miki, pray for us that we may always be willing to talk about Jesus and to forgive those who hurt us. Amen.

For a multimedia glossary of Catholic Faith Words, Sunday readings, seasonal and Saint resources, and chapter activities go to **aliveinchrist.osv.com**.

Chapter 9 Review

Ⓐ Work with Words Match each description in Column 1 with the correct term in Column 2.

Column 1	Column 2
1. founded the Missionaries of Charity in Calcutta, India	Matrimony
2. asked the women at the tomb why they were seeking Jesus among the dead	Paschal Mystery
3. refers to the suffering, Death, Resurrection, and Ascension of Jesus	Blessed Mother Teresa
4. rising to new life in a family as you become one with another	Eucharist
5. the greatest celebration of the Paschal Mystery	Angels

Ⓑ Check Understanding Cross out any incorrect answers you find in the items below.

6. Christ communicates the saving effects of his Paschal Mystery through the Seven Sacraments, such as (**Baptism, Confirmation, Thanksgiving, Reconciliation**).

7. (**Baptismal fonts, bread and wine, the Cross and shroud, Paschal candles**) are images of the Paschal Mystery.

8. All people need Christ the Redeemer to free them from (**bondage to sin, the reign of death, mistakes they have made**).

9. Jesus' suffering and Death on the Cross means that you can (**avoid all suffering in this life, live forever with God, share in the Paschal Mystery**).

10. Jesus' Resurrection is (**remembered at Mass every Sunday, less important than other truths of the Catholic faith, a part of the Paschal Mystery**).

Go to **aliveinchrist.osv.com** for an interactive review.

Unit Review

A **Work with Words** Match each description in Column 1 with the correct term in Column 2.

Column 1

1. Christ's work of redemption through his suffering, Death, Resurrection, and Ascension

2. By this you die to selfishness and live in compassion as the Holy Spirit moves you to acts of charity and service

3. Stories that make comparisons in order to teach a lesson

4. The mystery that the Son of God took on a human nature in order to save all people

5. God's Reign of justice, love, and peace

Column 2

Kingdom of God

parables

Incarnation

Paschal Mystery

Confirmation

B **Check Understanding** Complete the statement or answer the question with the correct word or phrase.

6. "The Divine" is another way of saying

_____.

7. Miracles help you see the presence of

_____.

8. When you have _____, God calls you to conversion.

9. What was the purpose of the Magi's gift of myrrh?

_____

10. Who received the first news of the Resurrection?

_____

Complete each sentence with the correct term from the Word Bank.

11. You can be _____ as you gather with the Church community to hear the Word of God and experience the power of the Holy Spirit through the words and actions of the Sacraments.

12. The Church calls the Incarnation a mystery because it can be understood only through _____.

13. Your human _____ as a child of God becomes clearer the more you become like Jesus.

14. Saint Paul Miki was a _____.

15. Every _____ is a day of joy as the Church remembers the Resurrection.

Word Bank

Sunday

dignity

martyr

changed

faith

C **Make Connections** Write a response to each statement.

16-18. Explain why Jesus himself was a proclamation of God's Kingdom, using the following terms:

forgiveness   signs and wonders   preached

_____

_____

_____

_____

_____

_____

_____

_____

19. Choose one of the following images of the Paschal Mystery, and explain what it means:

Cross and shroud   **Paschal Candle**   **victorious lamb**

_____

_____

_____

_____

_____

_____

_____

20. Explain why the story of the sower is a parable.

_____

_____

_____

_____

_____

_____

_____

_____

_____

The Church

Our Catholic Tradition

- The Church is one, holy, catholic and apostolic. (CCC, 811)

- As members of the Church, we are called to show God to others. Together, we continue Christ's mission in the world. (CCC, 871)

- We are united by our belief in Christ, one Baptism, and the Holy Spirit. (CCC, 866)

- With the guidance of the Holy Spirit, the Pope and bishops continue the Apostles' mission to lead, teach, and make holy, proclaiming the Good News to all. (CCC, 857)

How does the Holy Spirit, acting through the teaching office of the Church, help you grow in holiness?

The Church's Message

 Let Us Pray

Leader: Make us one in your love, O God.

"How good and how pleasant it is,
    when people live together in unity!"
Based on Psalm 133:1

All: God of all, make us one for all; fill us with your Spirit;
unite us in your Son. Amen.

 Scripture

...Live in a manner worthy of the call you have received, with all
humility and gentleness, with patience, bearing with one another
through love, striving to preserve the unity of the spirit through the
bond of peace: one body and one Spirit, as you were also called to the
one hope of your call; one Lord, one faith, one baptism; one God and
Father of all, who is over all and through all and in all. **Ephesians 4:1–6**

? What Do You Wonder?

- What sort of sign would we be to
  others if we lived as Saint Paul asked
  in his letter to the Ephesians?

- How can we as a Church be a sign of
  unity to the world?

A Time of Renewal

Why was the Second Vatican Council important?

The years from 1962 to 1965 were years of a renewal in the Catholic Church. Pope Saint John XXIII gathered the bishops in Rome to discuss the meaning of the Church and its role in modern society. Here is how the opening of the council might have been reported in a school newspaper of that time.

Underline one of the goals of the Council and talk with a partner about why it was important.

Pope John XXIII Opens Vatican Council

Today in Rome, Pope John XXIII opened the Second Vatican Council, a meeting of bishops from Africa, Asia, Europe, Australia, and the Americas. Such a gathering has not occurred since 1870.

Goals of the Council

The goals of the council are to renew the Church's liturgy; to help the Church respond to the problems of today's world, especially the need for peace and justice; to promote unity among all believers; and to find new ways to spread the Gospel. Pope John surprised everyone by asking for this meeting, which will go on for many months. The work of this council is sure to influence the Church in many ways.

Bishops and observers at the closing ceremony of the Second Vatican Council in St. Peter's Basilica in Rome in 1965. Pope John XXIII (inset) welcomed participants almost three years before.

Observers at the Council

Some people who are not bishops will come to the council as observers. Those people will share ideas and help the bishops make decisions. The observers represent Orthodox churches, Protestant denominations, and various other groups. Some women have also been invited to participate.

The Wider World

The Second Vatican Council will be reported worldwide by television, radio, and newspapers. The council's opening address, "Message to Humanity," begins with these words: "We take great pleasure in sending to all [people] and nations a message concerning the well being, love, and peace which were brought into the world by Christ Jesus ... and entrusted to the Church." The Church is confident that she has a message of Good News to share. The world is watching.

United States Cardinals Meyer, Cushing, Spellman, McIntyre, and Ritter attend the Second Vatican Council in 1962.

Share Your Faith

Reflect Imagine that you are a news reporter assigned to cover a new council. Write three questions that you think are important.

_____

_____

_____

Share Work in a small group to decide which questions you would ask the Pope, bishops, and observers.

Essential Characteristics

In what ways do you help fulfill the Church's mission?

Catholic Faith Words

Marks of the Church the essential characteristics that distinguish Christ's Church and her mission: one, holy, catholic, and apostolic

Body of Christ a name for the Church of which Christ is the head. All the baptized are members of the body.

The Second Vatican Council was a sign to the world of the Church's mission to point people toward God's Kingdom. The Church is one, holy, catholic, and apostolic. These are the **Marks of the Church** by which all can see the Kingdom at work in the Church. You, too, are a sign of God's Kingdom when you help those in need, forgive those who have hurt you, and welcome new Church members. Together, we live the faith and witness to God's Reign when we put God first through prayer and participation in the Sacraments, and when we reflect Jesus' self-giving love.

The Church is an assembly, a gathering of the People of God. This Church is also called the **Body of Christ** because, through her, Christ is present in the world. The Church is like a building in which the Holy Spirit lives. People are like the stones of the walls and floor. Jesus is the cornerstone that holds the building together.

Scripture

God's House and People

Come to [Jesus], a living stone, rejected by human beings but chosen and precious in the sight of God, and, like living stones, let yourselves be built into a spiritual house to be a holy priesthood to offer spiritual sacrifices acceptable to God through Jesus Christ.

1 Peter 2:4–5

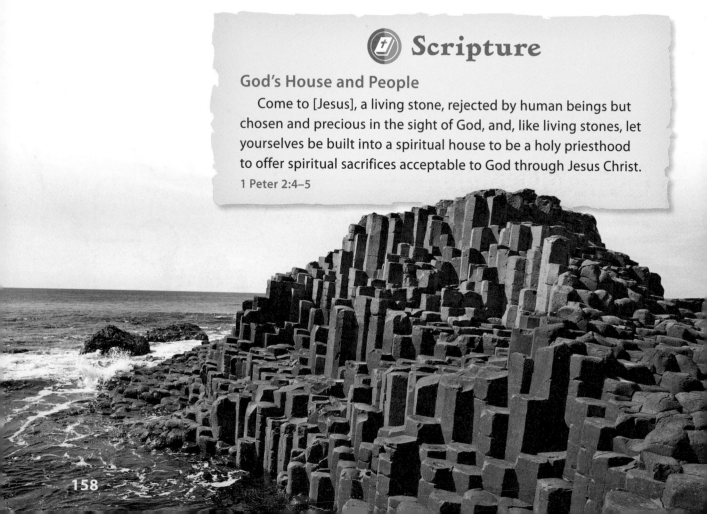

Marks of the Church

one	The Church is one because the power of the Holy Spirit unites all the members in one faith. (See this chapter.)
holy	The Church is holy because she is called by God for a specific purpose. God makes her holy to be a sign of God to the world. (See Chapter 12.)
catholic	The Church is catholic because Jesus sent the Church out to tell the Good News to the whole world. (See Chapter 19.)
apostolic	The Church is apostolic because the Apostles worked with Jesus to begin the Church. The Church today teaches what the Apostles taught, and the bishops are the direct successors of the Apostles. (See Chapter 11.)

Signs of Unity

The first of the Marks of the Church is unity—the Church is *one*. Just as many materials are needed to construct a single building, so are many people brought together to become one in faith. Important signs of the Church's unity are:

- The oneness of her faith
- Her common celebration of worship, especially in the Sacraments
- Her close connection to the Apostles, whose authority has been handed down to the Pope and bishops through the Sacrament of Holy Orders

Throughout history and to this day, divisions in the Church have weakened her as a sign to the world. Therefore, perfect unity is a goal for which the Church must constantly pray and toward which she must work. The Holy Spirit continues to help the Church achieve this goal of oneness by bringing together all the faithful. In the gathering of people of all backgrounds and ways of life, the Church works to create one People of God.

➔ **In what ways do you show unity as a member of the Church at home and in school?**

Connect Your Faith

Praise God for Unity Working in small groups, write a slogan that explains to others some part of the Church's unity. As a group, be ready to explain your slogan for the other groups.

Our group slogan is

_____

_____

_____

_____

_____

Our Catholic Life

What images make you think of the Church?

The Bible includes a variety of images that describe and help people understand the Church. Each of these reveals a part of the nature of the Church. Together, the images give a clearer picture of the mystery of the Church.

Match the term used in the Bible on the left with the descriptions on the right.

The Church in the Bible

Body of Christ	Christ loves and remains with the Church.
People of God	We are called and chosen by God and we share in Christ's mission.
Pilgrim People	Christ remains present in the world through his Body, the Church. Just as the parts of a human body need one another to be whole, so the Church needs each of her members.
Bride of Christ	The Church is on a prayerful journey to a holy place, journeying to her true home—eternal life with God.

Christian pilgrims take part in a Good Friday procession at the Church of the Holy Sepulchre in Jerusalem.

People of Faith

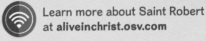

September 17

Saint Robert Bellarmine, 1542–1621

Saint Robert Bellarmine, an Italian priest, lived at a time when Catholics and Protestants were fighting each other. He spent his life explaining and defending Catholic teaching. He wrote a catechism explaining what Catholics believe. But he also knew that God loves all people. He prayed daily for unity in the People of God. Saint Robert understood that even when we disagree with someone, we must still remember them in prayer. He knew that God wants all people to be happy with him in Heaven.

Discuss: In what ways can you respectfully help people understand the Church and her teachings?

Learn more about Saint Robert at **aliveinchrist.osv.com**

Live Your Faith

Explain to a partner what is happening in the picture. How is the young person an example of Christ's love?

Illustrate one way you can show that you are a sign of Christ's love in the world.

Let Us Pray

Prayer of Petition

This is a prayer of petition asking the Holy Spirit for guidance. It is a prayer that was prayed during the Second Vatican Council. Today, we join with the voices before us as we add our hopes to theirs.

Gather and begin with the Sign of the Cross.

Leader: Today, we too will ask the Holy Spirit to help us be faithful witnesses to Christ and his Church.

Reader 1: Knowing you are always with us, in our failings and our goodness, we are united in your holy name.

All: Come, and remain with us. Enter our hearts.

Reader 2: Guide our actions. Point us to the path we should take. Show us what we must do, so that with your help, all we do may be pleasing to you.

All: Amen.

Reader 3: O Holy Spirit, you are never-ending justice. Do not let us disturb or interrupt justice. Unite our hearts to yours. Do it powerfully, so we may be one in you; so we are always united with you in truth.

Adapted from "Prayer of the Council Fathers"

All: Amen.

Leader: We are a sign of God's Kingdom when we love God above all things and share his love with our neighbor. The Holy Spirit lives and works within each baptized person to continue Jesus' mission in the Church. Our prayer-song helps us to remember our commitment to our mission.

 Sing "Loving God"

FAMILY+FAITH
LIVING AND LEARNING TOGETHER

YOUR CHILD LEARNED >>>

This chapter identifies the Marks of the Church, describes the characteristics of unity, and examines the Holy Spirit's movement and presence in the Church and her mission.

Scripture

 Read **Ephesians 4:1–6** to find out what Saint Paul wrote about the importance of unity.

Catholics Believe

- As members of the Church, we are all united in living out the mission of Christ.
- The Church's unity is expressed in the images of the Body of Christ and the People of God.

To learn more, go to the *Catechism of the Catholic Church #738, 775, 776, 813–816, 820* at **usccb.org**.

People of Faith

This week, your child learned about Saint Robert Bellarmine, who was known as much for his rigorous defense of the Catholic faith as he was for praying for his enemies.

CHILDREN AT THIS AGE >>>

How They Understand Christian Unity The number of different churches is often puzzling to children who are in fifth grade. Their black-and-white style of reasoning might lead them to focus on who is "right" and who is "wrong." As Catholics, we recognize that we can experience unity in diversity, both in the Catholic Church and as we work with other Christians to live the teachings of Jesus in our world. Discussing similarities in beliefs as well as differences can be important when helping fifth-graders attain this sense of unity with others.

CONSIDER THIS >>>

Recall a time when you experienced a deep sense of oneness with someone.

These experiences of oneness, of union in our lives, find their source in the presence and power of the Holy Spirit. From the same Holy Spirit the Church experiences union and communion. As Catholics, we know that "the Holy Spirit, the bond of love between the Father and the Son, unites all the members of the Church as the one People of God. The Church professes one Lord, one faith, and one Baptism and forms one body" (*USCCA, p. 127*).

LET'S TALK >>>

- Ask your child to name the four Marks of the Church.
- Talk about why the Church is called the Body of Christ.

LET'S PRAY >>>

 Saint Robert Bellarmine, help us to remember to pray for the unity of all Christians. Amen.

 For a multimedia glossary of Catholic Faith Words, Sunday readings, seasonal and Saint resources, and chapter activities go to **aliveinchrist.osv.com**.

Chapter 10 Review

A **Work with Words** Circle True if a statement is true, and circle False if a statement is false. Correct any false statements.

1. The People of God is another name for the Church, called by Christ to share in his mission. **True/False**

   _____

2. Jesus' followers are the head of the Body of Christ. **True/False**

   _____

3. One, holy, catholic, and apostolic are the Theological Virtues. **True/False**

   _____

4. The followers of Jesus are called to be "living stones," just as Jesus himself is. **True/False**

   _____

5. The Second Vatican Council was primarily concerned with the role of the Church in the United States. **True/False**

   _____

B **Check Understanding** Write a brief response to each statement or question.

6. What did Pope Saint John XXIII do to renew the Church?

   _____

   _____

7. What are the bonds of unity in the Church?

   _____

8. How is it possible for people of all backgrounds and ways of life to form one Church?

   _____

Name and explain two of the four images of the Church.

9. _____

10. _____

Go to **aliveinchrist.osv.com** for an interactive review.

The Teaching Church

❤ Let Us Pray

Leader: Loving God, grant us knowledge of your teaching.

"Make known to me your ways, Lord;
   teach me your paths.
Guide me by your fidelity and teach me,
   for you are God my savior…" **Psalm 25:4–5**

All: Help us learn to follow the way of Jesus, the one we call *rabbi* and *teacher*, the one we name *Lord*. Amen.

📖 Scripture

Then Jesus approached [the Apostles] and said to them, "All power in heaven and on earth has been given to me. Go, therefore, and make disciples of all nations, baptizing them in the name of the Father, and of the Son, and of the holy Spirit, teaching them to observe all that I have commanded you. And behold, I am with you always, until the end of the age." **Matthew 28:18–20**

❓ What Do You Wonder?

- How does the Church teach as Jesus taught?
- Who are the successors of the Apostles and the key teachers in the Church?

The Church on Earth

Who teaches you about being a follower of Jesus?

We are all curious about many things. Do you remember how many times you have asked the question, "Why?" Your teachers encourage you to ask questions so you can learn. And often our teachers ask us questions to help us really understand the meaning of what they teach.

Scripture

Peter's Confession about Jesus

Jesus asked the Apostles this question: "Who do you say that I am?"

Peter replied, "You are the Messiah, the Son of the living God." Jesus knew that only God could have shown Peter this truth.

He said to Peter, "I say to you, you are Peter, and upon this rock I will build my church." Jesus also promised Peter the keys to the Kingdom of Heaven.   Based on Matthew 16:15–19

➺ What do you think Jesus wanted the Apostles to learn from this?

➺ If Jesus asked you this question today, how would you answer him?

The Apostles' Mission

When Jesus sent the Apostles out to spread the Good News of his Father's Kingdom, he also established the mission and authority of their successors. In this way, the teaching authority of the Apostles is passed on through the ages.

The successors of the Apostles are the bishops, in union with the **Pope**. They carry on the Apostles' mission to witness to the truth of Jesus. With the assistance of priests, the bishops proclaim the Good News and teach in Jesus' name. Because the Church is built on the foundation of the Apostles, she is apostolic.

Faithful to the Truth

Teaching and learning are wonderful abilities when you use them in harmony with God's plan and in the light of God's truth. Members of your family and of your parish community help you come to know about God and trust in his love and guidance.

As your teacher, the Church faithfully passes on what God has revealed through his Son, Jesus. The Church teaches by example and by handing on her beliefs and traditions to her members.

Catholic Faith Words

Pope the successor of Peter, the bishop of Rome, and the head of the entire Catholic Church

Share Your Faith

Reflect Think about those who have taught you about the Catholic faith and what you have learned from them. Write two examples here.

1. Person: _____

   What you learned: _____

   _____

2. Person: _____

   What you learned: _____

   _____

Share With a partner, discuss some of the things you have learned about your faith from teachers.

Pope Francis visits Saint Maria Maggiore Basilica in Rome with cardinals after his first appearance as the new Pope.

The Teaching Office

Who are the teachers in the Catholic Church?

Together, the Pope and the bishops make up the **Magisterium**, or "body of teachers."

- The Pope is the successor of Peter, the bishop of Rome and head of the entire Church.

- Each bishop is also the leader of a particular diocese. Bishops have received the fullness of the Sacrament of Holy Orders and work together with the Pope to guide, teach, and make the Church holy.

With the guidance of the Holy Spirit, the Magisterium protects and explains the Word of God and safeguards it for future generations as part of the Church's Sacred Tradition. Because the Holy Spirit guides the Church in the right direction in crucial matters, the Magisterium officially declares that her most important teachings are free from error. This is called the doctrine of **infallibility**.

Catholic Faith Words

Magisterium the teaching office of the Church, which is all of the bishops in union with the Pope. The Magisterium has the teaching authority to interpret the Word of God found in Scripture and Tradition.

infallibility a gift of the Holy Spirit to the Church by which the Pope and the bishops in union with him may declare definitively that a matter of faith or morals is free from error and must be accepted by the faithful

Highlight what the Magisterium does for the Church.

Guidance of the Holy Spirit

Guided by the Holy Spirit, the Church's leaders settle certain important questions of faith and morals in order to help deepen understanding of the teachings of Jesus and the Apostles. This understanding also helps the People of God make right choices in living good moral lives.

Infallibility is connected to another important fact about the Church. The Holy Spirit guides the People of God to the truth. When the People of God—the Pope, the bishops, and all the faithful—come to a common understanding about an important or central truth, they can be sure that they are correct. This is called the "sense of the faithful." The Holy Spirit works through the community of the faithful, giving the community itself a faith-filled understanding of the truth.

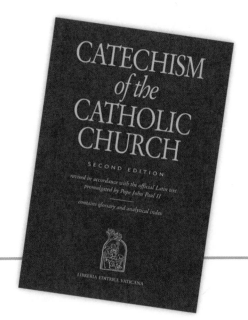

Connect Your Faith

Fill Your Toolbox With a partner, add to this group of "tools" you will need to build your lifelong journey of faith. How can the Church help you use these tools more effectively?

_____

_____

_____

Our Catholic Life

How does the Church speak about her teaching?

The Catholic Church uses several terms and titles when it speaks about her teaching. These ways of talking about the Church allow all her members to be precise and to avoid misunderstanding. They will also be helpful to you in learning about the Church.

Words for Understanding

- Remember that a **doctrine** or **dogma** is an important teaching revealed by Christ and taught by the Church's Magisterium. As a Catholic, you are required to believe these revealed truths.

- Name one Church doctrine you know.

  _____

- Recognize that an important ministry of the **Pope** and **bishops** is to teach with the guidance of the Holy Spirit. It is their duty to interpret the Catholic faith and explain it to all people.

- What is the name of the current Pope?

  _____

- Appreciate that a **catechist** or **teacher** is someone who teaches the faith and helps people learn how to live according to the faith.

- Most catechists are lay people. How did your catechist discover his or her calling to teach?

  _____

- Understand that **priests** and **deacons** assist the bishops in carrying out the teaching ministry. They do so by preaching, celebrating the Sacraments, and guiding the people.

- What have you learned about the Church from your parish's priest or deacons?

  _____

People of Faith

October 22

Pope Saint John Paul II, 1920–2005

One of the jobs of the Pope is to help explain the Catholic faith to all people. Pope Saint John Paul II traveled to 129 different countries around the world telling everyone about God's love and mercy. He went to some countries that a Pope had never visited before, like Mexico and Haiti. Pope John Paul also knew another one of his jobs as Pope was to teach the People of God how to make right choices in living good moral lives. To do that, he wrote many special letters, called encyclicals, telling us about Jesus, Mary, and God.

Discuss: How can you tell people about God's love?

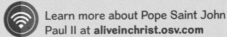 Learn more about Pope Saint John Paul II at **aliveinchrist.osv.com**

Live Your Faith

Name one thing about the Catholic faith that you would like to teach to someone else. How will you do this?

_____

_____

_____

_____

Name something about your faith that you do not understand.

_____

_____

_____

_____

_____

Over the next week, talk with someone in your parish about it.

Let Us Pray

Celebration of the Word

Gather and begin with the Sign of the Cross.

Leader: Blessed be the name of the Lord.

All: Now and forever.

Reader: Jesus is our teacher. He knows our needs and answers our longing for wisdom and truth. Listen to Jesus' teaching from the Sermon on the Mount.

Read Matthew 5:17–20.

The Gospel of the Lord.

All: Praise to you, Lord Jesus Christ.

Leader: Grateful for the teachings of Jesus, we turn to God in prayer.

Read or recite the prayers you seek. After each prayer, pray together, "Lord, hear our prayer."

To conclude our prayers, lift your hands and pray the prayer that Jesus taught us.

Pray the Lord's Prayer aloud.

Go in peace, glorifying the Lord by your life.

All: Thanks be to God.

 Sing "Lead Me, Lord"
Lead me, Lord, lead me, Lord,
by the light of truth
to seek and to find the narrow way.
Be my way; be my truth;
be my life, my Lord,
and lead me, Lord, today.
Text: Based on Matthew 5, 7, John 14;
John D Becker. Text and music
© 1987 John D Becker.
Published by OCP. All rights reserved.

FAMILY+FAITH

LIVING AND LEARNING TOGETHER

YOUR CHILD LEARNED >>>

This chapter describes the Magisterium as the teaching office of the Church, explains apostolic succession, and defines dogma as teachings revealed by Christ and taught by the Church.

Scripture

 Read **Matthew 28:18–20** to find out what Jesus asked the disciples to do.

Catholics Believe

- The Apostles proclaimed Christ's Good News and spread the Reign of God as Jesus commanded.
- Under the guidance of the Holy Spirit, the Pope and the bishops continue the Apostles' mission to teach.

To learn more, go to the *Catechism of the Catholic Church #84–86, 88, 424, 551–553, 857–863* at **usccb.org**.

People of Faith

This week, your child learned about Pope Saint John Paul II. As Pope, he traveled to 129 different countries.

CHILDREN AT THIS AGE >>>

How They Understand the Teaching Church Fifth-graders understand that they don't yet know everything. They are still looking to an authority to tell them about the aspects of life with which they have limited experience. They will look especially to parents and other significant adults in their lives, and the esteem with which children hold the teaching of the Church will depend on what they hear from these adults.

CONSIDER THIS >>>

Think of the best teacher you ever had. How did they help you to learn?

A good teacher helps us to learn and, maybe even more importantly, helps us to understand how much more there is to learn. Through Baptism we are called to a lifelong journey of faith formation. The Church is our teacher and helps us to know and love Jesus more intimately. As Catholics, we know that "living out one's Baptism is a lifelong responsibility. Growing in holiness and discipleship involves a willingness to continue to learn throughout one's whole life about the faith and how to live it" (*USCCA*, p. 196).

LET'S TALK >>>

- Ask your child to explain how the Pope is the successor of Peter.
- Share with each other one person who has taught you about your faith.

LET'S PRAY >>>

 God our Father, thank you for Pope Saint John Paul II. Help us always show God's love to the world as he did. Amen.

For a multimedia glossary of Catholic Faith Words, Sunday readings, seasonal and Saint resources, and chapter activities go to **aliveinchrist.osv.com**.

Chapter 11 Review

A Work with Words Write the answers to the questions in the boxes below. Unscramble the letters that appear in the circle boxes to find the answer to the last question.

1. Which Apostle did Jesus call the "rock," and to whom did Jesus give the keys to the Kingdom of God?

2. What is the quality of being error-free in matters of faith and morals?

3. What is the Church's teaching office called?

4. Who guides the People of God to the truth and preserves them from error in crucial matters?

5. Whom did Christ send out to teach and baptize all nations?

1. ⬚⬚⬚⬚⬚

2. ⬚⬚⬚⬚⬚⬚⬚⬚⬚⬚⬚⬚

3. ⬚⬚⬚⬚⬚⬚⬚⬚

4. ⬚⬚⬚⬚ ⬚⬚⬚⬚⬚

5. _____

B Check Understanding Match each description in Column 1 with the correct term in Column 2.

Column 1

6. learning to be like Jesus

7. assist the Pope and bishops

8. successors of the Apostles

9. important teaching revealed by Christ, taught by the Magisterium

10. teacher of the faith, often a lay person

Column 2

doctrine

catechist

your lifelong task

priests and deacons

Pope and bishops

Go to aliveinchrist.osv.com for an interactive review.

Lives of Holiness

Let Us Pray

Leader: Gracious God, we have been made in your image and have received a breathtaking calling:

"Be holy, just as your heavenly Father is holy."
Based on Matthew 5:48

All: Help us, holy God, to live up to that image and calling. Amen.

Scripture

Blessed be the God and Father of our Lord Jesus Christ, who has blessed us in Christ with every spiritual blessing in the heavens, as he chose us in him, before the foundation of the world, to be holy and without blemish before him. In love he destined us for adoption to himself through Jesus Christ, in accord with the favor of his will. **Ephesians 1:3–5**

? What Do You Wonder?

- What do you think it means to be holy?
- How can Mary and the other Saints help us grow in holiness?

Models of Virtue

Why is it important to know about the Saints?

Saints are known for heroic virtue, or the exemplary practice of Christian virtues. Saints are excellent examples of discipleship and of living as a follower of Jesus. Some are heroes or heroines because they took a stand against those who did not believe in what Jesus had taught. They are signs of hope for us. Most Saints are ordinary people, gifted with God's grace at Baptism, as are all of the faithful. What makes them Saints is how they lived their lives. Saints let the grace of God shine through them, and they become living signs of God's love.

On Being a Saint

Choose one of these Saints. What would each person want you to understand about God's love?

Catholic Faith Words

salvation the loving action of God's forgiveness of sins and the restoration of friendship with him brought by Jesus

holy unique and pure; set apart for God and his purposes

Fruits of the Holy Spirit the qualities that can be seen in us when we allow the Holy Spirit to work in our hearts

Saint Juan Diego

While Juan Diego was walking to Mass, the Virgin Mary appeared to him and asked him to have a church built on the site. With a miracle from the Virgin Mary, he was able to convince the local bishop and the church was built.

Saint Teresa of Ávila

Known for her spiritual life, Teresa taught that in prayer the important thing is not to think much, but to love much. She explained that love is "the desire to please God in everything."

Saint Frances Xavier Cabrini

The first American citizen to become a Saint, she founded the Missionary Sisters of the Sacred Heart to care for poor children in schools. She came to the United States in 1889. Filled with trust in God and endowed with administrative ability, this remarkable woman founded schools, hospitals, and orphanages.

Respond to the Holy Spirit

You cannot buy or earn **salvation**. Salvation is a gift from God that is yours because of the sacrifice of Jesus. Your good works show that you accept and thank God for his generosity. They are also a means by which you grow in holiness, through God's grace and Christ's merit. Good works are a response to the prompting of the Holy Spirit's calling you to goodness.

Saints are models for you because they listened and responded to the Holy Spirit's call. By their example of faithful living, Saints remind you that God is the source of all life and holiness.

One of the Marks of the Church is that she is **holy**. The Saints point to Jesus, who sacrificed himself to make the Church holy. An important work of the Holy Spirit, who dwells in the Church, is to sanctify, or make holy. As members of the Church, all Catholics are called to be holy through the Holy Spirit. When we allow the Holy Spirit to work in our lives, characteristics called the **Fruits of the Holy Spirit** (see page 317) can be seen in our lives.

(see page 317)

Share Your Faith

Reflect Look at the images of some of the Saints on these pages.

Share Choose one of the images, and tell a partner what qualities of the Saint you can see from the image.

Saint Kateri Tekakwitha
Saint Kateri became the first Native American to be canonized, in 2012. She learned about Jesus from Jesuit missionaries. Because she lived so close to nature and found God in the natural world and the wonders of creation, she is the patron Saint of ecology, nature, and the environment.

Saint Pio of Pietrelcina
Many penitents flocked to Saint Padre Pio for confession. He used the confessional to bring both sinners and devout believers closer to God. When giving counsel or encouragement, he relied on the Holy Spirit to know what each person needed to hear.

Mary, Queen of Saints

How does the Church name and honor Saints?

The Church honors Saints because of their lives of holiness. Many Saints have feast days. Parishes and people are often named for them. Saints are chosen to be patrons of persons, countries, and organizations. Saints help you by their prayers and example. These models of holiness show the obedience of faith that Mary, the **Mother of God**, the greatest Saint and known as the Queen of Saints, showed by saying "yes" to God. Read part of the **Annunciation** below.

Catholic Faith Words

Mother of God a title given to Mary because she is the Mother of the Son of God who became man

Annunciation the Angel Gabriel's announcement to Mary that she was called to be the Mother of God

Assumption the teaching that after her earthly life, Mary was taken into Heaven, body and soul, to be with Jesus

 Scripture

The Handmaid of the Lord

Then the angel said to her, "Do not be afraid, Mary, for you have found favor with God. Behold, you will conceive in your womb and bear a son, and you shall name him Jesus." ... Mary said, "Behold, I am the handmaid of the Lord. May it be done to me according to your word." Then the angel departed from her. Luke 1:30–31, 38

The Church teaches the truth that from the beginning of her existence, God kept Mary free from sin. This doctrine is called the Immaculate Conception. From the time that he was born, Jesus, the Son of God made man, was the center of Mary's life. Catholics believe in Mary's **Assumption**—that after her earthly life she was taken into Heaven, body and soul, to be with Jesus.

By honoring Mary, Catholics show their belief that all of God's faithful people will share in the glory of Christ's Resurrection.

➤ How do you say "yes" to God in your daily life?

Honor and Intercession

The New Testament refers to all members of the Church as Saints because they have been baptized by the power of the Holy Spirit into the Paschal Mystery. The Church today has a process of **canonization** to publicly recognize certain people of faith who have died as Saints. **Beatification** is one step in the process of canonization. The community is encouraged to ask these Saints for prayer and look to them as examples. Just as we might ask a person who we know is close to God to pray for us, we can also ask the Saints, who are with God in Heaven, to pray for us. Scripture tells us that the "prayer of a righteous person is very powerful" (James 5:16). Worship is reserved for God alone. But by honoring the Saints and praying for their intercession, the Church also honors God.

➡ **In what ways do you honor Mary and other Saints?**

Catholic Faith Words

canonization a declaration by the Pope naming a person as a Saint. Canonized Saints have special feast days or memorials in the Church's calendar.

beatification the second step in the process of becoming a Saint, in which a venerable person is recognized by the Church as having brought about a miracle through his or her prayers of intercession

Connect Your Faith

Honor Mary and the Saints How does the Church celebrate Mary and the other Saints during the year?

_____

What is your favorite feast day?

_____

Our Catholic Life

How do you pray the Rosary?

The Rosary is a prayer honoring Mary. It is also a sacramental, a sacred symbol and object that helps us respond to the grace received in the Sacraments. Sacramentals help us pray and remember God's love for us. The rosary has five sets of ten beads. Each set is called a decade. When people pray the Rosary, they keep in mind important events in the lives of Jesus and his Mother. These events are called the Mysteries of the Rosary.

How to Pray the Rosary

- Hold the crucifix, and pray the Apostles' Creed.

- Then say the Our Father and three Hail Marys, followed by a Glory Be to the Father.

- The Rosary is divided into five decades. Each decade is made up of an Our Father, ten Hail Marys, and a Glory Be to the Father. Use the beads as you pray each of the five decades. During each decade, think about the mystery it represents.

- Close the Rosary by praying Hail, Holy Queen.

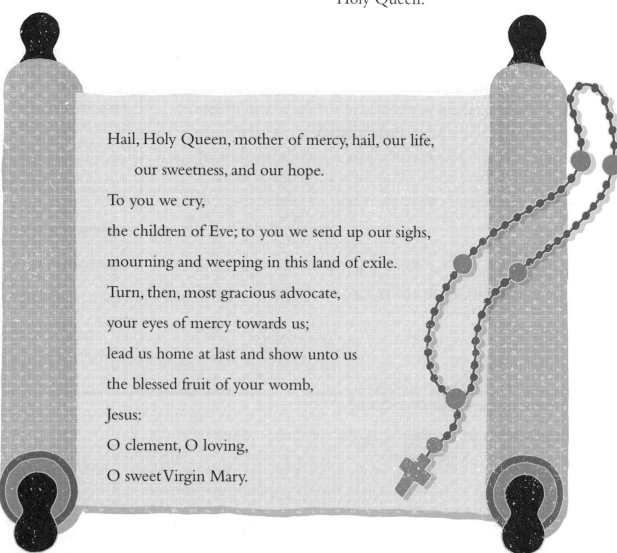

Hail, Holy Queen, mother of mercy, hail, our life,

   our sweetness, and our hope.

To you we cry,

   the children of Eve; to you we send up our sighs,

   mourning and weeping in this land of exile.

   Turn, then, most gracious advocate,

   your eyes of mercy towards us;

   lead us home at last and show unto us

   the blessed fruit of your womb,

Jesus:

O clement, O loving,

O sweet Virgin Mary.

People of Faith

August 22

Queenship of Mary

Although all of the Saints rejoice in God's presence, Mary enjoys a special place among them. We honor Mary, the Mother of Jesus, as Queen of Heaven and Earth. Calling her "Queen" reminds us that she is as close to her Son in Heaven as she was when he lived on Earth. We recall Mary's coronation each time we pray the last of the Glorious Mysteries of the Rosary. But Mary is not just a queen. She is also our mother. When we ask for her help, she always takes our prayers to Jesus.

Discuss: What is your favorite prayer to Mary?

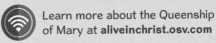 Learn more about the Queenship of Mary at **aliveinchrist.osv.com**

Live Your Faith

Choose one Saint whom you will honor by learning more about him or her.

_____

Tell one thing you learned about him or her that surprised you.

_____

_____

Write a prayer, asking for your chosen Saint's help, and pray it throughout the week.

Saint _____,

pray for me,

that I _____

_____.

 **Let Us Pray**

Litany to Mary

Gather and begin with the Sign of the Cross.

Leader: Loving God, we thank you for the gift of your Saints. We ask Mary, the Mother of Jesus, to pray for us so that we may be faithful, as she was.

All respond "Pray for us" after each title of Mary.

Hail Mary,	Cause of our joy,
Mother of Christ,	Help of Christians,
Virgin most faithful,	Queen of Angels,
Mirror of justice,	Queen of all Saints,
Seat of wisdom,	Queen of Peace,

Leader: Pray for us, O holy Mother of God,

All: That we may be worthy of the promises of Christ.

Leader: Let us pray.

Bow your heads as the leader prays.

All: Amen.

 Sing "Mary, a Woman of Faith"
Mary, Mother of God,
teach us in your ways.
Mary, Mother of God,
lead us to your Son.
Living in faith, always trusting in God.
All generations call her blessed.
Mary, Mother of God,
Mary, Mother of God.

FAMILY+FAITH
LIVING AND LEARNING TOGETHER

YOUR CHILD LEARNED >>>

This chapter identifies the Holy Spirit as sanctifier, describes personal holiness and canonization, and presents key teachings about Mary, the Mother of God and the greatest of Saints, and how we honor her.

Scripture

 Read **Ephesians 1:3–5** to find out what Saint Paul wrote about holiness.

Catholics Believe

- Mary and the Saints provide the Church with models of heroic virtue and holiness.
- Canonization declares that a model Christian is enjoying eternity with God.

To learn more, go to the *Catechism of the Catholic Church #828, 829, 1173, 2013, 2030* at **usccb.org**.

People of Faith

This week, your child learned about Mary, the Mother of Jesus, who is honored as Queen of Heaven and Earth.

CHILDREN AT THIS AGE >>>

How They Understand the Call to Holiness A popular concept today is the "personal best." Unfortunately, we are often tempted to think we have done our "personal best" when we persisted until we felt challenged or until trying hard to do something became inconvenient. Fifth-graders might sometimes think that they could not be as holy as the men and women we call Saints, but God calls all of us to holiness, and he gives us the grace we need to accomplish what he has called us to do.

CONSIDER THIS >>>

As a parent, how often have you wished that you had a child psychologist on speed dial?

We yearn for the knowledge and insight of an expert when we are swimming in uncharted waters. When it comes to living our faith, we may often feel the same way. The Church puts us in touch with some great role models—the Saints. As Catholics, we know that "when we read the lives of the saints, their teachings and witness, we can be motivated to holiness by their example which was shaped by the Holy Spirit" (*USCCA*, p. 106).

LET'S TALK >>>

- Ask your child to explain canonization as a public recognition of a person as a Saint.
- Share with each other the name of a favorite Saint.

LET'S PRAY >>>

 Hail Mary, Mother of God and Queen of Heaven, pray for us now and all the days of our lives. Amen.

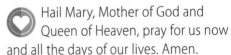 For a multimedia glossary of Catholic Faith Words, Sunday readings, seasonal and Saint resources, and chapter activities go to **aliveinchrist.osv.com**.

Chapter 12 Review

A **Work with Words** Fill in the circle next to the correct response.

1. Saints can help you by their _____.
   - ○ divinity and power
   - ○ prayer and example
   - ○ example and divinity

2. Mary showed the obedience of faith by saying _____ to God.
   - ○ "I AM"
   - ○ "yes"
   - ○ "I am afraid"

3. The Church is holy because of the presence of the _____ within the Church.
   - ○ candles
   - ○ Holy Spirit
   - ○ liturgical calendar

4. Those who follow Jesus are called _____.
   - ○ disciples
   - ○ sanctifiers
   - ○ handmaids

5. During the year, the Church celebrates Saints with _____.
   - ○ Sacraments
   - ○ worship
   - ○ feast days

Solve the crossword puzzle.

Across

7. To declare that a person is named a Saint

9. The Angel Gabriel's announcement to Mary that she was to be called the Mother of God

10. The loving action of God's forgiveness of sins

Down

6. The Holy Spirit, who makes the Church holy

8. Mary's being taken into Heaven, body and soul

Go to **aliveinchrist.osv.com** for an interactive review.

Unit Review

A **Work with Words** Find ten important terms from this unit in the word search below, and write them on the lines next to the clues.

1. Gabriel's announcement to Mary _____

2. Jesus is the head of the _____ of Christ.

3. To declare a person a Saint is to _____.

4. A prayer honoring Mary is the _____.

5. All Catholics are called to _____.

6. The _____ 's gift to the Church is infallibility.

7. These were promised to Peter. _____

8. The _____ Vatican Council was called in 1962.

9. Jesus is the _____.

10. An important work of the Holy Spirit is to be a _____.

S	N	N	I	E	N	D	C	X	D	L	I
S	N	O	N	R	Z	O	O	W	J	E	R
E	L	I	H	K	L	I	R	F	V	B	E
N	L	T	O	O	B	B	N	U	U	Y	I
I	U	A	L	P	W	L	E	O	R	C	F
L	A	I	Y	U	G	K	R	A	N	G	I
O	Z	C	S	K	E	Y	S	O	E	A	T
H	F	N	P	L	E	O	T	M	B	A	C
K	Z	U	I	A	R	B	O	D	Y	Y	N
V	D	N	R	V	X	L	N	E	Q	C	A
G	S	N	I	F	Z	B	E	J	I	P	S
P	P	A	T	S	E	C	O	N	D	H	U

B Check Understanding Match each description in Column 1 with the correct term in Column 2.

Column 1

Column 2

11. built on the lasting foundation of the Apostles

People of God

12. the Pope and the bishops

one, holy, catholic, and apostolic

13. studied the Church's role in modern society

apostolic

14. assembly called by Christ to share in his mission

Second Vatican Council

15. these marks describe God's Kingdom at work in the Church

Magisterium

C Make Connections Write a response to each statement.

Explain the role of individuals as members of the Pilgrim People, using the following terms:

16. Catechist

_____

_____

_____

_____

17. Doctrine

_____

_____

_____

_____

18. Priest

_____

_____

_____

_____

19. Choose one of the other images of the Church (People of God, Body of Christ, or Bride of Christ), and explain what it means.

_____

_____

_____

_____

_____

20. Name the image that best describes your participation in the Church, and give the reasons for your choice.

_____

_____

_____

_____

_____

Morality

Catholic devotees hold lit candles during a midnight Easter vigil Mass in Hyderabad, India.

Our Catholic Tradition

- Evil is a result of humans turning away from God's goodness. (CCC, 385)

- We are redeemed from the power of evil and sin through the power of Jesus' Death and Resurrection. (CCC, 1741)

- We experience the salvation of God's grace through the Sacraments. (CCC, 1084)

- We receive God's forgiveness especially through the Sacrament of Penance and Reconciliation. (CCC, 1440)

What does the Sacrament of Penance and Reconciliation teach us about human beings and God?

Evil in the World

 Let Us Pray

Leader: Good and gracious God, hear us as we do our best to answer your call to choose what is good over what is evil, what is right over what is wrong.

"Turn from evil and do good;
    seek peace and pursue it." **Psalm 34:15**

All: Lead us not into temptation, but deliver us from evil. Amen.

Scripture

But God proves his love for us in that while we were still sinners Christ died for us. For just as through the disobedience of one person the many were made sinners, so through the obedience of one the many will be made righteous. **Romans 5:8, 19**

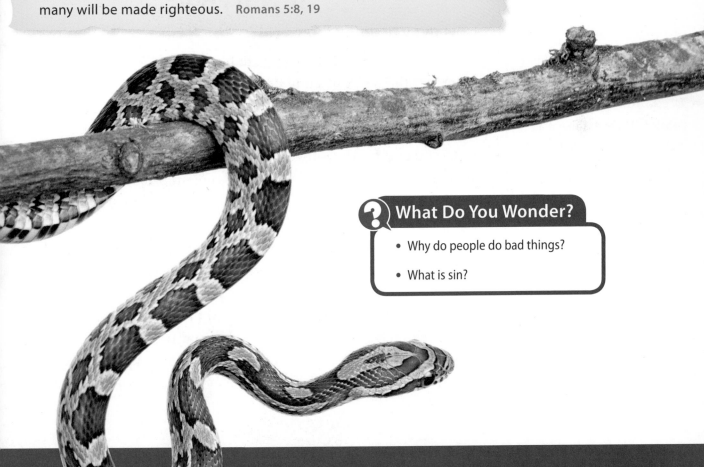

? What Do You Wonder?

- Why do people do bad things?

- What is sin?

The Source of Sorrow

How did evil enter the world?

Some bad things that happen are beyond human control. But others are the result of sinful decisions and actions.

Sin Enters the World

God is good and desires only good for people. Yet sin and evil are found in human life. The Book of Genesis teaches that Adam and Eve's choice to disobey God ended the **Original Holiness** that God had created. The disobedience of our first parents, and its effects on all humans, is known as Original Sin. With Original Sin, the harmony between humans and God, between humans and nature, and among all people was destroyed. Death entered the world, and people became subject to the inclination to sin. All humans have been affected by Adam and Eve's decision, and all share in the human condition of Original Sin. As you listen to this Scripture passage, recall how much God truly loves and cares for you.

Catholic Faith Words

Original Holiness the state of goodness that humanity enjoyed before our first parents, Adam and Eve, chose to sin against God

Underline what happened as a result of Original Sin.

 **Scripture**

The Sacrifice of Jesus

For Christ did not enter into a sanctuary made by hands, a copy of the true one, but heaven itself, that he might now appear before God on our behalf. ... once for all he has appeared at the end of the ages to take away sin by his sacrifice. Just as it is appointed that human beings die once, and after this the judgment, so also Christ offered once to take away the sins of many, will appear a second time, not to take away sin but to bring salvation to those who eagerly await him. **Hebrews 9:24,26–28**

➜ **What does this passage tell you about Jesus' care for you?**

Share Your Faith

Reflect Read the story of the Fall as told in Genesis 3:1–6. Write one thing you learned about sin and one thing you have learned about God from the reading.

About Sin

_____

_____

About God

_____

_____

_____

_____

Share your responses with a partner.

Turning from God

What are mortal sin and venial sin?

The presence of evil and of innocent suffering in the world are two of the hardest things for humans to face. Why evil exists is the hardest question to answer. Only faith can provide an adequate explanation.

As Catholics, we know that no evil, and no suffering, is more powerful than God. The Father so wanted us to know this that he sent his Son to this world. Jesus' suffering on the Cross and his Resurrection are sure signs that God is more powerful than evil. Jesus conquered **sin** by offering us a way back to his Father. He conquered everlasting death by giving us eternal life.

Sin is a deliberate thought, word, deed, or omission that is contrary to the law of God. Sins of omission occur when we do not do what we should, even when we know it is right. Sins of commission occur when we do something we should not have, even when we know it is wrong.

Mortal Sin

Mortal sin is the most serious form of personal sin. Someone who commits mortal sin breaks his or her relationship with God. Mortal sin involves complete selfishness. For a sin to be mortal, it must be a serious matter, done with a person's full knowledge and complete consent. Examples of such serious matters are murder and extreme forms of injury, and wishing grave harm on others. Even in these cases, the other two conditions of full knowledge and consent must be met before a sin is mortal. A person who has tried to live in friendship with God does not easily choose to sin so seriously.

To restore friendship with God after committing mortal sin, the sinner must repent (turn away from sin) and seek forgiveness through the Sacrament of Penance and Reconciliation. God's grace helps the sinner do this.

Underline what is necessary for friendship with God to be restored after a mortal sin has been committed.

Jesus conquered the power of sin and death by rising to new life in the Resurrection.

Venial Sin

Venial sin weakens a person's relationship with God. A sin is venial when it involves disobeying God's law in a less serious matter than one associated with mortal sin. For example, someone who makes fun of another because of gender, physical or mental abilities, or appearance causes harm to that person's dignity and worth. This lack of respect can be a venial sin.

Venial sin may sometimes lead to mortal sin. A person who lies about or steals small things may be establishing a pattern of behavior that can lead to more serious sins. Small acts of discrimination can lead to extreme forms that could be mortally sinful if a person chooses to show only hate rather than love. Mortal sin occurs when selfishness wins out completely.

The Forgiveness of Sins

Even in cases of serious sin, God always forgives sinners when they are truly sorry and wish to turn their hearts to him again. Through the grace of the Sacrament of Penance and Reconciliation, people can have their sins forgiven and rebuild a loving relationship with God.

Catholic Faith Words

sin a deliberate thought, word, deed, or omission contrary to the law of God. Sins hurt our relationship with God and other people.

mortal sin the most serious form of personal sin, through which a person breaks his or her relationship with God

venial sin a sin that weakens a person's relationship with God but does not destroy it

Connect Your Faith

The Wrong Choice Think of one movie or television program you have seen that showed an example of one person's sinful choice and the consequences that everyone else had to suffer.

Name of movie or show:

_____

Sinful choice:

_____

Consequences of the choice:

_____

_____

Our Catholic Life

How do you express pain and sorrow?

From the Bible, you learn that in the face of tragedy, God's People bring their feelings of sorrow and anger to God. Such prayers of sorrow and anger are called lamentations. They express the need for God's presence in times of difficulty. Psalm 55 is an example of a prayer of lamentation. Use it to understand how you can pray in this way.

1. Follow these steps in order to tell God about your feelings of anger and sorrow.

2. Place a check mark by the things you have trouble expressing.

Prayer of Lamentation

☐	**Express your feelings honestly.** Describe the feeling you wish to pray about.	• Tell God how you really feel. • Remember that he already knows and wants to help you, but you should try to express and share your needs with God.
☐	**Name the painful situation clearly.** In Psalm 55, the psalmist has been betrayed by a friend. The violent city is also mentioned.	• In your prayer, include every aspect of the situation you wish to pray about. • What is the event? Who or what caused it? What would you like to do about it?
☐	**Express your hope and trust in God.** In this part of the prayer, it is important to express your trust in God's power and goodness.	• Like the psalmist who was looking for freedom and peace (see Psalm 55:19), you will find strength when you affirm your faith in God. • What do you believe God has already done for you? What do you believe he is doing right now? What do you believe he will do?

People of Faith

Saint Gemma Galgani, 1878–1903

Saint Gemma Galgani was a beautiful Italian girl who loved Jesus from the time she was very little. When she wanted to send someone a message, she would sometimes ask her Guardian Angel to deliver it for her. When she prayed, her Angel would kneel and pray with her. She felt him always at her side, even when she was afraid or sick. Saint Gemma said the best way to always do the right thing is to pray to Jesus and Mary for help.

Discuss: When do you pray to Jesus or Mary for help?

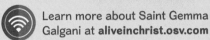

Learn more about Saint Gemma Galgani at **aliveinchrist.osv.com**

Live Your Faith

Look through newspapers or magazines for stories of people who made good choices to avoid personal sin. Choose one and make notes below on how you think the person you chose would explain the mystery of evil.

_____

_____

_____

_____

_____

_____

_____

_____

_____

_____

Compare your notes with a partner and discuss the similarities and differences between your chosen people.

Let Us Pray

Litany of Repentance

Gather and begin with the Sign of the Cross.

Leader: God our loving Father, you are always ready to forgive us.
Let us reflect on how we have sinned.

 All: Sing "God of Mercy"

God of mercy, you are with us.

Fill our hearts with your kindness.

God of patience, strong and gentle,

fill our hearts with your kindness.

Lord, have mercy. Lord, have mercy.

Lord, have mercy upon us. (repeat)

© 1995, 1999, Bernadette Farrell. Published by OCP. All rights reserved.

All pray the Act of Contrition together. It is found in the Our Catholic Tradition section of your book, page 323.

Leader: Let us pray.

Bow your heads as the leader prays.

All: Amen.

ACT OF CONTRITION

My God,
I am sorry for my sins with
all my heart.
In choosing to do wrong
and failing to do good,
I have sinned against you
whom I should love above
all things.
I firmly intend, with your
help,
to do penance,
to sin no more,
and to avoid whatever leads
me to sin.
Our Savior Jesus Christ
suffered and died for us.
In his name, my God have
mercy.

Amen

4295 © J.B. CO.

YOUR CHILD LEARNED >>>

This chapter describes Jesus' Death and Resurrection as God's plan for redemption, and examines the relationship between sin and the Sacrament of Penance and Reconciliation.

Scripture

 Read **Romans 5:8, 19** to find out about God's love for us through the obedience of Jesus.

Catholics Believe

- Evil is the result of humans' turning away from God's goodness.
- God sent his Son to redeem people from the power of sin and evil.

To learn more, go to the *Catechism of the Catholic Church #309, 311, 312, 397, 1855* at **usccb.org**.

People of Faith

This week, your child learned about Saint Gemma Galgani, who had a special devotion to her Guardian Angel, asking him to help protect her from evil.

CHILDREN AT THIS AGE >>>

How They Understand the Mystery of Evil Because of their tendency to think in absolutes, fifth-graders might think that evil actions only come from "evil people." When they understand that there is the potential for good or for evil in each of us, they can become more aware of times in which they might be tempted to turn away from God's goodness. This will help them to prepare for the challenges of increased peer pressure in the coming years.

CONSIDER THIS >>>

Do you find that gossiping becomes easier the more you do it?

The more we move away from what is good, the easier it becomes to move toward what is evil. Committing a less serious sin can lead to committing a more serious sin or developing a pattern of sin. As Catholics, we know that "every sin has consequences. It disrupts our communion with God and the Church, weakens our ability to resist temptation, and hurts others. .... Christ, acting through the Church, brings about the healing of the consequences of sin" (*USCCA, p. 244*).

LET'S TALK >>>

- Ask your child to explain the origin of sin.
- Talk about how through the grace of the Sacrament of Penance and Reconciliation our sins can be forgiven.

LET'S PRAY >>>

Dear Jesus, sometimes it is hard to be good, but I know that with your help, I can always do the right thing. Amen.

 For a multimedia glossary of Catholic Faith Words, Sunday readings, seasonal and Saint resources, and chapter activities go to **aliveinchrist.osv.com**.

Chapter 13 Review

A **Work with Words** Match each description in Column 1 with the correct term in Column 2.

Column 1

1. the sin of our first parents and the sinful human condition

2. disobedience to God's law in a serious matter with complete knowledge and full consent

3. the state of goodness humanity enjoyed before Adam and Eve chose to sin against God

4. prayer of sorrow and anger

5. disobedience to God's law in a matter that is not deeply serious

Column 2

mortal sin

lamentation

venial sin

Original Holiness

Original Sin

B **Check Understanding** Fill in the circle next to the correct response.

6. Through the grace of the Sacrament of _____, people can have their sins forgiven.
   ○ Matrimony
   ○ Penance and Reconciliation
   ○ Holy Orders

7. Only _____ can provide a sufficient answer to the question of evil.
   ○ faith
   ○ the Church
   ○ wisdom

8. To restore friendship with God after committing mortal sin, the sinner must _____.
   ○ repent and receive penance
   ○ receive Communion
   ○ write a psalm

9. Venial sin may sometimes lead to _____.
   ○ mortal sin
   ○ repentance
   ○ eternal life

10. The Book of Genesis teaches that Adam and Eve's choice to disobey God ended the _____ that he created.
    ○ free will
    ○ Original Holiness
    ○ shame

Go to **aliveinchrist.osv.com** for an interactive review.

New Life in Christ

 Let Us Pray

Leader: Loving God, fountain of life, you quench all thirsts in the living waters of Baptism.

[Jesus said,] 'the water I shall give will become in him a spring of water welling up to eternal life.'"
John 4:14

All: Flood us with mercy, O Lord, and wash away our faults in the torrent of your love. Amen.

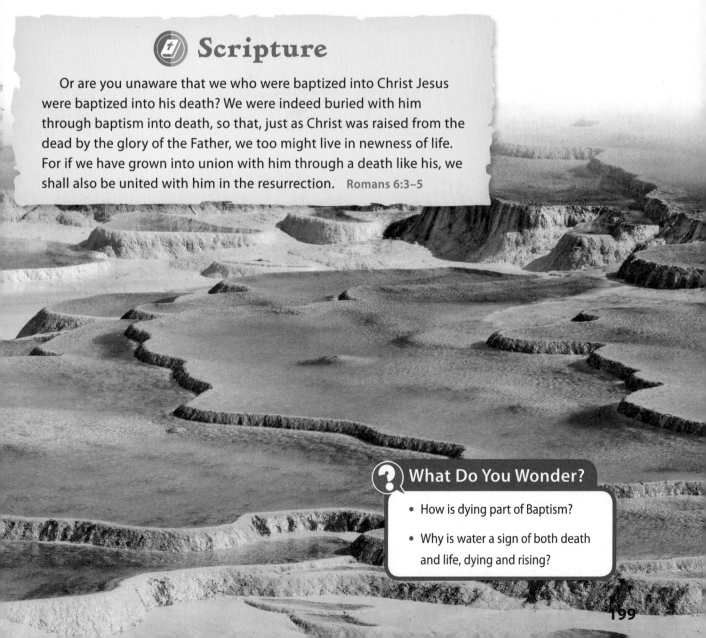

Scripture

Or are you unaware that we who were baptized into Christ Jesus were baptized into his death? We were indeed buried with him through baptism into death, so that, just as Christ was raised from the dead by the glory of the Father, we too might live in newness of life. For if we have grown into union with him through a death like his, we shall also be united with him in the resurrection. Romans 6:3–5

What Do You Wonder?

• How is dying part of Baptism?

• Why is water a sign of both death and life, dying and rising?

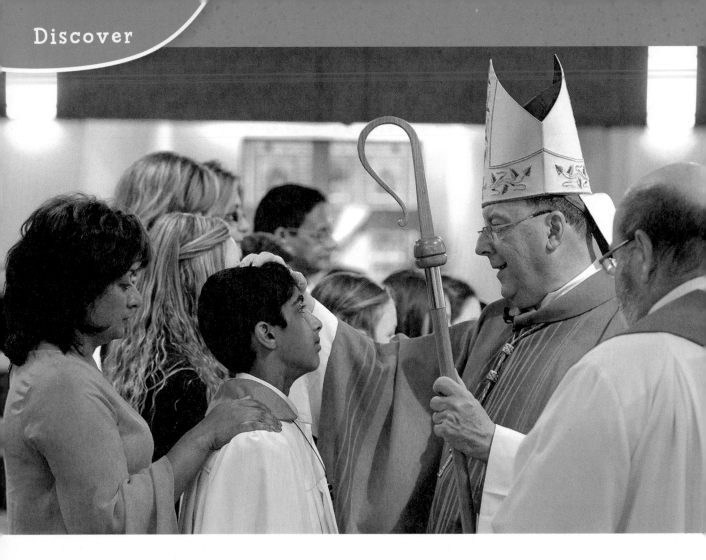

Sacraments of Initiation

What new life is given in Baptism?

At Baptism, you first received grace and began a new way of life. The Sacraments of Confirmation and Eucharist complete your initiation as a member of the Catholic Church, but they do not mark the end of your journey of faith. They are the beginning of this journey. The Sacraments of Initiation include Baptism, Confirmation, and Eucharist. Through these Sacraments, you are initiated into a relationship with Christ and celebrate membership in the Catholic Church. Through these Sacraments, we share in Christ's role as priest, prophet, and king.

As priests, we praise God, offer our lives to God, and pray with and for others. As prophets, we know the Church's teachings on morality and justice, stand up for what is right, and follow God's Word. As kings, we behave responsibly, act as leaders, and act with justice, mercy, and love.

Most Christians are baptized as infants, which is the customary practice of the Catholic Church. At Baptism, a person is reborn in Christ and freed from both Original Sin and personal sin. Through the Church, the grace of the Sacraments is given to sustain this new life. The Sacrament of Confirmation deepens the grace of Baptism. In both Baptism and **Confirmation**, we are anointed with **Sacred Chrism**.

The New Life of Grace

Paul compares the new life of Baptism with the Resurrection of Jesus. When a person is baptized, he or she is said to have "died" to sin. Paul points out that the baptized person then "rises" to new life in Christ in the community of the Church.

ⓣ Scripture

Freedom from Sin; Life in God

As to his death, [Jesus] died to sin once and for all; as to his life, he lives for God. Consequently, you too must think of yourselves as [being] dead to sin and living for God in Christ Jesus. **Romans 6:10–11**

Grace and Conversion

Through the Sacraments of the Church, God shares his divine life with you. The grace given in the Sacraments is not earned. It is a gift from God. You respond to God's gift of grace by turning away from sin and living according to the law of love that Jesus taught. The movement away from sin and into the mystery of God's love is called conversion. It begins with God's call and is sustained through life by your cooperation with God's grace.

Share Your Faith

Reflect How does the Catholic Church help you become closer to Christ?

_____

_____

_____

_____

_____

Share your answer with a partner.

One Step at a Time

How are the Sacraments of Initiation celebrated for adults?

Just as it takes time to become part of a family, so it takes time to prepare to be baptized and to be initiated into the Church. The Church welcomes new adult members through a step-by-step process called the **Rite of Christian Initiation of Adults**, or the Order of Christian Initiation.

United to Christ and to the Church

Although Jeremy was twenty-three years old, he still felt nervous when he rang the doorbell of Saint Benedict's. As soon as Father Paul sat down with him, Jeremy said, "I'd like to become a Catholic. What tests do I have to take?" The priest smiled and said, "Let's take this one step at a time. The process of becoming a member of the Church, which we call initiation, takes time." He invited Jeremy to a gathering where he would meet people who were on a similar faith journey.

Catholic Faith Words

Rite of Christian Initiation of Adults (RCIA) the process by which adults and some children become members of the Catholic Church through the Sacraments of Initiation

catechumen a "learner," or person preparing to celebrate the Sacraments of Initiation

sponsor a representative of the parish community who supports a catechumen celebrating the Sacraments of Initiation

Becoming an Elect

After a few months, Jeremy decided he wanted to prepare for Baptism, and he became a **catechumen**. During this time, the lives of those committed to the faith were an example to him. Jeremy also had support from his **sponsor**, Ed. Ed came to sharing sessions at the church with Jeremy. He prayed with Jeremy and told him what being Catholic was like. Jeremy came to know and love the Christian way of life and the Catholic Church.

Many months later, on the First Sunday of Lent, Jeremy became one of the elect. This meant that he would celebrate the Sacraments of Initiation at the Easter Vigil on Holy Saturday.

A Night to Remember

Finally, Holy Saturday arrived. At the baptismal pool, Father Paul asked Jeremy to declare his faith in God the Father, God the Son, and God the Holy Spirit. As Father Paul immersed Jeremy in the water three times, he said, "I baptize you in the name of the Father, and of the Son, and of the Holy Spirit." Jeremy was given new life in Christ.

After a prayer to the Holy Spirit, Father Paul placed his hands on Jeremy's head and confirmed him with Sacred Chrism, saying, "Jeremy, be sealed with the Gift of the Holy Spirit."

At last, the moment came to receive the Eucharist. Jeremy stood before Father Paul to receive Holy Communion. "The Body of Christ, the Blood of Christ" echoed in his mind and heart as he returned to his

place after receiving Communion for the first time. Now, Jeremy felt truly united to Christ and to the Church.

➡ Have you ever wanted to join a group? Why?

➡ How did you go about joining?

 Underline how Jeremy's sponsor supported him.

Connect Your Faith

Continue the Journey Write a thank-you note to your godparents or to someone in your parish community who has helped you on your journey of faith. Be sure to say how the person or persons have helped you.

Our Catholic Life

What can help you deepen your faith?

The Sacraments of Initiation bring you to new life as a Catholic and prepare you to continue your journey of faith. Here are some practices that can help you along.

Add your own ideas in the spaces provided.

The Tools

Focus on Your Faith

- Base your decisions on the Commandments and Jesus' teachings.
- Count on the guidance of the Holy Spirit.
- Pray to God, who is always ready to listen.
- _____

Participate at Mass

- Actively participate at Mass; it strengthens your bond with Jesus and with your parish.
- Take part in the Eucharist. Through it, God gives you his grace to sustain you on your journey.
- _____

Rely on Your Faith Community

- Allow Church members to help you on your way. These people may include your family, your pastor, or your religion teacher.
- Talk to people whom you know and trust about questions or problems.
- _____

Set an Example

- Learn by doing.
- Participate in the life of the Church, and make a habit of service to others.
- Through your actions, strengthen your love and commitment to the Church and give witness to the truth of your faith.
- _____

People of Faith

Saint Cyril of Jerusalem, 315–386

Saint Cyril was a great teacher. He lived in the same country that Jesus did. After he became a priest, the bishop of Jerusalem asked him to prepare catechumens for Baptism. Saint Cyril explained the beliefs of the Church to those wanting to join. We still have his lectures today. They tell us how people prepared for Baptism in the early Church. They also tell us how the Mass was celebrated. Years later, when he became the bishop of Jerusalem himself, Cyril continued to give these lectures. He knew it was very important for people to understand exactly what happens when they are baptized.

Discuss: Talk about a time when you watched a Baptism.

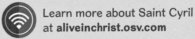

Learn more about Saint Cyril at **aliveinchrist.osv.com**

Live Your Faith

Think of a time when you really made an effort to live as a follower of Jesus in your parish, school, or neighborhood. Over the next week, make that effort again, but with a different group of people. Make notes on what you did, how you accomplished this, and how you felt afterward.

_____

_____

_____

_____

_____

_____

_____

_____

_____

_____

_____

Let Us Pray

Baptismal Promises

Gather and begin with the Sign of the Cross.

Leader: Let us pray. Loving God, we sing your praise, for you have given us new life through the grace of Baptism. Enfold us within your Church, through Christ our Lord.

All: Amen.

Reader: A reading from the holy Gospel according to John.

Read John 3:1–21.

The Gospel of the Lord.

All: Praise to you, Lord Jesus Christ.

Leader: Let us renew the promises of our Baptism.
Do you reject Satan, all his works, and all his empty promises?

All: I do.

Leader: Do you believe in God, the Father Almighty?

All: I do.

Leader: Do you believe in Jesus Christ, his only Son?

All: I do.

Leader: Do you believe in the Holy Spirit, the holy Catholic church, the communion of saints, the forgiveness of sins, and life everlasting?

All: I do.

Leader: Let us pray.

Bow your heads as the leader prays.

All: Amen.

 Sing "Yes, Lord, I Believe/Sí Señor Yo Creo"

FAMILY+FAITH
LIVING AND LEARNING TOGETHER

YOUR CHILD LEARNED >>>

This chapter identifies the Sacraments of Initiation and the steps of the RCIA process, and explains that through the Seven Sacraments God shares his divine life.

Scripture

 Read **Romans 6:3–5** to find out what Saint Paul wrote about Baptism.

Catholics Believe

- Through the Sacraments of Initiation—Baptism, Confirmation, and Eucharist—we enter into a relationship with Christ and celebrate membership in the Catholic Church.

- Confirmation seals us with the Gift of the Holy Spirit and deepens the grace of Baptism.

To learn more, go to the *Catechism of the Catholic Church #1212, 1213, 1229–1233, 1316, 1391* at **usccb.org**.

People of Faith

This week, your child learned about Saint Cyril of Jerusalem, who is known for instructing catechumens preparing for Baptism.

CHILDREN AT THIS AGE >>>

How They Understand the Sacraments of Initiation

Most fifth-graders do not remember their Baptism because it happened when they were babies. Because of this, they might miss the idea of conversion as applied to Christian Initiation. It is helpful for them to know the promises their parents made when they were baptized and how they can choose to "live out" their Baptism as children of God.

CONSIDER THIS >>>

How would you fill in this blank? _____ changed everything.

We can all think of a life-changing event or two in our lives. Spiritual conversion is truly life-changing. It is a turning away from sin and moving toward deeper union with God. As Catholics, we know that "sin harms our relationship with God and damages our communion with the Church. Conversion of heart is the beginning of our journey back to God ....Conversion must involve a change of heart as well as a change of actions" (*USCCA, p. 237*).

LET'S TALK >>>

- Ask your child to name the three Sacraments of Initiation.

- Share a story about the Sacrament of Baptism in your family.

LET'S PRAY >>>

 Dear God, bless all those who are getting ready to become Catholic and all who want to be baptized. Amen.

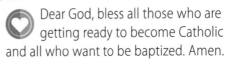 For a multimedia glossary of Catholic Faith Words, Sunday readings, seasonal and Saint resources, and chapter activities go to **aliveinchrist.osv.com**.

Chapter 14 Review

A **Check Understanding** Circle True if a statement is true, and circle False if a statement is false. Correct any false statements.

1. A catechumen is a person who acts as a sponsor for someone who wishes to become a Catholic. **True/False**

   _____

   _____

2. Focusing on faith, participating at Mass, relying on the faith community, and setting an example are all ways to welcome a new family member. **True/False**

   _____

3. Confirmation is the Sacrament that deepens the grace of Baptism, and strengthens us to give witness to Christ in the world. **True/False**

   _____

4. The grace of the Sacraments must be earned. **True/False**

   _____

5. Sacred Chrism is used in anointing in the Sacraments of Initiation. **True/False**

   _____

Using the words in the Word Bank, describe the Rite of Christian Initiation of Adults.

6–10. _____

_____

_____

_____

_____

_____

_____

_____

Word Bank

· · · · · · · · · · · ·

conversion

Easter Vigil

catechumen

Sacraments of Initiation

sponsor

Go to **aliveinchrist.osv.com** for an interactive review.

Forgiveness and Healing

♥ Let Us Pray

Leader: Forgiving Father, remind us always of your amazing promise of pardon and peace, that we can always come home to you.

"Bless the LORD, my soul;
 and do not forget all his gifts,
Who pardons all your sins,
 and heals all your ills …" **Psalm 103:2–3**

All: Father, thank you for being a God who forgives, heals, and welcomes your wayward children with open arms. Amen.

📖 Scripture

The Pharisees and their scribes [asked], "Why do you eat and drink with tax collectors and sinners?" Jesus said to them in reply, "Those who are healthy do not need a physician, but the sick do. I have not come to call the righteous to repentance but sinners." **Luke 5:30–32**

❓ What Do You Wonder?

- How do you know if you really need forgiveness?
- Why is it sometimes hard to ask for forgiveness?

A detail of *Return of the Prodigal Son*, by Julie Ribault

Reconciliation and Forgiveness

How can you bring forgiveness and reconciliation into your relationships?

Jesus understood that anger can have a negative effect on even close relationships. In this story of forgiveness and reconciliation, Jesus taught his followers a lesson that he also lived.

Catholic Faith Words

confession an essential element of the Sacrament of Penance and Reconciliation when you tell your sins to the priest; another name for the Sacrament

reparation the action taken to repair the damage done from sin

contrition being sorry for your sins and wanting to live better

absolution words spoken by the priest during the Sacrament of Penance and Reconciliation to grant forgiveness of sins in God's name

 **Scripture**

The Parable of the Lost Son

Jesus told a story about a man with two sons. The younger son said, "Father, give me the share of your estate that should come to me." The father did so, and the son went far away. He wasted his money and was soon starving. Desperate, he decided to return to his father's house. He went home, where his forgiving parent greeted him with joy and love. The father told his servants to prepare a feast to celebrate his son's return. When the older son heard about this, he was angry and complained to his father. But the father, who loved his sons equally, replied, "My son, you are here with me always; everything I have is yours. But now we must celebrate … because your brother was dead and has come to life again; he was lost and has been found."

Based on Luke 15:11–32

➜ What does the older son learn after expressing his anger to his father?

A Generous Father

Like the father in the story that Jesus told, God always wants you to come home to his love. No one is ever far from God's mercy. Christ continues to share God's forgiving and healing love through the Church in the Sacraments of Healing, which include Penance and Reconciliation, sometimes called the Sacrament of Confession or simply **confession**, and Anointing of the Sick. In these Sacraments, God's forgiveness and healing are given to those suffering physical and spiritual sickness.

Catholics who commit serious sin are required to celebrate the Sacrament of Reconciliation, but the Church encourages all to celebrate it. Sin wounds or destroys relationships with God, the Church, and others. Reconciliation heals these relationships. After you confess your sins to the priest, he gives you a penance, which helps you repair the damage done from your sin by doing something good; it also helps you turn away from sin in the future. This action is called **reparation**.

After you have confessed your sins, the priest will ask you to pray the Act of Contrition (see page 323 in the Our Catholic Tradition section of your book). This prayer helps you express **contrition**, or sorrow, for your sins and your intention to do better. It reminds you that God, who always hears your prayers, is forgiving, just, and merciful. Your confession of sins and the **absolution**, or words spoken by the priest to grant forgiveness of sins in God's name, bring you God's peace and grace.

Penance and Reconciliation

Parts

Acts of the Penitent
- Contrition
- Confession
- Penance

Act of the Priest
- Absolution

Signs
- Confession by penitent
- Priest's words of absolution
- Extension of priest's hands

Effects
- Forgiveness of sins
- Reconciliation with God and the Church
- Peace and spiritual strength

Share Your Faith

Reflect Think of an idea for a modern parable of forgiveness. Begin by thinking of situations in which people find it hard to forgive.

Share With a partner, decide whether you would tell your story as a play, a poem, or a short story. Write the form you would use and three to five sentences telling what the situation would be or what your parable would be.

A Healing Sacrament

Why is the Anointing of the Sick called a Sacrament of Healing?

In the Hawaiian Islands of the late 1800s, no healing was available for those stricken with Hansen's disease, or leprosy. All victims were exiled to Molokai, one of the Hawaiian Islands.

Saint Damien and the Lepers

Belgian missionary priest Damien de Veuster volunteered to serve on Molokai. When he arrived, conditions in the settlement were horrible. Disorder and despair were everywhere.

Father Damien cared for the outcasts and taught them to help one another. He built homes for orphans. He baptized people and brought them the other Sacraments. Because of his great faith, he was inspired to love these very sick people and to stay with them to the end. This compassionate priest eventually contracted leprosy himself and thereafter referred to himself and his flock as "we lepers."

➨ **What do you think it meant to the people that Father Damien said "we lepers"?**

Compassion for Those Who Are Sick

Father Damien could not cure illness, but he could ease pain, help restore dignity, and bring hope to those he served. Through the Sacraments, Father Damien brought people God's healing and forgiveness. Although Molokai's exiles had been separated from family and friends, they learned from this good priest the truth that they could never be separated from the love of God in Jesus Christ. Father Damien was canonized by Pope Benedict XVI in 2009.

During his life on Earth, Jesus showed compassion for those who were sick and often healed them. Through the Sacrament of the Anointing of the Sick, the Church continues to bring Jesus' healing touch to strengthen, comfort, and forgive the sins of those who are seriously ill or close to death. Anyone who is seriously ill, at an advanced age, or facing surgery can receive this Sacrament. It should also be celebrated when someone is thought to be near death.

Highlight what Father Damien taught the exiles of Molokai.

A priest performs the laying on of hands during the Sacrament of the Anointing of the Sick.

Anointing of the Sick

Signs

Laying on of hands, prayer, anointing of the forehead and hands with the oil of the sick

Effects

The strength to bear illness, the forgiveness of sins, preparation for eternal life, peace, courage, union with the sufferings of Christ, sometimes physical healing

Connect Your Faith

Share Healing Love Make a list of what Saint Damien did to care for the lepers. Then discuss in small groups how you can use some of these ideas to care for the sick.

Our Catholic Life

How do you prepare yourself to receive forgiveness?

God's love and goodness help you see your need for forgiveness and healing. He gives us the gift of our conscience, an inner voice that helps us to judge whether actions are right or wrong. It is important for us to know God's laws so our conscience can help us make good decisions. Examining your conscience regularly helps you recognize your sin as well as bad habits that can lead to sin. It is a prayerful reflection on and assessment of your own words, attitudes, and actions. It prepares you to receive the Sacrament of Penance and Reconciliation.

Examine Your Conscience

Take time to think about each step. You do not need to share your thoughts. Be honest with yourself and with God.

1. **Pray to the Holy Spirit for help in recalling your sins.** Ask him to guide you in acknowledging sins and expressing sorrow. Do you understand how actions can hurt? What things are hard for you to feel sorry for?

2. **Reflect on your life.** Have you neglected your relationship with God or with others? How have you misused what you have been given? Have you forgiven those who have hurt you?

3. **Think about the Commandments, the Beatitudes, the teachings of the Church, and the command to love.** Cheating, spreading rumors, disobeying, and stealing are against the Commandments. How have you lived by the Beatitudes? Have you thought of others' needs or avoided fights? Have you been helpful at home? Have you stood up for what is right or treated others with respect?

4. **Ask for help.** Ask God to give you the grace to live a life that mirrors his love and goodness. Ask for humility.

5. **Decide to do better.** Do something positive to make up for your sins.

6. **Thank God.** Praise God for loving you even when you fail to love him or others as you should.

7. **Pray an Act of Contrition.** Ask God for forgiveness.

People of Faith

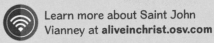

August 4

Saint John Vianney, 1786–1859

Saint John Vianney found school difficult. He had a very hard time with Latin. Because of that, he almost wasn't allowed to become a priest. But he was so good and kind, he was finally ordained. He became the priest of a small church in a French town called Ars. John had a special gift of knowing exactly what to say to people who confessed their sins. Within a few years, thousands of people would come to Ars just to go to confession. John often spent sixteen hours a day hearing confessions and counseling people on how to be closer to God.

Discuss: How do you prepare to go to confession?

Learn more about Saint John Vianney at **aliveinchrist.osv.com**

Live Your Faith

Compose your own short prayer to the Holy Spirit or an Act of Contrition for use in an examination of conscience.

Let Us Pray

Prayer of Peace

Gather and begin with the Sign of the Cross.

 All: Sing Dona Nobis Pacem together.

Dona nobis pacem, pacem.

Dona nobis pacem.

Leader: A reading from the holy Gospel according to John.

Read John 14:27.

The Gospel of the Lord.

All: Praise to you, Lord Jesus Christ.

Sing Dona Nobis Pacem together.

All pray the Lord's Prayer together
and exchange a sign of peace
at the conclusion of the hymn.

 All: Sing "Heal Us, Lord"

Heal us, Lord.

We feel the power of your love.

Let your Spirit come unto us.

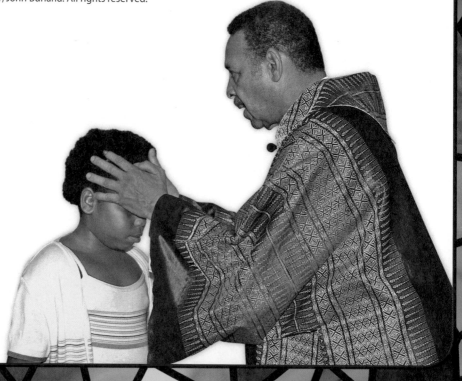

YOUR CHILD LEARNED >>>

This chapter defines contrition and absolution and identifies the Sacraments of Healing as Christ's actions through the Church to share God's healing and forgiving love.

Scripture

 Read **Luke 5:30–32** to find out what Jesus says about sinners.

Catholics Believe

- The Church receives God's forgiveness through the Sacraments of Healing.
- The Sacrament of Reconciliation includes contrition, confession, penance, and absolution.

To learn more, go to the *Catechism of the Catholic Church #1421, 1491, 1527, 1531* at **usccb.org**.

People of Faith

This week, your child learned about Saint John Vianney, whose special ministry was hearing confessions and counseling sinners.

CHILDREN AT THIS AGE >>>

How They Understand the Sacraments of Healing Even though many of them have already received the Sacraments of Penance and Reconciliation for the first time, fifth-grade children might still struggle with the idea of confession to a priest. ("Why do I have to confess my sins to a priest?") With some guidance, they are capable of understanding that the Church is a family, and that we are all connected in the Body of Christ. When one of us sins, it affects everyone. The priest serves as a representative of Christ but also of the Catholic community.

CONSIDER THIS >>>

Have you ever wondered why there is sickness and death in this world?

Sickness and death are unavoidable in human life. To strengthen us and unite our suffering with Christ's suffering on the Cross, the Church celebrates the Sacrament of the Anointing of the Sick. As Catholics, we know that "when the Sacrament of Anointing of the Sick is given, the hoped-for effect is that, if it be God's will, the person be physically healed of illness. But even if there is no physical healing, the primary effect of the Sacrament is a spiritual healing by which the sick person receives the Holy Spirit's gift of peace and courage to deal with the difficulties that accompany serious illness or the frailty of old age" (*USCCA, p. 254*).

LET'S TALK >>>

- Ask your child to retell the Bible story of the Prodigal Son in his or her own words.
- Share a story of forgiveness in your own family.

LET'S PRAY >>>

 Dear God, forgive us our sins and help us to always do your will. Amen.

 For a multimedia glossary of Catholic Faith Words, Sunday readings, seasonal and Saint resources, and chapter activities go to **aliveinchrist.osv.com**.

Chapter 15 Review

A Work with Words Complete each sentence with the correct term from the Word Bank. Not all terms will be used.

1. _____ refers to the words spoken by the priest during the Sacrament of Penance and Reconciliation to grant forgiveness of sins in God's name.

2. The father in the parable celebrated the return of his son with a _____.

3. _____ is sincere sorrow for having sinned.

4. Absolution is part of the Sacrament of _____.

5. The strength to bear illness is an effect of _____.

Word Bank
· · · · · · · · · · ·

contrition

Penance and Reconciliation

feast

the Anointing of the Sick

absolution

prayer

service

B Check Understanding Cross out any incorrect answers you find in the items below.

6. The signs of the Sacrament of the Anointing of the Sick are (**laying on of hands, anointing with oil, doing penance**).

7. The basic elements of the Sacrament of Penance and Reconciliation are (**contrition, confession, penance, Communion, absolution**).

8. Some steps to take in examining your conscience are (**to reflect, to think about the Commandments, to sing hymns, to decide to do better**).

9. Contrition for sins (**is unnecessary, must be sincere, helps restore damaged relationships with God and the Church**).

10. Saint Damien is a heroic example of reconciliation and healing because he (**found a cure for Hansen's disease; devoted himself to the care of those exiled on Molokai; brought comfort, dignity, and hope to those in his care**).

Go to aliveinchrist.osv.com for an interactive review.

A Work with Words Complete each sentence with the correct terms from the Word Bank. Not all terms will be used.

Word Bank

catechumen   absolution   Penance
contrition   witness   Holiness
consent   mortal   beginning
Original   sincere   Initiation

1. A _____, or "learner," is a person preparing

   to celebrate the Sacraments of _____.

2. For a sin to be _____, it must be a serious
   matter, done with full knowledge and complete

   _____.

3. _____ Sin is the sin of Adam and Eve,
   which led to the sinful condition of the human race from its

   _____.

4. _____ is

   _____ sorrow for having sinned.

5. _____ refers to the words spoken by the

   priest during the Sacrament of _____
   and Reconciliation to grant forgiveness of sins in God's name.

B **Check Understanding** Circle the letter of the choice that best completes each sentence.

6. We should always remain confident and hopeful, even though sin and evil are in the world, because _____.

   a. of Baptism

   b. a, c, and d

   c. of Reconciliation

   d. of God's power over sin

7. Baptism is like the Resurrection because _____.

   a. Jesus had both

   b. both are Sacraments

   c. new life begins

   d. both need water

8. The Sacraments of the Anointing of the Sick and Penance and Reconciliation both use _____ to show God's grace.

   a. Sacred Chrism

   b. repentance

   c. signs

   d. a pall

9. The Church celebrates the Sacraments of Baptism, Confirmation, and Eucharist all together _____.

   a. at Pentecost

   b. never

   c. every Sunday

   d. during the Easter Vigil

10. Venial sin _____ but does not _____ a person's relationship with God.

   a. weakens / destroy

   b. improves / deny

   c. changes / weaken

   d. reverses / change

C Make Connections Write a response to each statement or question.

11. What is the purpose of a prayer of lamentation?

   _____

   _____

12. What will solve the problem you express in a lamentation?

   _____

   _____

13. When you are faced with the problem of evil, what helps you?

   _____

   _____

   _____

14. How are sins forgiven?

   _____

   _____

   _____

Name three of the steps in an examination of conscience.

15. _____

16. _____

17. _____

Describe three ways that you can get help to deepen your faith.

18. _____

19. _____

20. _____

Sacraments

Our Catholic Tradition

- In the liturgy, the Holy Spirit forms the community as an assembly. (CCC, 1112)

- The Eucharist unites Christ's followers to him and to one another. (CCC, 1396)

- In the Eucharist, the bread and wine become the Body and Blood of Christ. He is really and truly present in the Eucharist—Body, Blood, soul, and divinity. (CCC 1374)

- In worship and daily living, the community shows that through the Eucharist, Christ lives in us, and we live in Christ. (CCC, 1076)

What do we celebrate in the Mass?

Gathered as One

♥ Let Us Pray

Leader: Gather us together, O Lord. Welcome us to your house.

"I rejoiced when they said to me,
   'Let us go to the house of the LORD.'"
   Psalm 122:1

All: Thank you, God, for your presence among us. Thank you for making us a people who need to be made one. Amen.

📖 Scripture

Call an assembly!
Gather the people,
   sanctify the congregation;
Assemble the elderly;
   gather the children,
   even infants nursing at the breast.
Joel 2:15b–16

❓ What Do You Wonder?

- How is praying as an assembly different from praying alone?

- Why do we have to go to Mass every Sunday?

United in Christ's Body

How are we united in the Mass?

We read in the Acts of the Apostles that the very first Christians gathered together to break bread and praise God.

Catholic Faith Words

Real Presence a phrase used to describe the teaching that Jesus Christ is really and truly with us in the Eucharist—Body, Blood, Soul, and Divinity

Communion of Saints everyone who believes in and follows Jesus: people on Earth, and people who have died and are in Purgatory or Heaven

 Scripture

Communal Life

Every day they devoted themselves to meeting together in the temple area and to breaking bread in their homes. They ate their meals with exultation and sincerity of heart, praising God and enjoying favor with all the people. And every day the Lord added to their number those who were being saved. **Acts 2:46–47**

As Jesus commanded at his Last Supper, we continue to gather as the Church today. At Sunday Mass, Sally sees Billy Yuan with his grandfather, who is in his wheelchair. Father Burke is talking with Deacon Tom, and Sister Teresita is with the Dixon family. Sally says hello to DJ and waves to Zoe, who comes early to pray the Rosary. Happy or sad, people come. All are welcome.

In His Name

The worshippers at Sally's church have come from different places to assemble as one community of faith. When the opening hymn begins and all raise their voices in song and prayer, they become more than just a group of individuals. They become a liturgical assembly gathered in Christ's name, doing the most important thing that Catholics can do—participating in the Eucharist.

When a parish community comes together to participate in the Eucharist, you can see that all kinds of people make up the Body of Christ. Rich and poor, old and young, healthy and frail, people come together from all nations and cultures to share in the Mass, the celebration of their salvation through Christ. Together they become an assembly of the People of God brought together by the Holy Spirit with Christ in their midst.

The Real Presence

The Mass is central to Catholic life because it unites us more closely to Christ and to one another. During the liturgy, Catholics celebrate the presence of Christ.

He is present in the assembly, the priest, and the Word of God. Most importantly, Jesus is really and truly present in the Eucharist. Our gifts of bread and wine truly become Christ. The Church teaches that in the Eucharist, Jesus Christ is really and truly present: Body, Blood, Soul, and Divinity. This unique, true presence of Christ in the Eucharist under the appearance of bread and wine is called the **Real Presence**.

In the Eucharist, the bread and wine become the Body and Blood of Christ. In the celebration, we remember, give thanks for, and share in his life, Death, and Resurrection through prayer, song, active participation, and reception of Holy Communion. All are united to the sacrifice of Christ through which new life comes. And we are not just united with those at Mass with us. Because we are part of the **Communion of Saints**, we are joined more closely to all those who believe. We remember in a special way those who have died, praying that they will have eternal happiness and life with God in Heaven.

→ How and with whom are we united in the celebration of the Mass?

Share Your Faith

Reflect What sights, sounds, and actions make you feel welcome at Mass?

_____

_____

_____

Share With a partner, share these things and why they make you feel welcome. Discuss how you can welcome others as you gather for the Mass.

Participation in the Community

Why do we celebrate the Lord's Day?

When Sally joins the parish community for Mass on Sunday, she may not be aware that she is stepping into a tradition many centuries old. In the time of the early Christians, Sunday was the Lord's Day, the day on which the community celebrated the Resurrection of Jesus. The Church continues this practice today.

The Eucharist is the high point of a life of faith shared by a community. The Christian community must be built day by day, as Saint Paul advised an early Church community.

 Scripture

Church Order

"We urge you, brothers, admonish the idle, cheer the fainthearted, support the weak, be patient with all. See that no one returns evil for evil; rather, always seek what is good [both] for each other and for all. Rejoice always. Pray without ceasing. In all circumstances give thanks, for this is the will of God for you in Christ Jesus." **1 Thessalonians 5:14–18**

Sunday Observance

According to Jewish custom, the Sabbath began on Friday evening. The early Jewish Christians adopted this custom. Similarly, the Church begins its observance of Sunday on Saturday evening. Because of this, Saturday evening Mass is considered part of the Sunday observance.

For Catholics, participation in the Sunday Eucharist is a privilege and a duty. It offers the opportunity to meet God the Father in a dialogue through Christ and the Holy Spirit, to pray, and to give offerings. To deliberately stay away from Mass on Sunday without a very good reason is a serious matter.

Role and Responsibilities

Within the Church, certain members are called to special service as ordained ministers—baptized men who, through the grace of the Sacrament of Holy Orders, serve God and the Church as bishops, priests, and deacons. By the power of the Holy Spirit, bishops and priests preside, or lead the Eucharistic celebration. The priest acts *in persona Christi,* representing Christ as he presides over the assembly in worship. Deacons assist in many ways, such as proclaiming the Gospel, and distributing Holy Communion.

Other members called by the community also have distinct roles in the liturgy. They are greeters, choir members, cantors, musicians, readers, altar servers, and extraordinary ministers of Holy Communion. All of these people help the assembly worship as one community.

Underline two of these liturgical roles that interest you or that you would like to know more about. Explain your choice.

Connect Your Faith

Share an Invitation Imagine that you have been asked to give a talk at the end of Sunday Mass, inviting others to serve in any of these liturgical roles. What three reasons would you give for joining a particular ministry?

1. _____

2. _____

3. _____

Our Catholic Life

What are the specific responsibilities of people who serve in the celebration of the Mass?

All members of the parish are invited to participate in the Eucharist. Priests and deacons assist the bishops in teaching, preaching, and celebrating the Sacraments. Led by these ordained ministers, other members of the Church serve the assembly. Think about the skills and qualities required for each one listed.

Place a check mark by the roles that could share your God-given gifts and talents with your parish community.

Roles and Responsibilities

☐ **Choir member** Enhances worship by singing in a group and supporting the singing of the assembly.

☐ **Extraordinary minister of Holy Communion** Helps distribute Communion at Mass or to those who are sick.

☐ **Cantor** Leads the people in song and sings the verses of the psalm and other sacred texts in the liturgy.

☐ **Greeter or usher** Greets and seats people, passes out worship programs and bulletins, and takes up the collection.

☐ **Reader or Lector** Proclaims the Word of God in the first and second readings of the Mass. A reader may also read the Prayer of the Faithful.

☐ **Altar server** Assists the priest by holding the book of Mass prayers and bringing items to the altar as needed. A server also carries the cross, candles, and incense in processions.

People of Faith

April 28

Saint Louis de Montfort, 1673—1716

Saint Louis de Montfort was a French priest. He told people to pray every day and to believe that God answers all prayers. He knew that Jesus used stories to invite us to become part of God's Kingdom. So Saint Louis did the same thing. He wrote many books to proclaim the Good News of God's love. Saint Louis had a special love for Jesus' Mother, Mary, so he told people about her, too. He said that she loves us even more than our own mothers do. People still read his books and learn about Jesus from his writings.

Discuss: What story can you tell about Jesus?

Learn more about Saint Louis de Montfort at **aliveinchrist.osv.com**

Live Your Faith

Name someone who makes you feel welcome at your parish during the Sunday celebration of the Lord's Day. Work in small groups to write thank you notes to the person each group member named. Outline your note below.

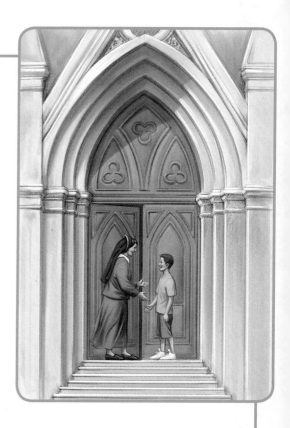

♡ Let Us Pray

Lectio Divina

This ancient prayer of the Church is a slow praying of the Scriptures in which we listen for what the Holy Spirit wants us to hear.

Gather and begin with the Sign of the Cross.

Leader: Come Holy Spirit. Open our ears;

All: open our minds; open our hearts.

Scripture Reading: 1 Thessalonians 5:14–18
First Reflection
Think of one word or phrase from the reflection
that stands out to you.

Scripture Reading: 1 Thessalonians 5:14–18
Second Reflection
Think about why your chosen word or phrase means
something important to you.

Scripture Reading: 1 Thessalonians 5:14–18
Third Reflection
Consider what God is saying or asking you to do
through the word or phrase.

All: Our Father, who art in heaven,
hallowed be thy name;
thy kingdom come,
thy will be done
on earth as it is in heaven.
Give us this day our daily bread,
and forgive us our trespasses,
as we forgive those who trespass against us;
and lead us not into temptation,
but deliver us from evil.

FAMILY+FAITH
LIVING AND LEARNING TOGETHER

YOUR CHILD LEARNED >>>

This chapter explains that the Mass is central to Catholic life because it unites Christ's followers more closely to him and to one another, including those who have died in God's friendship.

Scripture

 Read **Joel 2:15b–16** to find out about calling an assembly of believers.

Catholics Believe

- The wheat bread and grape wine become the Body and Blood of Christ in the Sacrament of the Eucharist.
- Participation in the Mass is a duty and privilege,

To learn more, go to the *Catechism of the Catholic Church #1141, 1373–1381* at **usccb.org.**

People of Faith

This week, your child learned about Saint Louis de Monfort, who influenced Pope Saint John Paul II's devotion to Mary.

CHILDREN AT THIS AGE >>>

How They Understand Sunday Mass Fifth-grade children may sometimes complain of being bored in Mass. They may see Mass as primarily an adult activity, not something geared toward them. However, they are at an age at which they can participate in Mass more than ever before. They can prepare by reading the Sunday readings before Mass, sing the hymns, and often can even participate in liturgical ministries, such as being an usher or altar server or singing in the choir. This participation can help children feel more a part of the community and more engaged in the liturgy.

CONSIDER THIS >>>

Have you ever experienced someone's presence after they died?

We hear about those experiences of presence in poetry, plays, and movies. We hear them from family and friends. These experiences confirm for us that love is stronger than death. Jesus' love for us conquered death. He gave us his Real Presence in the Eucharist so that we can continue to experience God's love—a love that is stronger than death. As Catholics, we recognize that "by the power of the Holy Spirit, Christ is present in the proclamation of God's Word, in the Eucharistic assembly, in the person of the priest, but above all and in a wholly unique manner in the Eucharist" (*USCCA, p. 223*). The true presence of Christ in the Eucharist under the appearance of bread and wine is called the Real Presence.

LET'S TALK >>>

- Ask your child to explain why the Eucharist is central to Catholic life.
- Talk about how your family celebrates the Lord's Day.

LET'S PRAY >>>

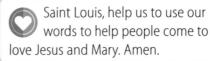 Saint Louis, help us to use our words to help people come to love Jesus and Mary. Amen.

For a multimedia glossary of Catholic Faith Words, Sunday readings, seasonal and Saint resources, and chapter activities go to **aliveinchrist.osv.com.**

Chapter 16 Review

A **Work with Words** Match each description in Column 1 with the correct term in Column 2.

Column 1

1. ordained men who proclaim the Gospel, serve at the altar, and distribute Holy Communion

2. called together by God to celebrate the liturgy

3. presides at the Eucharist

4. community built up by the Eucharist

5. has a role in the Eucharistic celebration

Column 2

bishop or priest

assembly

Body of Christ

each individual

deacons

B **Check Understanding** Fill in the circle next to the choice that best completes the sentence.

6. The true presence of Jesus Christ in the Eucharist, Body, Blood, Soul, and Divinity, is called the _____.
- ○ Paschal Mystery
- ○ Communion of Saints
- ○ Real Presence

7. The _____ is everyone who believes in and follows Jesus: people on Earth, and people who have died and are in Purgatory or Heaven.
- ○ Holy Trinity
- ○ catechumen
- ○ Communion of Saints

8. During Mass, Christ is present in all of these except _____.
- ○ the bells and incense
- ○ the Word of God
- ○ the Eucharist

9. Participation in the Sunday Eucharist is _____.
- ○ a privilege and an option
- ○ merely a duty
- ○ a privilege and a duty

10. All these are particular roles in the liturgy except _____.
- ○ reader
- ○ greeter
- ○ catechumen

Go to aliveinchrist.osv.com for an interactive review.

Liturgy of the Word

 Let Us Pray

Leader: Gracious Father, you are the author of all words
of truth.

"Your word, LORD, stands forever;
    it is firm as the heavens.
Through all generations your truth endures."
Psalm 119:89–90

All: Open our ears, and minds, and hearts, O God, to your
holy Word.

 **Scripture**

While [Jesus] was speaking, a woman from the crowd called out
and said to him, "Blessed is the womb that carried you and the breasts
at which you nursed." He replied, "Rather, blessed are those who hear
the word of God and observe it." **Luke 11:27–28**

? What Do You Wonder?

- How do you observe God's Word?

- What do you think Jesus means when
  he says that those who observe God's
  Word are "blessed"?

The Power of God's Message

Why is God's message important?

Jesus lived long ago, but his message is for all people of all times. Following Jesus helps us transform our lives. Here is a story about how learning about Jesus changed one man's life.

Saint Ignatius of Loyola

Ignatius of Loyola led a life of wealth and adventure. In 1507, when he was sixteen, he became a messenger in an important home in Spain. He often visited the Spanish court. As he grew older, he became a swordsman and a soldier.

In 1521, Ignatius was hit by a cannonball in a battle against the French army. One of his legs was wounded; the other was broken. The French soldiers admired his courage, so they took Ignatius back to his home, the castle of Loyola, to recover.

Ignatius spent months in bed while his legs mended. He asked for books to read, hoping that the castle had some adventure novels. The castle only had a book about Jesus' life and stories about Saints. Disappointed, he read what was brought to him.

To his surprise, the adventures of the Saints captured his imagination. Reading about the Saints taught Ignatius that his goals of fame and glory were empty. Instead, he decided to follow Jesus' teachings. He gave away his weapons and elegant clothes and dressed like a beggar.

Underline what helped lead Saint Ignatius to God.

Ignatius patterned his spiritual training after his military training. He wrote a book called the *Spiritual Exercises*, which outlines how to follow Jesus.

With a group of friends, Ignatius followed the exercises. They decided to share the Gospel throughout the world. They started the Society of Jesus, also called Jesuits. The Jesuits are a religious community of priests and religious brothers that still educates people about the Gospel. It is the largest male community in the Catholic Church. Today, there are approximately 19,000 Jesuits in the world.

Beginning the Mass

Saint Ignatius was moved by God's message. We, too, are moved by it. But we also must be prepared to listen to it. That is why the Mass begins by gathering the people together. The Introductory Rites focus our attention and prepare us to hear the Liturgy of the Word.

While we can be moved by the stories of the Saints, we are especially formed by God's Word. We must, however, open our hearts to allow God to change our lives. At Mass, we gather as Jesus' Body, the Church, and through the Introductory Rites, the Holy Spirit prepares our hearts to listen together to God's Word.

A Jesuit priest and professor unravels scrolls for study at the University of San Francisco's Center for the Pacific Rim.

Share Your Faith

Reflect Read Proverbs 16:16. Reflect silently on its meaning.

Share With a partner, take turns telling what the passage means to each of you. Write two sentences about why Saint Ignatius of Loyola would agree with this Bible verse. Explain your answer.

_____

_____

_____

_____

_____

God Speaks to Us

Why is the Liturgy of the Word important?

The process by which God makes himself known to us is called Divine Revelation. The chief sources of this Revelation are Sacred Tradition and Sacred Scripture. Every time you open the Bible, you discover a treasure—the Word of God. The Old Testament begins with the creation of the world. It tells about God's relationship with his People until the time of Jesus. The New Testament is about Jesus' life, teaching, and saving work. It also contains writings by Jesus' followers. Sacred Scripture was written long ago, but it continues to reveal God's truth today.

The inspired Word of God in Scripture is not something you can interpret on your own. The Church's understanding of the message of Jesus comes to you from the Apostles and from the life of the Church and her teachers. God's Word to the Church, safeguarded by the Apostles and their successors, the bishops, and handed down verbally to future generations is called Sacred Tradition. Scripture and Tradition have one common source: the Word of God conveyed through God's revelation.

Catholic Faith Words

Book of Gospels the book containing the Gospel readings from which the priest or deacon proclaims the Gospel during Mass

psalms poems and hymns that were first used in the liturgy of the Israelites. Today, the psalms are also prayed and sung in the public prayer of the Church.

Creed a formal statement of what we believe about the Holy Trinity and the Church. The word *creed* comes from the Latin for "I believe."

Scripture

Gratitude in Your Hearts

"Let the word of Christ dwell in you richly, as in all wisdom you teach and admonish one another, singing psalms, hymns, and spiritual songs with gratitude in your hearts to God." **Colossians 3:16**

Honoring God's Word

Ritual actions let the assembly know the importance of the Word of God. The readings are proclaimed from the ambo, the podium-like structure beside the altar. A lighted candle is usually placed near the ambo. After the first and second readings, the reader pauses and then says, "The word of the Lord," and you reply, "Thanks be to God."

➔ How do you express your gratitude to God during the liturgy?

Sometimes incense is used to reverence the **Book of Gospels**. The assembly stands for the Gospel reading. After the priest or deacon reads the Gospel, he raises the book and kisses it to show honor and love of God's Word.

Proclaimed and Preached

The Liturgy of the Word is the first of the two main parts of the Mass. It begins with the first reading from the Old Testament, followed by a response from one of the **psalms**, and ends after the profession of the Nicene or Apostles' **Creed** with the Prayer of the Faithful. In readings from the Old and New Testaments, God speaks to us as the assembly gathered, as well as to the heart of each person. We respond to him with our prayer.

The Liturgy of the Word

First Reading	The first reading is from the Old Testament or from the Acts of the Apostles.
Responsorial Psalm	The assembly usually sings a response taken from the psalm, and the choir sings the verses.
Second Reading	The second reading is from one of the New Testament Letters or from the Book of Revelation.
Acclamation	An Alleluia is sung, except during Lent, to express the assembly's anticipation of the Gospel.
Gospel Reading	Each person traces a cross on forehead, lips, and heart before the Gospel is proclaimed.
Homily	A talk given by the priest or deacon about the readings proclaimed and how God speaks to us today in his Word. The homilist encourages us to live faithfully.
Creed	Usually, the Nicene Creed is professed. During Easter and at other times, it's the Apostles' Creed.
Prayer of the Faithful	The assembly prays for the needs of Church leaders, the faithful, and the world.

Connect Your Faith

Respond to God Write three ritual actions during Mass that show the importance of the Word of God.

1. _____

2. _____

3. _____

_____

Our Catholic Life

How do you live God's Word?

The Word of God nourishes the Christian community in the liturgy. By reflecting on the Sunday readings either before or after Mass, you allow God's Word to become a real part of your life. When that happens, you live God's Word.

The exercise below is based on the Church's practice of *lectio divina*, "divine reading." It is a reflective way of reading Scripture that leads us to prayer.

Respond to the questions or statements in the space provided.

Reflect on the Word

Begin with a prayer:

- Ask the Holy Spirit to open your heart to hear God's Word.

- Read the Gospel or one of the other readings aloud. Write down the passage you will read.

_____

Ask yourself these questions:

- What words in the reading are important to me?

_____

- If I were going to tell someone the message of this reading, what would I say?

_____

_____

- How does this message apply to my life today?

_____

_____

- What action can I take today that will make the message of God's Word come alive in the world in which I live?

_____

_____

People of Faith

Saint Jerome, c. 341–420

When Saint Jerome was alive, most people spoke Latin. Because the Bible was written in Greek or Hebrew, most people couldn't read it. Jerome thought that everyone should be able to discover the Word of God, so he spent the rest of his life translating the Bible into Latin. His translation was called the *Vulgate*. The Church used it as the main Bible for almost 1,500 years. Jerome also wrote explanations about parts of the Bible that are hard to understand. These explanations are called commentaries. Saint Jerome wrote many other things, including history books and stories about Saints.

Discuss: What do you know about the Bible?

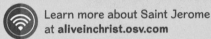 Learn more about Saint Jerome at **aliveinchrist.osv.com**

Live Your Faith

Listen carefully to the Sunday readings this week at Mass. In the space below, write how their messages will help you run the race of faith this week.

_____

_____

_____

_____

_____

_____

_____

_____

_____

_____

_____

Let Us Pray

Psalm Prayer of Praise

In this prayer, using a psalm from the Old Testament, we give praise to God for his everlasting love.

Gather and begin with the Sign of the Cross.

Side 1: I bow down before you.
I will give thanks to your name for your kind love
that never fails.

Side 2: When I prayed to you, you answered me.
You made me brave and strong.

All: I thank you, Lord, with all my heart.
I will sing your praises forever.

Side 1: All the rulers in the world will thank you, Lord.
They have heard the promises that you have made.
That is why they will thank you.

Side 2: They will sing about what you have done.
They will sing because of your great glory.

All: I thank you, Lord, with all my heart.
I will sing your praises forever.

Side 1: You keep me safe when there is trouble around me.
You save me with your love and protection.

Side 2: You will do everything you have promised.
Lord, your kind love will always continue.
Finish the work of your hands.

All: I thank you, Lord, with all my heart.
I will sing your praises forever. **Based on Psalm 138**

 Sing "Malo! Malo! Thanks Be to God"

YOUR CHILD LEARNED >>>

This chapter describes the elements of the Liturgy of the Word and the need to reflect on Scripture, and identifies Sacred Tradition as the message of Jesus that comes from the Apostles and the life of the Church.

Scripture

 Read **Luke 11:27–28** to find out what Jesus said about those who hear and observe the Word of God.

Catholics Believe

• Sacred Scripture is the Word of God written by humans.

• The Word of God is proclaimed and preached in the first of two main parts of the Mass: the Liturgy of the Word.

To learn more, go to the *Catechism of the Catholic Church #84, 108, 1088, 1100* at **usccb.org**.

People of Faith

This week, your child learned about Saint Jerome. Jerome translated the Bible from Greek and Hebrew into Latin.

CHILDREN AT THIS AGE >>>

How They Understand the Liturgy of the Word Because of the dramatic increase in reading and writing work that occurs in most educational settings beginning in fourth grade, many fifth-graders are better able than before to read and understand the language used in our Lectionary.

This can help to open up a new level of understanding of Scripture and of the Mass, especially if children can learn to look for connections between the readings used. Talk with your child about the readings after Mass. Ask them to share what teachings, words, attitudes, and beliefs they heard.

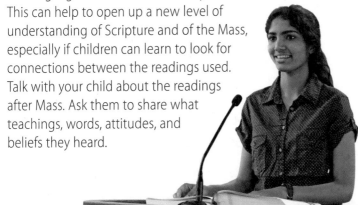

CONSIDER THIS >>>

Who is the person in your life you go to when you want to be heard?

To be heard is a very precious gift. God invites us to hear his Word at Mass. God enters into a dialogue with us and opens our hearts to hear his precious Word. As Catholics, we know that "the Liturgy of the Word is an important part of every liturgy because the proclamation of the Word of God and the response of faith to it help give meaning to the celebration" (*USCCA, p. 177*).

LET'S TALK >>>

• Ask your child to explain the importance of the Liturgy of the Word in the Mass.

• Share how your family honors God's Word.

LET'S PRAY >>>

 Saint Jerome, pray for us that we may love the Word of God as you did. May we always find wisdom and comfort in God's Word. Amen.

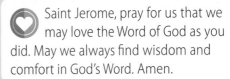 For a multimedia glossary of Catholic Faith Words, Sunday readings, seasonal and Saint resources, and chapter activities go to **aliveinchrist.osv.com**.

Chapter 17 Review

A
Work with Words Complete each sentence with the correct term from the Word Bank. Not all terms will be used.

> ### Word Bank
> Acclamation   Nicene Creed
>
> Sacred   candle
> Scripture
>   ambo
>
> Sacred
> Tradition   homily

1. The Bible is also called

   _____.

2. God's Word to the Church, safeguarded by the Apostles and their successors, the bishops, and handed down verbally to future generations comes from

   _____.

3. The _____ explains the reading in the Liturgy of the Word.

4. Readings are proclaimed from the _____ near the altar.

5. The homily is usually followed by the _____.

B
Check Understanding Fill in the circle by the choice that best completes the sentence or answers the question.

6. The Responsorial Psalm is said or sung after the _____.
   - ○ first reading
   - ○ Creed
   - ○ second reading

7. The word *creed* means _____.
   - ○ "I need"
   - ○ "I think"
   - ○ "I believe"

8. Participation in the Liturgy of the Word includes all of these except _____.
   - ○ listening
   - ○ fasting
   - ○ responding

9. Scripture and Tradition have one _____ source.
   - ○ historical
   - ○ biblical
   - ○ common

10. _____ actions show the assembly the importance of the Word of God.
   - ○ Holy
   - ○ Ritual
   - ○ Reverent

Go to aliveinchrist.osv.com for an interactive review.

Liturgy of the Eucharist

💜 Let Us Pray

Leader: Generous God, you satisfy our hungry hearts.

"Then I will thank you in the great assembly;
I will praise you before the mighty throng."
Psalm 35:18

All: You feed us, Lord, with the Bread of Life and the
Chalice of Salvation. We are full—full of thanks. Amen.

📖 Scripture

The cup of blessing that we bless, is it not a
participation in the blood of Christ? The bread
that we break, is it not a participation in the
body of Christ? **1 Corinthians 10:16**

❓ What Do You Wonder?

- How is the Mass a meal and a sacrifice?

- How do you participate in the Body of Christ?

Jesus Feeds Us

What hunger does the Eucharist satisfy?

Crowds followed Jesus around the countryside to hear him speak and to be healed. One time, the crowds followed Jesus to a town called Bethsaida. After a long day, the crowd was getting hungry. Yet, they showed no signs of leaving.

Scripture

The Feeding of the Five Thousand

As the day was drawing to a close, the Twelve approached [Jesus] and said, "Dismiss the crowd so that they can go to the surrounding villages and farms and find lodging and provisions; for we are in a deserted place here."

[Jesus] said to them, "Give them some food yourselves."

They replied, "Five loaves and two fish are all we have, unless we ourselves go and buy food for all these people."

Now the men there numbered about five thousand. Then he said to his disciples, "Have them sit down in groups of [about] fifty."

They did so and made them all sit down. Then taking the five loaves and the two fish, and looking up to heaven, [Jesus] said the blessing over them, broke them, and gave them to the disciples to set before the crowd. They all ate and were satisfied. And when the leftover fragments were picked up, they filled twelve wicker baskets.   Luke 9:12–17

➜ How did Jesus feed the crowd?

➜ How does Jesus feed us today?

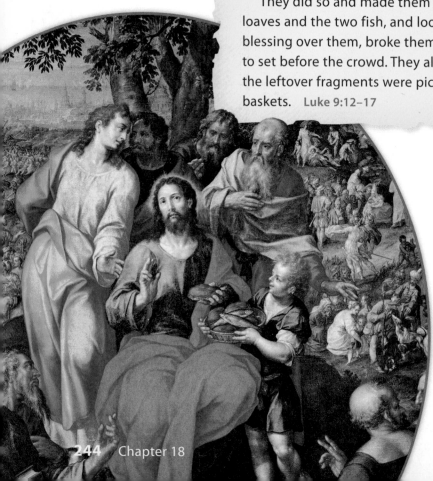

In this painting, the artist depicts the Apostles and others reacting to Jesus' command to feed the five thousand people gathered. What is their reaction?

Bread of Life

No matter what the cause, the hunger that people suffer is real. But those who hunger for bread also hunger for spiritual food. This hunger is as real as physical hunger. It is the hunger for happiness and love. Only God can feed this hunger, for God alone is the source of true happiness. God gave people a taste of true happiness in Jesus, the Savior.

In the Sacrament of the Eucharist, you share the Bread of Life and the Cup of Salvation. You taste the happiness you will one day experience with God in Heaven. The bread you eat at meals and the Eucharist are similar because both offer nourishment. The Eucharist, however, offers lasting spiritual nourishment and the promise of eternal life.

Share Your Faith

Reflect Think of ways in which the Eucharist is food for others.

Share Imagine that you are producing a movie called *Bread of the World*. With a partner, write a script for one scene of your movie. Act out your scene for the group.

The Eucharistic Mystery

Why is the Eucharist a sacrifice?

At the Last Supper, Jesus' words and actions changed the traditional Passover meal into something new. It became a living memorial of the sacrifice Jesus was about to make by his Death.

Catholic Faith Words

consecration the part of the Eucharistic Prayer in which the priest prays the words of Jesus over the bread and wine, and these elements become the Body and Blood of Christ

transubstantiation the process by which the power of the Holy Spirit and the words of the priest transform the bread and wine into the Body and Blood of Christ

Blessed Sacrament the Holy Eucharist, especially the Body of Christ, reserved in the Tabernacle

 Scripture

The Lord's Supper

While they were eating, Jesus took bread, said the blessing, broke it, and giving it to his disciples said, "Take and eat; this is my body." Then he took a cup, gave thanks, and gave it to them, saying, "Drink from it, all of you, for this is my blood of the covenant, which will be shed on behalf of many for the forgiveness of sins." Matthew 26:26–28

→ In what part of the Mass do you hear these words?

In order to give himself to his followers as the Bread of Life, Jesus died on the Cross. His Death was a perfect sacrifice of love. It brought salvation and the abundance of God's grace to the world. In the Eucharist, Christ unites his followers to his own sacrifice so that they can experience salvation.

The Liturgy of the Eucharist

Every time you participate in the Eucharist, you share both in the meal and in the sacrifice of Jesus. Throughout the Mass, the assembly is gathered and led by God's Spirit. In the Eucharistic Prayer, the people, led by the priest, ask the Father to send his Holy Spirit. This great prayer is at the heart of the second main part of the Mass during which we receive Jesus' Body and Blood—the Liturgy of the Eucharist.

The priest calls on the Holy Spirit to make holy the assembly and the gifts of bread and wine. In the part of the prayer called the **consecration**, the priest prays Jesus' own words from the Last Supper to consecrate the bread and wine. By the words of the priest and the power of the Holy Spirit, the wheat bread and grape wine are transformed into the Body and Blood of Christ. The Church refers to this mystery as **transubstantiation**. Through the action of the priest, Christ himself offers the sacrifice. Prayers for the whole Church follow. The Eucharistic Prayer ends with praise for the Trinity, and the assembly responds with the Great Amen.

Underline the meaning of transubstantiation.

When you truly believe and respond in faith, you can be transformed by the Body and Blood of Jesus. Through the Eucharist, you live in Christ, and Christ lives in you.

Outside of Mass, many Catholics participate in Eucharistic Adoration. They pray prayers of adoration before the **Blessed Sacrament.** The Blessed Sacrament is another name for the Holy Eucharist, especially the Body of Christ reserved in the Tabernacle.

Connect Your Faith

Talk About Sacrifice Write your responses to the following questions:

1. What did Jesus sacrifice for us? Why?

2. How does the Church celebrate and participate in that sacrifice?

Our Catholic Life

What does it mean to live the Eucharist?

Having received Christ in the Eucharist, the assembly is sent forth in the Concluding Rites with the responsibility to live the Eucharist. There are ways to be more active in living the Eucharist in your daily life.

Place check marks next to the things you will do this week.

Share the Gift of Love

☐	**Give thanks**	Every day, think about the gifts that you and your friends and family have been given and thank God for them.
☐	**Communicate**	When you are with a friend or family member, listen to what that person is saying. When it is your turn, share your thoughts and feelings.
☐	**Go forth**	Observe your school and neighborhood. Identify people who need help or situations that you could improve, and take some action.
☐	**Sacrifice**	Once each day, do something to help someone else, but do not tell anyone about it.
☐	**Remember**	Set aside some special time to read the stories of Jesus in the New Testament. Think about what they are saying about your own life.

People of Faith

Saint Clare of Assisi, 1194–1253

August 11

Saint Clare was one of the first people to follow the teaching of Saint Francis of Assisi. She lived with a group of women who were very poor and prayed all the time. Despite their hard life, Clare and the other women were very happy because they knew God loved them. Saint Clare believed that Jesus was really and truly present in the Eucharist. Two times, when enemies wanted to attack the town of Assisi, the people asked Clare for help. She came to the walls of the city, holding the Blessed Sacrament in her hands. Both times the enemy ran away in fear.

Discuss: How do you show your devotion to the Eucharist?

Learn more about Saint Clare of Assisi at **aliveinchrist.osv.com**

Live Your Faith

Write and illustrate a story board in the space below that shows how people your age can live out the Eucharist. Make sure to include yourself in your illustration.

Let Us Pray

Prayer of Gratitude

This prayer of gratitude helps us to be grateful for the Eucharist and to live the Eucharist in our lives.

Gather and begin with the Sign of the Cross.

Leader: In his great gift to us, Jesus, the Bread of Life, gave us his very life and love. We gather to thank him.

Reader 1: Because there are times we are worried or discouraged,

All: thank you for coming to us, O Bread of Life.

Reader 2: Because we can do nothing alone,

All: thank you for coming to us, O Bread of Life.

Reader 3: When others are lonely or left out,

All: we will be bread of life for others.

Reader 4: When people are in need of kindness, care, or a helping hand,

All: we will be bread of life for others.

Reader 5: When we give thanks to family and friends who have been there for us,

All: we will be bread of life for others.

Leader: Jesus, Bread of Life, you nourish us. Teach us, through this nourishing, to be nourishment for others.

All: Amen.

 Sing "Blest by Your Sacrifice"

FAMILY+FAITH
LIVING AND LEARNING TOGETHER

YOUR CHILD LEARNED >>>

This chapter explains the significance of the bread and wine becoming the Body and Blood of Christ, expressing the Mass as a holy meal and a sacrifice.

Scripture

 Read **1 Corinthians 10:16** to see what Saint Paul wrote about the Body and Blood of Christ.

Catholics Believe

- In Sunday worship and daily living, we show that the Eucharist is the source and the summit of the Catholic Church.

- The power of the Holy Spirit and the words of the priest transform the bread and wine into the Body and Blood of Jesus.

To learn more, go to the *Catechism of the Catholic Church #1324, 1372, 1398* at usccb.org.

People of Faith

This week, your child learned about Saint Clare of Assisi, one of the first followers of Saint Francis of Assisi. Clare's devotion to the Blessed Sacrament saved her town from attack two times.

CHILDREN AT THIS AGE >>>

How They Understand Transubstantiation The process of transubstantiation, by which our gifts of bread and wine become the Body and Blood of Jesus, is a mystery to most adult Catholics, and even more of a mystery to children. With the trust and openness of young children, First Communicants (often second-graders) can accept this doctrine on faith. Fifth-graders are sometimes more skeptical. It helps them to know that Jesus promised in Scripture that he would be with us in this way, that early Christians professed this belief, and that the Catholic Church has upheld this doctrine for 2,000 years.

CONSIDER THIS >>>

How focused are you on what you eat?

Everywhere in our culture we see and hear messages about food. One of those familiar messages is "you are what you eat." Saint Augustine proclaimed that when we consume the Eucharist, "we become what we eat." Our need to be nourished and fed by God in the Eucharist is essential and central to our lives. As Catholics, we know that "Holy Communion increases our union with Christ. Just as bodily food sustains our physical life, so Holy Communion nourishes our spiritual life. This Communion moves us away from sin, strengthening our moral resolve to avoid evil and turn ever more powerfully toward God" (*USCCA, p. 223*).

LET'S TALK >>>

- Ask your child to explain the Liturgy of the Eucharist, the second main part of the Mass.

- Share how your family lives the Eucharist.

LET'S PRAY >>>

 Saint Clare, pray for us that we may share your faith and trust in God's love, and your respect and love for the Eucharist. Amen.

 For a multimedia glossary of Catholic Faith Words, Sunday readings, seasonal and Saint resources, and chapter activities go to **aliveinchrist.osv.com**.

Chapter 18 Review

A **Work with Words** Fill in the circle by the choice that best completes the sentence.

1. The Eucharist is both a _____ and a _____.
   - ○ Sacrament/commandment
   - ○ sacrifice/sacred meal
   - ○ sacrifice/Tabernacle

2. Living the Eucharist means having gratitude for God's gifts and showing it through _____.
   - ○ meditation
   - ○ sacrificing for others
   - ○ doing penance

3. The changing of bread and wine into the Body and Blood of Christ is called _____.
   - ○ redemption
   - ○ celebration
   - ○ transubstantiation

4. In the Eucharistic Prayer, the words and activities of the priest and the power of the Holy Spirit bring about the _____ of the bread and wine.
   - ○ consecration
   - ○ sacrifice
   - ○ celebration

5. Jesus gave himself _____.
   - ○ to change the Third Commandment
   - ○ as a perfect sacrifice of love
   - ○ to consecrate a Tabernacle

B **Check Understanding**
In the boxes provided, write the words that complete the sentences. If your other answers are correct, the answer to number 10 will appear in the shaded boxes.

6. Jesus fed the crowd with two fish and five _____ of bread.
7. The Bread of the Eucharist offers lasting spiritual _____.
8. When you truly believe and respond in faith, you can be _____ by the Body and Blood of Jesus.
9. "This is my blood of the _____, which will be shed on behalf of many for the forgiveness of sins."
10. In the Sacrament of the Eucharist, you share the Bread of _____ and the Cup of Salvation.

Go to aliveinchrist.osv.com for an interactive review.

A Work with Words Match each description in Column 1 with the correct term in Column 2.

Column 1

Column 2

1. words the priest prays over the bread and wine so that they become Christ's Body and Blood

Sacred Tradition

2. community of believers who come together for public worship

Eucharistic Prayer

3. God's Word to the Church, safeguarded by the Apostles and their successors, the bishops, and handed down verbally to future generations

Real Presence

4. the heart of the second half of the Mass

the consecration

5. the real and true presence of Christ in the Eucharist

assembly

Complete each statement.

6. The bread you eat at meals and the Bread of Life in the

_____ are similar in that both offer nourishment.

7. By the power of the Holy Spirit, bishops and priests,

_____ ministers, preside or act as leaders of the Eucharistic assembly.

8. During the Concluding Rites, the assembly is _____.

9. At the _____ Jesus' words and actions changed the traditional Passover meal into a living memorial of the sacrifice he was about to make by his Death on the Cross.

10. _____ is the holy writings of the Old and New Testaments, the inspired Word of God written by humans.

B Check Understanding **Complete each sentence with the correct term.**

11. Through the _____, you live in Christ, and Christ lives in you.

12. Jesus is present in the _____ as it is proclaimed and preached in the liturgy.

13. The _____ is another name for the Holy Eucharist, especially the Body of Christ reserved in the Tabernacle.

14. In the liturgy, the people remember with thanksgiving the

   _____ Mystery of the Lord through prayer, song, Sacrament, listening, active participation, and reception of Communion.

15. Rich and poor, old and young, healthy and frail, people come together

   from all nations and cultures to share in the _____, the celebration of their salvation through Christ.

C Make Connections **Write a response to each of the statements.**

Explain the best way for you to participate in the Liturgy of the Word, using the following terms:

| reader | reflection | God's Word |

16–18. _____

_____

_____

_____

_____

_____

Use the following terms to explain what living the Eucharist means:

give   thanks   sacrifice

19-20. _____

_____

_____

_____

_____

_____

_____

_____

_____

_____

_____

_____

Kingdom of God

Our Catholic Tradition

- Answering God's call through the Sacraments at the Service of Communion helps to build up the People of God. (CCC, 1534)

- Faith in the Resurrection is the basis of our hope in eternal life with God in Heaven. (CCC, 989)

- As we wait for Christ's Second Coming, we must pray and live justly. (CCC, 2859)

- The Works of Mercy are actions that address the physical and spiritual needs of others. (CCC, 2447)

How does faithfully living your vocation affect life in this world and the next?

The Call to Serve

Let Us Pray

Leader: Lord, help us hear your call to service.

"I heard the voice of the Lord saying, 'Whom shall I send? Who will go for us?' 'Here I am,' I said; 'send me!'" Isaiah 6:8

All: Servant Lord, help us remember that the only way into your Kingdom is through the servants' entrance. Amen.

Scripture

"Whoever serves me must follow me, and where I am, there also will my servant be. The Father will honor whoever serves me."

[Then Jesus] rose from supper and took off his outer garments. He took a towel and tied it around his waist. Then he poured water into a basin and began to wash the disciples' feet and dry them with the towel around his waist.

So when he had washed their feet [and] put his garments back on and reclined at table again, he said to them, "Do you realize what I have done for you? You call me 'teacher' and 'master,' and rightly so, for indeed I am. If I, therefore, the master and teacher, have washed your feet, you ought to wash one another's feet. I have given you a model to follow, so that as I have done for you, you should also do."

John 12:26; 13:4–5, 12–15

❓ What Do You Wonder?

- What kind of servant leader was Jesus?
- What kind of service does Jesus expect from you?

Responding to God's Call

How do vocations serve God and others?

Catholic Faith Words

vocation a particular way to answer God's call, whether as a lay person (married or single), a religious, or a member of the ordained ministry

Jesus makes it clear that you must live your life in service of others if you want to be his disciple. We answer God's call to service through our **vocation**. All Christian vocations flow from the grace received in Baptism. Every person has the responsibility to answer the call from God and to choose a vocation in which they cooperate with God as he makes his Kingdom visible on Earth.

Any vocation to which you are called by God involves work. Your work is a reflection of your goodness and good acts. You participate in creation and God's Reign through honest and useful work. When Jesus saw the needs of the people around him, he wanted to help them. Through his disciples, Jesus reached out to people everywhere.

Scripture

The Compassion of Jesus

Jesus went around to all the towns and villages, teaching in their synagogues, proclaiming the gospel of the kingdom, and curing every disease and illness. At the sight of the crowds, his heart was moved with pity for them because they were troubled and abandoned, like sheep without a shepherd. Then he said to his disciples, "The harvest is abundant but the laborers are few; so ask the master of the harvest to send out laborers for his harvest." Matthew 9:35–38

➤ **What is the mission of all baptized followers of Jesus?**

Serve God and Others

The mission of the Church is to be catholic, or universal, and to welcome every person who wishes to be a disciple of Jesus. Through Baptism, all of us are called to spread the Gospel and build up the Body of Christ. Here is a story about two disciples who looked for ways to serve others in their daily lives.

Saints Isidore and Maria

Near the end of the eleventh century, a humble farm laborer named Isidore lived in Spain with his wife, Maria. After their only son died young, the couple lived a life of complete devotion to God. Although Isidore and Maria remained poor, they were good people who worked hard and prayed often. They became known as champions of the poor and sick.

It is said that Isidore shared his meals so generously that often he had only scraps left for himself. Another story relates that some fellow workers complained that Isidore was always late to work in the fields because he went to Mass in the morning. But Isidore explained that he had to report first to a higher Master.

➜ **What activities do you offer to God?**

➜ **How does doing this help you?**

Share Your Faith

Reflect Think of a person whom you particularly admire because of his or her service to others.

Share With a partner, discuss the qualities you admire in such persons. In the space below, write words that describe some of these qualities. Circle one quality that each of you will practice this week.

Building Up the Body of Christ

How do people live the Sacraments at the Service of Communion?

Isidore and Maria served God as a married couple. Marriage is one of the particular ways to answer God's call, or vocation. Isidore and Maria lived a simple life of work and daily prayer. They dedicated themselves to each other, just as Christ dedicated himself to the Church and to the service of God and his Kingdom. In the Church, the building up of the People of God is accomplished with God's grace through the efforts of both ordained ministers—baptized men who, through the Sacrament of Holy Orders, serve God and the Church as bishops, priests, and deacons teaching, guiding, and leading the assembly in worship—and the **laity**, also known as laypeople.

These ordained men, as well as those in **consecrated religious life**, are given charisms, special gifts or graces, to live out the Christian life and to serve the common good in building up the Church.

Lay men and women have a special responsibility to bring the Good News of Jesus to the world around them through work, public service, and family life. Other men and women are called to consecrated religious life. They take **vows**, or make solemn promises, to dedicate their lives in service to God. Some deacons, priests, and bishops belong to religious communities.

➔ How do the ordained ministers and laity in your parish build up the People of God?

Two young nuns await the arrival of the Pope during a papal visit to Barcelona, Spain.

Sacraments at the Service of Communion		
Sacrament	Minister of the Sacrament	Signs
Holy Orders	The bishop	The laying on of hands and prayer of consecration
Matrimony	The couple (in Eastern Rite Churches, the priest)	The exchange of promises

The Church celebrates two Sacraments that particularly help Catholics answer the call to service. These Sacraments at the Service of Communion are the Sacrament of Holy Orders and the Sacrament of Matrimony. Both celebrate people's commitment to serve God and the community and to build up the People of God.

In Matrimony, a baptized man and a baptized woman promise to love and be faithful to each other throughout their lives. They receive grace that will help them lead lives of love that reflect Christ's love for his Church. They commit to sharing married love only with each other. The man and woman also promise to be open at all times to the possibility of having children and to love, care for, and educate any children God gives them. The Sacrament of Matrimony is celebrated publicly before a priest or deacon, witnesses, and the gathered assembly.

In Holy Orders, baptized men are ordained to serve the Church faithfully as deacons, priests, or bishops. Priests and deacons promise to obey the bishop, and bishops promise to exercise their authority in accordance with other bishops and the Pope.

Connect Your Faith

Answer the Call Design an advertisement that encourages people to live out their vocations as single people, married couples, ordained ministers, or men and women religious. Think about the vocation to which God may be calling you.

Our Catholic Life

What does a religious vocation require?

Religious communities dedicate themselves to lives of service. Those who are called to a religious vocation can join one of a large number of communities. Each community has its own gift, or charism, that determines the kind of service to which the members of the community give their lives.

A variety of features distinguish one religious community from another. You can learn about the communities by looking at these aspects.

Choose a religious community to research and fill in the chart with the information you find.

Many Ways to Serve

Identify the ministry. Often a community is identified with its ministry. Some are devoted to prayer. Others are known for teaching, health care, or missionary work.

Trace the history. Who founded the community? Some were founded by Saints like Benedict and Francis. Others have been founded by groups or little-known individuals.	**Who?** _____ _____

Examine the way of life. Like the early Christians, religious communities often share a simple life and have developed special ways of praying, working, and living together. They may follow a common, unifying rule of life.

Find the motivation. Some communities were started in order to meet certain needs. Monastic communities began when many Christians felt called to leave the busy life of the world and live a life of contemplation. Other groups came into being to serve a specific need in the world or in the Church.	**Why?** _____ _____ _____

Understand the commitment. Many religious take vows of poverty, chastity, and obedience. Others take additional vows.

See the changes. How has the community developed over time? Many communities change their purpose as needs or social conditions change.	**How?** _____ _____

People of Faith

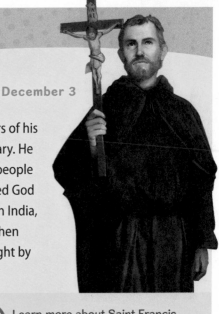

Saint Francis Xavier, 1506—1552

December 3

Everyone expected Saint Francis Xavier to be a teacher like other members of his family. Instead, he listened to God's call to become a priest and a missionary. He knew his vocation was to tell people about Jesus. He was one of the first people to follow Saint Ignatius of Loyola, the founder of the Jesuit order. He served God by leaving his home in Spain and going to Asia. He preached the Gospel in India, Indonesia, and Japan. Many people became Christians because of him. When Saint Francis didn't know the language of the people he was with, he taught by using pictures of Mary and Jesus.

Discuss: How can you share the Gospel with others?

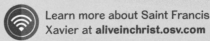 Learn more about Saint Francis Xavier at **aliveinchrist.osv.com**

Live Your Faith

Write three interview questions for a priest or deacon who serves your parish. Schedule a time to talk to him about his work and ask your questions. After your interview, send the priest or deacon a thank you note for what he does in your community.

1. _____
   _____
   _____

2. _____
   _____
   _____

3. _____
   _____
   _____

Let Us Pray

Celebration of the Word

Gather and begin with the Sign of the Cross.

Leader: God our Father, you call us in Baptism to continue the work of your Son. Help us hear your word to us today.

Reader: A reading from the First Book of Samuel.

Read 1 Samuel 3:1–10.

The word of the Lord.

All: Thanks be to God.

Leader: Let us pray.

Bow your heads as the leader prays.

All: Amen.

 Sing "Somos el Cuerpo de Cristo/We Are the Body of Christ"
Somos el cuerpo de Cristo.
We are the Body of Christ.
Hemos oído el llamado;
we've answered "Yes" to the call of the Lord.
Somos el cuerpo de Cristo.
We are the Body of Christ.
Traemos su santo mensaje.
We come to bring the Good News
to the world.
© 1994, Jaime Cortez. Published by OCP.
All rights reserved.

YOUR CHILD LEARNED >>>

This chapter identifies vocation as the particular way we respond to God's call to serve him and others and examines consecrated religious life and the Sacraments at the Service of Communion.

Scripture

 Read **John 12:26; 13:4–5, 12–15** to find out what Jesus did for the disciples at the Last Supper.

Catholics Believe

- Through Baptism, all of us are called to spread the Gospel and build up the Body of Christ.
- The Sacraments at the Service of Communion are Holy Orders and Matrimony.

To learn more, go to the *Catechism of the Catholic Church #1534, 1653* at **usccb.org**.

People of Faith

This week, your child learned about Saint Francis Xavier, who was the one of the first Jesuit missionaries in Asia. He used pictures of Mary and Jesus to help teach the Gospel.

CHILDREN AT THIS AGE >>>

How They Understand God's Call We often ask fifth-graders what they would like to be when they grow up. Seldom are they asked what God is calling them to be. God made us, and he knows us better than we know ourselves. We cannot be happier than when we are doing what we were made for. Children this age are ready to begin to consider, based on their interests, talents, and opportunities, where God might be leading them.

CONSIDER THIS >>>

How much influence do you have on helping your child discover God's plan for his or her life?

According to research, parents are the number one influence in their child's life. The Church recognizes the role of parents as not only influential, but the primary influence in helping their child grow in faith. As Catholics, we know that "the Christian family is called to be a community of faith, hope, and love in an environment of prayer. Aided by a number of other virtues, such as prudence, justice, fortitude, and temperance, the family that practices them begins to actualize its spiritual calling as a domestic church" (*USCCA, p. 377*).

LET'S TALK >>>

- Ask your child to name the two Sacraments at the Service of Communion.
- Share a family story about the Sacrament of Matrimony.

LET'S PRAY >>>

 Saint Francis Xavier, pray for us that we may know what God wants us to do with our lives and have the courage to follow God's call. Amen.

For a multimedia glossary of Catholic Faith Words, Sunday readings, seasonal and Saint resources, and chapter activities go to **aliveinchrist.osv.com**.

Chapter 19 Review

A Work with Words Match each description in Column 1 with the correct term in Column 2.

Column 1

1. vocation

2. dedicated to God and a community by vows

3. ordination of bishops, priests, and deacons

4. members of the Church who are not ordained

5. Sacrament joining a baptized man and a baptized woman

Column 2

Matrimony

Holy Orders

men and women religious

particular way to respond to God's call

lay people

B Check Understanding Circle True if a statement is true, and circle False if a statement is false. Correct any false statements.

6. Religious life refers to the lives of men and women in religious communities who make vows of fidelity, hopefulness, and love. **True/False**

   _____

7. Ordained men serve God and the Church through the Sacrament of Matrimony. **True/False**

   _____

8. Rather than being bitter about the loss of their son, Isidore and Maria devoted their lives to God. **True/False**

   _____

9. Charisms are graces that forgive sins. **True/False**

   _____

10. The minister of Holy Orders is the bishop. **True/False**

    _____

Go to aliveinchrist.osv.com for an interactive review.

The Last Things

 Let Us Pray

Leader: Lord of life and death, we trust in your everlasting love.

"For my soul has been freed from death,
    my eyes from tears, my feet from stumbling.
I shall walk before the LORD
    in the land of the living." **Psalm 116:8–9**

All: Lord of life and death, we trust in your everlasting love. Amen.

 Scripture

Jesus told the Sadducees: "That the dead will rise even Moses made known in the passage about the bush, when he called 'Lord' the God of Abraham, the God of Isaac, and the God of Jacob; and he is not God of the dead, but of the living, for to him all are alive." **Luke 20:37–38**

Pilgrims at an Easter sunrise service pray and proclaim their belief in the Resurrection.

? What Do You Wonder?

- How is everyone alive for God?
- How does the Church help her members at the time of death?

Choosing Love and Life

What does the Church teach about life after death?

Do you ever wonder what Heaven, Hell, and Purgatory are like? Jesus teaches us that the choice between Heaven and Hell is freely made. Those who choose not to believe and show love will suffer eternal separation from God. Those who have faith and accept grace will choose love and be welcomed into the life of the Holy Trinity, for the Trinity is love itself.

The Last Judgment is God's final triumph over evil that will occur at the end of time when Christ returns and judges all the living and the dead. Then, all will fully see and understand God's plan for creation.

This stained glass artwork shows Jesus separating the lambs from the goats, as he will separate those who have loved from those who have not at the time of the Last Judgment (see Matthew 23:32).

ⓕ Scripture

The Judgment of the Nations

When the Son of Man comes again, those who have loved will be separated from those who have not.

Then the king will say to those on his right, "Come, you who are blessed by my Father. Inherit the kingdom prepared for you from the foundation of the world. For I was hungry and you gave me food, I was thirsty and you gave me drink, a stranger and you welcomed me, naked and you clothed me, ill and you cared for me, in prison and you visited me." Then the righteous will ask when they did any of these things. And the king will say to them, "Amen, I say to you, whatever you did for one of these least brothers of mine, you did for me."   **Based on Matthew 25:31–40**

➔ **What does Jesus teach us about Heaven and Hell?**

Eternal Life

As Catholics, we believe that **Heaven** is how the souls of the just experience the full joy of living eternally in God's presence. **Hell** is eternal separation from God because of a choice to turn away from him and not seek forgiveness. We know that Jesus promised his followers **eternal life**. We prepare for eternal life by growing in friendship with God. God's gift of eternal life is free—we can't earn it on our own. We receive that gift through faith in God. When we have real faith, we will follow Jesus faithfully, doing our very best to show love to God and to others.

But we know how often we fail to do what God asks of us. We sin and do harm to others, ourselves, and our relationship with God. When we die, we take with

us the effects of our sin. The individual judgment by God at the time of a person's death is called **Particular Judgment**. God decides where a person will spend eternity according to their faith and works. **Purgatory** is a final purification after death and before Heaven.

Catholic Faith Words

Heaven the full joy of living eternally in God's presence

Hell eternal separation from God because of a choice to turn away from him and not seek forgiveness

eternal life life forever with God for all who die in his friendship

Purgatory a state of final cleansing after death and before entering into Heaven

Particular Judgment the individual judgment by God at the time of a person's death; when God decides, after a person's death, where that person will spend eternity according to his or her faith and works

Share Your Faith

Reflect Think of some ways that you can work together with God as he builds his Kingdom.

Share With a partner, brainstorm some of the ways you can make small, loving choices day by day.

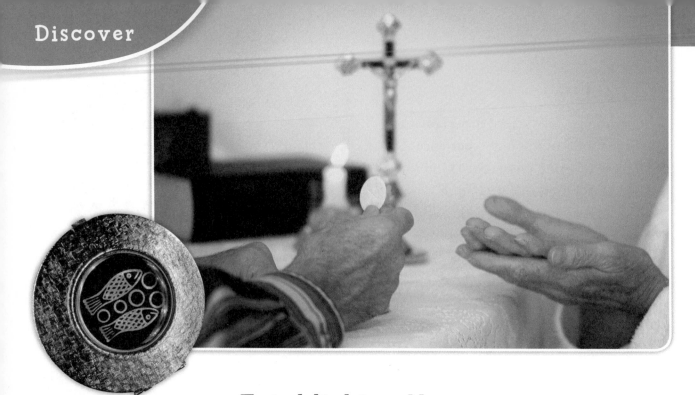

A pyx, such as the one above, is used to carry the Eucharist to someone who is ill and unable to attend Mass.

Establishing Hope

What happens at the end of your mortal life?

Humans suffer bodily death because of Original Sin. But the Death and Resurrection of Jesus establish hope for a happy death and for eternal life with God.

Faith and Baptism are necessary for salvation for all who have heard the Good News of Jesus. If infants die without Baptism, the Church trusts in God's merciful love to bring them to salvation. Those who have not heard the Gospel can be saved if they are doing their best to follow God's will. For a catechumen, the desire for the Sacrament and repentance for sins is enough for salvation.

Care for the Dying

The Church helps people prepare for death through prayer and rites. These rites include the Anointing of the Sick, the final Eucharist, called **viaticum**, or "food for the journey," and sometimes the Sacrament of Penance and Reconciliation. The Rite of Christian Funerals reflects the community's belief and hope that those who die in faith will enter eternal life with the Trinity. In the Eucharist, the Church continues to pray for those who have died. Every Mass is offered not only for the souls of the living but also for the souls of those who have died.

The Journey Home

After a person has died, the Church celebrates a Mass of Christian Burial. The Church community gathers to proclaim the message of eternal life and to pray that the one who has died will experience its joy. The coffin containing the body or the urn containing the cremated remains of the person who has died is met by the presider at the church entrance. The presider blesses the coffin or urn with holy water. The lighted Easter candle reminds those gathered of the person's dying and rising in Christ. The pall, a white cloth like the garment received in Baptism, is draped over the coffin.

The Scripture readings at a funeral Mass focus on God's mercy and forgiveness. The homily offers words of consolation, or comfort, based on the Paschal Mystery. During the Liturgy of the Eucharist, the assembly remembers the sacrifice of Jesus' Death and the glory of his Resurrection.

In the final farewell before burial, the Church commends, or gives, to God the person who has died. Then the Church calls upon choirs of angels to welcome the person into the paradise of God's heavenly Kingdom. There, all the faithful will be together in Christ.

Connect Your Faith

Prepare for Eternity Write three ways the Church helps people who are dying prepare for death.

1. _____

2. _____

3. _____

Our Catholic Life

How do you comfort the sorrowful?

To bury the dead is one of the Corporal Works of Mercy, and to comfort the sorrowful is one of the Spiritual Works of Mercy. As members of Christ's Body, Church members must support those who have lost loved ones. But it is often difficult to know what to do.

The Role of the Comforter

Here are a few steps you can take to help comfort those in your community who might be experiencing a loss.

- **Understand that grieving is a process that takes time.** When someone dies, those who mourn will experience many different feelings. There is no quick or easy way to get through the process of grieving and no set period of time in which grieving should be finished.

- **Gather with the community of faith to pray.** The most common occasions for communal prayer are the wake or prayer service, the funeral, and the graveside service.

- **Support those who mourn.** If you go to a wake or a funeral, tell the grieving family that you are sorry for their loss, or share something with them about the one who died. It helps those who have lost someone they love to know that they are not alone in missing the person. Offer your prayers, sympathy, and understanding throughout the year.

- _____

_____

_____

In the space above, write one more action that could comfort someone in a time of sorrow or loss.

People of Faith

December 26

Saint Stephen, martyred c. A.D. 36

Saint Stephen was the first Christian martyr. He lived just a few years after Jesus. He was a deacon chosen to distribute food to the Greek-speaking Christian community in Jerusalem. He was a great preacher whose views worried Jewish leaders. For example, he told Christians that they didn't have to worship at the Temple in Jerusalem. The Jewish leaders had Stephen stoned to death. Stephen wasn't afraid to die because he knew he was going to Heaven. As he was dying, Stephen forgave the people who killed him, just like Jesus did on the Cross.

Discuss: Why shouldn't Christians be afraid to die?

Learn more about Saint Stephen at **aliveinchrist.osv.com**

Live Your Faith

Name something you can do this week to remember someone you know who has died.

_____

_____

Write a short prayer for people you know who have died. Make a point to pray this prayer during the week.

_____

_____

_____

_____

_____

_____

_____

_____

_____

Let Us Pray

Celebration of the Word

Gather and begin with the Sign of the Cross.

Leader: God our Father, we remember today that you are our beginning and our end.

Reader: A reading from the Second Letter to the Corinthians.

Read 2 Corinthians 5:6–10.

The word of the Lord.

All: Thanks be to God.

Leader: Let us pray for those who have died, that they might experience fully the love of Christ. Trusting in God, let us pray for them and for those who may be close to death.

Pray silently for a few moments.

Leader: Let us conclude by praying together the following words from the funeral liturgy.

All: May the angels lead them into paradise;
may the martyrs come to welcome them.
From the Mass of Christian Burial

 Sing "I Know That My Redeemer Lives"

I know that my Redeemer lives,
that I shall rise again. (Repeat)

FAMILY+FAITH
LIVING AND LEARNING TOGETHER

YOUR CHILD LEARNED >>>

This chapter explains Heaven, Hell, and Purgatory, describes the Mass of Christian Burial, and identifies how we prepare for eternal life by serving God and one another right now.

Scripture

 Read **Luke 20:37–38** to find out what Jesus said about resurrection.

Catholics Believe

- Faith in the Resurrection is the source of hope in eternal life and happiness with God in Heaven.
- The Church cares for the dying through prayer and celebration of last Eucharist, known as viaticum.

To learn more, go to the *Catechism of the Catholic Church #989, 1012, 1024, 1523–1525* at **usccb.org**.

People of Faith

This week, your child learned about the first martyr, Saint Stephen, whose story is told in Acts 6, 7.

CHILDREN AT THIS AGE >>>

How They Understand the End of Life Fifth-graders, unlike much younger children, understand the permanence of death. They might also have some experience with death, such as a grandparent or relative who has died. What happens after death is still a mystery to them, but they may imagine Heaven as a world much like our own but better.

CONSIDER THIS >>>

Have you ever described a traffic jam, a three-hour dance recital, or waiting in a long line as Hell?

While we use the term lightly, we need to pay attention to what the Church teaches us. Because God created us with free will, we have a choice between Heaven and Hell. As Catholics, we understand that "freely chosen eternal separation from communion with God is called *hell*. While images of fire have been used traditionally to picture hell, for example in the Scriptures, the reality exceeds our ability to describe the pain of isolation that comes from rejecting God's love" (*USCCA, p. 155*).

LET'S TALK >>>

- Ask your child to explain how the Church helps people prepare for death.
- Share a family story about a time when the Church helped a friend or family member prepare for death.

LET'S PRAY >>>

 God, help us face death with courage and faith like Saint Stephen did. Amen.

 For a multimedia glossary of Catholic Faith Words, Sunday readings, seasonal and Saint resources, and chapter activities go to **aliveinchrist.osv.com**.

Chapter 20 Review

A **Work with Words** Match the description in Column 1 with the correct term in Column 2.

Column 1	Column 2
1. separation from God forever	Heaven
2. life forever with God for all who die in his friendship	Particular Judgment
3. full joy of living eternally in God's presence	Hell
4. cause of bodily death	eternal life
5. the individual judgment by God at the time of a person's death	Original Sin

B **Check Understanding** Write a brief response to each question.

6. How do Catholics prepare for eternal life?

_____

_____

7. What are the needs of a person who is grieving?

_____

_____

8. Why is the Easter candle lit during a funeral?

_____

_____

9. What will happen at the Last Judgment?

_____

_____

10. What is viaticum?

_____

_____

Go to aliveinchrist.osv.com for an interactive review.

Bring the Good News

 Let Us Pray

Leader: Christ, our Savior, come quickly. We stand ready and eager to welcome you.

"Sing praise to God, sing praise;
   sing praise to our king, sing praise.
For God is king over all the earth;
   sing hymns of praise." **Psalm 47:7–8**

All: Christ, our Savior, come quickly. We stand ready and eager to welcome you. May your Kingdom come. Amen.

Scripture

Blessed the one whose help is the God of Jacob,
   whose hope is in the LORD, his God,
The maker of heaven and earth,
   the seas and all that is in them,
Who keeps faith forever,
   secures justice for the oppressed,
   who gives bread to the hungry.
The LORD sets prisoners free;
   the LORD gives sight to the blind.
The LORD raises up those who are bowed down;
   the LORD loves the righteous.
The LORD protects the resident alien,
   comes to the aid of the orphan and the widow,
   but thwarts the way of the wicked.
The LORD shall reign forever,
   your God, Zion, through all generations!
Hallelujah! **Psalm 146:5–10**

? What Do You Wonder?

- What is one thing people your age can do to spread the Good News of Jesus?

- What have you learned this past year that makes you want to shout "Hallelujah!"?

Missionaries

What are the qualities of a missionary?

The Church has a mission to bring the Good News to all people everywhere. One woman accepted that mission fully.

Saint Frances Xavier Cabrini

Little Frances Cabrini loved to hear her father read stories of missions in China. Her greatest wish was to travel far from her native Italy to share God's Word. As a teenager, Frances could not join a convent because of poor health. She learned how to be a teacher. She taught for several years in small towns in Italy.

Priests and bishops saw that Frances was a talented teacher and manager. They asked her to take over an orphanage. At the orphanage, she and several companions studied and became the Missionary Sisters of the Sacred Heart.

Mother Cabrini heard that missionaries were needed in the United States, but she dreamed of going to China. Pope Leo XIII told her, "Not to the East, but to the West." So, she went to the United States. She began her work with poor Italians in New York. In time, Mother Cabrini's sisters also worked in Chicago, Seattle, Philadelphia, Des Plaines, New Orleans, and other cities. They set up hospitals, schools, shelters, and orphanages that served the poor.

Mother Cabrini became an American citizen in 1909. When she died in 1917, her order had founded 67 institutions. She was canonized in 1946. She was the first American citizen to be canonized.

 Circle the cities on the map where Mother Cabrini founded hospitals and other places that served the poor.

Move Toward the Kingdom

Like Jesus, Mother Cabrini was a teacher. She wanted to bring the Good News to the people of China, but ended up serving and sharing Jesus' message with the poor in the United States.

The message of Jesus is greater than any one person who proclaims it today. It takes holy people, such as **missionaries**, to proclaim it well, but the source of their holiness is the Holy Spirit dwelling in them through Baptism. God gives us the **Gifts of the Holy Spirit**—wisdom, counsel, understanding, fortitude, knowledge, piety, and fear of the Lord—and the ability to follow his guidance to live the Christian life. We are sealed with the Gifts of the Holy Spirit at Confirmation. Just as the Holy Spirit empowered Jesus, he gives us the courage to do Christ's work.

 ## Scripture

Fulfilled in Your Hearing

Jesus came to Nazareth, where he had grown up, and went into the synagogue on the sabbath day. He stood up to read and was handed a scroll of the prophet Isaiah...

"The Spirit of the Lord is upon me,
    because he has anointed me
    to bring glad tidings to the poor.
He has sent me to proclaim liberty to captives
    and recovery of sight to the blind,
    to let the oppressed go free,
and to proclaim a year acceptable to the Lord."

Rolling up the scroll,... he sat down...the eyes of all in the synagogue looked intently at him. He said to them, "Today this scripture passage is fulfilled in your hearing."   Based on Luke 4:16–21

Share Your Faith

Reflect Recall that through the power of the Holy Spirit, you can have the courage to continue Jesus' work.

Share Proclaim to a partner what Jesus read from the prophet Isaiah. Take turns explaining what Jesus meant when he said the Scripture passage had been fulfilled, and how you are trying to live this passage.

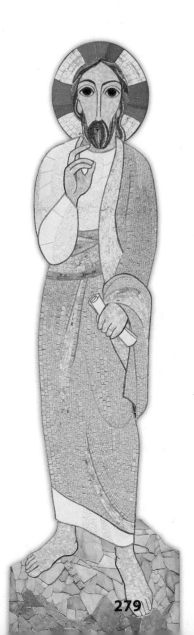

In Word and Action

How can you be a part of the mission of the Church?

The celebration of each Sacrament reminds us that the Reign of God is among us in Jesus Christ. God's Kingdom is embraced when we celebrate the Baptism of new birth in the Church and become brothers and sisters in Christ. When we receive the Sacraments, especially the Eucharist, we are given grace to become more like Christ—to love God and others better.

The Gospel message is the Good News of God's Kingdom and his saving love. Missionaries are people who answer God's call to bring the message of Jesus and announce the Good News of his Kingdom to people in other places. Even when those who have been reborn and nourished in Christ do not go to faraway lands to preach the Gospel, they are called to be disciples and missionaries in their daily lives. They share the Good News of Jesus by word and example, and they invite others to follow Christ. This sharing, or **evangelization**, has its origins in the first Pentecost, when the Holy Spirit came upon the followers of Jesus and strengthened them to take the Good News to every nation. When you live as a disciple of Jesus, you become a sign of God's Kingdom, wherever you are.

➔ **How are we sent forth after Mass to evangelization?**

Celebration of God's Reign

Following the command and example of Jesus, some people go to faraway places to teach the Gospel and to help meet the needs of others. Catholic Social Teaching is the Church's teaching about how we are to treat others and live in community. To feed the hungry, to give drink to the thirsty, to clothe the naked, to shelter the homeless, to visit the sick and the imprisoned—these are the **Corporal Works of Mercy**. Missionaries also care for the spiritual needs of people by performing the **Spiritual Works of Mercy**. They offer prayer, instruction, patience, forgiveness, counseling, and comfort. You can find the Corporal and Spiritual Works of Mercy listed on page 317 in the Our Catholic Tradition section of your book.

Equal Before God

The Works of Mercy are to be offered to all who are in need, without exception. All people are equal in God's eyes because he has created them in his own image and likeness.

Your works of mercy can be acts of charity or works of justice. Charity responds to short-term needs and provides direct services such as food, clothing, and shelter. Justice responds to long-term needs and promotes social change in institutions or political structures. When you perform an act of charity, you show Christ's love to another by helping lessen the suffering of body or spirit. When you act with justice, you give others what is their due. You work for social justice when you work to provide the framework that will protect the rights of those who are poor or cast out by society. All people have a right to food, shelter, health, and dignity. All societies have the responsibility to provide for the good of all.

Connect Your Faith

Bring Justice With a small group, brainstorm ways injustice in your local community could be corrected. Report the results of your discussion to the other groups. As a group, choose one step that you can take to improve the situation.

Our Catholic Life

How can you contribute to social justice?

The bishops of the United States named seven themes of Catholic Social Teaching that embrace the Gospel message. As Catholics, we may find it easier to live the Gospel message of social justice among people who are familiar to us. Social justice demands that we extend the same respect and love to those whom we don't know directly and who have a culture and outlook different from ours. Applying these themes will help you act justly.

Fill in the blanks with words from the Word List.

Living the Themes

1. Respect the **life and** _____ **of every person.** All policies and personal decisions must show a value for human life and dignity.

2. Value _____ , **community, and participation.** The well-being of individuals depends on community and family. All people have a right and a duty to participate in society.

3. Uphold **rights and responsibilities.** Human rights must be

   protected, and responsibilities to _____ must be met.

4. Evaluate actions in terms of how they affect **those who are**

   most _____ . A basic moral test is to ask whether an act will help those who are poor.

5. Honor the **dignity of work and the rights of workers.** Workers

   deserve a just wage and the _____ to form unions, to hold private property, and to act independently of outside influence or control.

6. Practice **solidarity** with others. Be committed to the

   _____ good—the good of everyone—globally as well as locally.

7. **Care for God's** _____ . To practice social justice, take care of the Earth's natural resources.

Word List
• • • • • • • • • •

family

common

vulnerable

dignity

creation

right

others

People of Faith

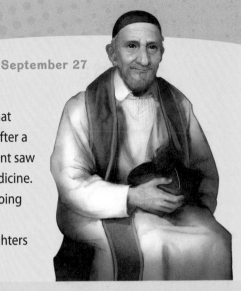

September 27

Saint Vincent de Paul, 1581–1660

Maybe there is a store in your town called "Saint Vincent de Paul" that sells secondhand things. That store and others like it were named after a French priest who lived more than 500 years ago. When Saint Vincent saw poor, sick children, he would give them food, clothes, toys, and medicine. He also taught them about Jesus. Other people saw what he was doing and wanted to help him, so he formed a group for men called the "Congregation of the Mission" and a group for women called "Daughters of Charity."

Discuss: How do you live the Corporal Works of Mercy?

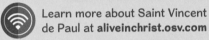

Learn more about Saint Vincent de Paul at **aliveinchrist.osv.com**

Live Your Faith

Choose one of the themes of Catholic Social Teaching and create an illustration that shows one way you can support that theme in your own life.

Let Us Pray

Guided Reflection

This is a guided scriptural reflection, during which we remember an event in Jesus' life and think about ourselves being a part of it.

Gather and begin with the Sign of the Cross.

Leader: We gather today in prayer, attentive once again to God's Word. Let us listen to a Scripture reading we heard and reflected upon.

Read Luke 4:16–21.

Because Scripture wasn't just for thousands of years ago, but is also for us today and every day, our guided reflection helps us to be part of this Scripture passage.
Holy Spirit, we know you are with us.

All: Holy Spirit, guide us.

Leader: Let us close our eyes, be very still, and use our imaginations.

After the reflection:

This Scripture passage calls us to the mission of the Church. Let us continue to pray. The Spirit of the Lord is upon us.

Side 1: We will bring Good News to our world,

Side 2: we will proclaim freedom to those who are captive,

Side 1: sight to the blind,

Side 2: let the oppressed go free,

All: and proclaim a year acceptable to the Lord.

 Sing "Holy Spirit"

Holy Spirit, come into our lives.
Holy Spirit, make us truly wise.

FAMILY+FAITH
LIVING AND LEARNING TOGETHER

YOUR CHILD LEARNED »»

This chapter explains Isaiah's proclamation of God's Kingdom, identifies the Works of Mercy, and describes evangelization as sharing the Good News of Jesus.

Scripture

 Read **Psalm 146:5–10** to find out about God as our source of strength.

Catholics Believe

- The Church's mission is to bring the Good News to all people everywhere.
- The Corporal and Spiritual Works of Mercy are actions that address the physical and spiritual needs of others.

To learn more, go to the *Catechism of the Catholic Church #849, 851, 2820* at **usccb.org**.

People of Faith

This week, your child learned about Saint Vincent de Paul, whose life mission was to aid the poor.

CHILDREN AT THIS AGE »»

Helping Your Child Understand Evangelization Fifth-graders might not have considered ways in which they can spread the Good News of Jesus. They might think this is something only adults would do. Hearing that Jesus has given this mission to every Christian and helping them consider practical, concrete ways they can do this in word and action will assist them in their understanding of this important work.

CONSIDER THIS »»

Have you ever thought you had enough to worry about with caring for your own family life and wondered why you should worry about the bigger injustices in the world?

One of the primary responsibilities of family life is to care for the needs of its members. Our Catholic faith, however, calls us to share God's love beyond our family. We are responsible for the needs of the world. As Catholics, we understand that "social justice is both an attitude and a practical response based on the principle that everyone should look at another person as another self. It is also a virtue that directs all other virtues of individuals toward the common good" *(USCCA, p. 326)*.

LET'S TALK »»

- Ask your child to explain the Corporal Works of Mercy.
- Share how your family lives the Corporal Works of Mercy.

LET'S PRAY »»

 Dear God, open our eyes to the poor and suffering in our midst. Help us learn to share what we have with all in need. Amen.

For a multimedia glossary of Catholic Faith Words, Sunday readings, seasonal and Saint resources, and chapter activities go to **aliveinchrist.osv.com**.

Chapter 21 Review

A **Check Understanding** Circle True if a statement is true, and circle False if a statement is false. Correct any false statements.

1. You are a disciple when you follow the example of Jesus. **True/False**

   _____

   _____

2. The sharing of the Good News of Jesus by word and example is called evangelization. **True/False**

   _____

   _____

3. The mission of the Church is to bring the Gospel of Jesus only to those who are good. **True/False**

   _____

   _____

4. Social justice requires a society to respect the dignity of its members. **True/False**

   _____

   _____

5. Those who are baptized have completed their mission of evangelization. **True/False**

   _____

   _____

Fill in the circle next to the correct response.

6. Works of Mercy can be works of _____.

   ○ justice only

   ○ charity only

   ○ both justice and charity

7. A _____ answers God's call to bring the message of Jesus to people who do not know it.

   ○ priest

   ○ missionary

   ○ martyr

8. Saint Frances Cabrini was the first _____ to be named a Saint.

   ○ Native American

   ○ North American

   ○ German

9. All of the following are Corporal Works of Mercy except _____.

   ○ pray for the dead

   ○ feed the hungry

   ○ visit the sick

10. The Spiritual Works of Mercy address _____.

    ○ physical needs

    ○ our own needs

    ○ the needs of the heart, mind, soul

Go to aliveinchrist.osv.com for an interactive review.

Unit Review

A **Check Understanding** Complete the word search to find the boldface words that appear in the phrases below the box. Then fill the spaces provided with the remaining letters, in order, and you will reveal the secret message.

R	E	S	U	R	R	E	C	T	I	O	N
T	T	H	I	S	I	S	O	W	H	Y	T
H	E	E	M	A	S	S	M	O	F	C	H
R	R	I	S	T	I	A	F	N	B	U	R
I	N	A	L	I	S	A	O	C	E	L	E
B	A	E	U	C	H	A	R	I	S	T	R
A	L	M	E	R	C	Y	T	T	I	O	N

1–2. A homily offers words of **comfort**, liturgy proclaims the message of **eternal** life,

3–4. Scripture readings tell of God's **mercy**, and the **Eucharist** reminds us that

5. we can all share in the glory of Jesus' **Resurrection**.

⬜⬜⬜⬜ ⬜⬜ ⬜⬜⬜ ⬜

⬜⬜⬜ ⬜⬜⬜⬜ ⬜⬜

⬜⬜⬜⬜⬜⬜⬜⬜⬜

⬜⬜⬜⬜⬜⬜ ⬜⬜ ⬜

⬜⬜⬜⬜⬜⬜⬜⬜⬜⬜

Name three reasons why Catholics should work for social justice.

6. _____

7. _____

8. _____

Name two ways to answer the call of God.

9. _____

_____

_____

10. _____

_____

_____

Match each description in Column 1 with the correct term in Column 2.

Column 1

11. life forever with God for all who die in his friendship

12. commitment, common life, a rule, ministries

13. helpful effect on those who are poor

14. the coming of the Holy Spirit upon the first disciples of Jesus

15. prayer, Reconciliation, Anointing of the Sick, and viaticum

Column 2

preparation for death

basic test of social justice

eternal life

consecrated religious life

Pentecost

B **Make Connections** Write a response to each question or statement.

Use the three terms below to explain how you would help a friend who is going through the grieving process.

understand   pray   support

16–18. _____

_____

_____

_____

_____

_____

19. How can you follow the example of Saints Isidore and Maria?

_____

_____

_____

_____

20. Explain one way in which you perform the Works of Mercy in your everyday life.

_____

_____

_____

_____

Life and Dignity of the Human Person

In Scripture, God tells us, "Before I formed you in the womb I knew you" (Jeremiah 1:5). God created each one of us. Every person is unique and unrepeatable. He has a special plan for each of our lives. He knows what he made us to be.

Because God made each person, we should treat each person with human dignity. Every life is valuable to God. We should take care of the bodies and minds God gave us and use them to do good things. We respect others because every life is important to God. We protect the lives of the unborn, the elderly and in ill health, and those with other needs, because we are all made in the image of God.

Life and Dignity

The Church teaches that the Commandments forbid sins against the dignity and rights of human beings. This means that people may not be abused. They must be free to follow God's will for them and to make choices about how they will live. Human dignity requires Christians to love others as they love themselves. All people are equally deserving of the benefits of God's creation.

Many citizens of the United States live comfortably. They have dreams and ambitions for the future. They pray and worship whenever and wherever they like.

But there are those who can't take these things for granted. In the world today, as many as 27 million people are being held as slaves. They cannot go to school, and so they have no hope for a better life. They cannot even choose to worship God. They have no one to protect them from danger in the work their owners force them to do.

≫ Why is it our responsibility to help those who are treated unjustly and without dignity?

Serve Your Community

Take some time to think very carefully about what slavery really is.

1. Read and reflect on Matthew 25:31–40. What does this passage say to you about how human beings should treat one another?

   _____

2. Slavery means that a person has no choice. Of the choices you have, which is most important? What would you most like to have a choice about?

   _____

   _____

As a group, decide on and plan one thing that you can do to increase awareness of one kind of slavery.

Call to Family, Community, and Participation

From the very beginning, God made people to be in relationship with one another. In Genesis 2:18, Scripture tells us, "The LORD God said: It is not good for the man to be alone. I will make a helper suited to him." God gave us communities of persons so that we could take care of one another.

The family is a very special type of community. Our Church teaches that the family is the "school of holiness" and the "domestic Church." These names reflect the Catholic teaching that the family is where we learn who God is, and how to live a Christian life. It is the first place where we learn what it means to live in a community. The family is where we learn how to love others.

Call to Community

The Church teaches that the family is the fundamental community in society. God created families in which you can grow as the person he wants you to be. Your role in the family helps you understand your role in society. As you grow and become a member of other communities, you have responsibilities to them as well. You should care for those who are young, old, disabled, or poor. Jesus spoke clearly about your responsibility to reach out. The Corporal Works of Mercy describe your responsibility.

You have many opportunities. Some neighborhoods have people living in poverty, most have elderly citizens, and some may have people who need homes or jobs. You know the discomfort of unfamiliar surroundings. Immigrants face problems that you can help them manage. Members of Catholic Social Services live the Corporal Works of Mercy each day as they help others.

≫ To what communities do you belong? What responsibilities do you have as a member of those communities?

Plan a Prayer Service

Jesus calls his followers not only to help those who are closest to them, but also to help others in this world. Take some time to think of needs you know about in your community.

1. A need you know about in your community:

   _____

2. A need you know about in the world:

   _____

With the help of your catechist, conduct a prayer service. Offer petitions you have written for help in your community. At the end of the service, choose something that you are willing to do to help, and commit yourself to it.

Rights and Responsibilities of the Human Person

Because God made every person, everyone has rights and responsibilities. Rights are the freedoms or things every person needs and should have. Responsibilities are our duties, or the things we must do.

Jesus tells us to "love your neighbor as yourself" (Mark 12:31). The *Catechism* teaches that when we respect the dignity of another person, we treat them as "another self." We respect the rights that come from their dignity as a human being (CCC, 1943–44). Everyone has a right to food, shelter, clothing, rest, and the right to see a doctor if they need one. We also have a responsibility to treat others well and work together for the good of everyone.

Women religious discuss their Catholic Relief Services work at Esperance Hospital in northern Haiti.

Respect Rights

When you love, act justly, and make peace, you are building the Kingdom of God. You are also respecting your own and others' right to live according to God's plan. Although you may not realize it, every day you meet situations that involve the rights of others.

- You respect your classmates' right to privacy when you respect their space and belongings.

- You respect your classmates' right to an education when you participate in class.

- You respect your classmates' right to a safe environment when you settle conflicts peacefully.

Dealing with conflict without violence, anger, or bullying is both a right and a responsibility. It is one way to follow God's law of love.

≫ In what ways can you see the rights of others being violated in your school and neighborhood?

≫ When is it difficult to see God's image in others?

Do It Differently

In the space below, write an example of a time when you felt a lack of respect from others. Describe to a partner how you felt when it happened.

_____

_____

With a partner, role-play your examples in the way you wish they had happened.

Now think of a time when you did not treat others with respect. Describe to a partner what happened. Explain below what you should have done differently.

_____

_____

_____

Option for the Poor and Vulnerable

In Scripture, Jesus says that "whatever you did for one of these least brothers of mine, you did for me" and "what you did not do for one of these least ones, you did not do for me" (Matthew 25:40, 45). This means we should treat people in need the same way we would treat Jesus himself. We should give special priority to people who are hungry, thirsty, homeless, or alone.

Saint Rose of Lima said, "When we serve the poor and the sick, we serve Jesus." Our Church teaches that we should have special love and care for those who are poor and put their needs first. This is called the *preferential option for the poor*. The *Catechism* teaches that "God blesses those who come to the aid of the poor" (CCC, 2443).

Option for the Poor

Scripture calls us to help those in need because every person is made in God's image. All people have a right to life and a right to secure the basic necessities of life.

Catholics must protect these rights and share their own resources to ensure that everyone has enough material goods to live in dignity.

Divisions between those who are rich and those who are poor are growing. Catholics must work for the good of those who are poor because the Eucharist makes all members one body. Pope Saint John Paul II points out that we are called to see a neighbor as an "other self," to pray for all who are poor, and to look for signs of poverty and work for change.

Catholics offer help not only because they are called to be charitable, but also because they are called to be just. The Society of St. Vincent de Paul is an organization that gives lay people a way to make a significant contribution to this mission of the Church.

>> How does the Eucharist encourage us to care for those who are poor?

Make a Difference

List some of your possessions. Put those that are true necessities in the "Need" column and all others in the "Want" column.

Need	Want
_____	_____
_____	_____
_____	_____

Imagine not having the items in your "Need" list for an entire week. How would that change the way you thought about your "Want" list? What would you be willing to change or give up to help more people get the things they need?

_____

_____

The Dignity of Work and Rights of Workers

All adults have a right and responsibility to work. Work helps people earn money to buy food and other necessities. It also helps to give their lives meaning as they cooperate with God's creation. Everyone should have access to meaningful work, whether it is within the home or outside the home.

Scripture and Catholic Tradition teaches that workers deserve to be treated with justice by their employers: "You shall not exploit a … hired servant" (Deuteronomy 24:14). They have a right to a fair wage for their work (see Leviticus 19:13; Deuteronomy 24:15). When there is a conflict between workers and employers, workers have a right to get together and express their opinion. Workers and their employers should treat one another with respect and solve conflicts peacefully.

The Dignity of Work

Because work is done by people created in God's image, it is holy. Work honors the skills and the talents we have from God. Your work is to study in school so that you can become a responsible member of society. Your parents work to provide for you.

Employers must respect the rights of their workers. Workers need fair pay to provide for their families. They also have the right to decent working conditions and the right to organize in order to protect themselves against unfair treatment.

People everywhere depend on farm workers for fruits and vegetables, and yet many are mistreated. Migrant workers earn less than the minimum wage. Many live with other workers or family members in one room. Some have no shelter at all. In the fields, they are often without water or toilet facilities. Many children cannot attend school because of moving and work. Many are immigrants and fear they will be sent out of the country if they complain.

≫ Why do you think employers don't pay more attention to the rights of farm workers?

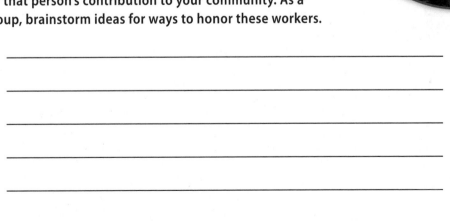

Show Appreciation

With your group, make a list of people and jobs to support. (Don't forget to consider the people who work in your school.) Your task will be to visit a person who does that job and show your respect and appreciation for that person's contribution to your community. As a group, brainstorm ideas for ways to honor these workers.

_____

_____

_____

_____

_____

_____

Solidarity of the Human Family

Our world includes people of different nations, races, cultures, beliefs, and economic levels. But God created each one of us. We are one human family. In fact, Scripture tells us that the differences that we see between ourselves and others are not important to God: "There is no partiality with God" (Romans 2:11). God calls everyone to be his children.

Because God created all people, we have an obligation to treat everyone with love, kindness, and justice. In the Beatitudes, Jesus calls us to be peacemakers, "for they will be called children of God" (Matthew 5:9). Working for justice among all people will help us to live in peace with one another.

Priests and brothers of the Missionaries of the Poor repair roofs in a poor district of Kingston, Jamaica.

Solidarity

The Church teaches that as children of God, all people are united in the spirit of solidarity, or dedication to the good of all. However, the people of God have a special responsibility in justice to ensure that all humans can live in freedom and dignity. Those who live in richer countries must work to help those who live in poorer countries. People have more wealth than ever before, yet many of the world's people still suffer hunger, poverty, and lack of education. Christians must work to change this situation.

Many organizations within the Catholic Church reach out to people in need. It is the work of everyone who follows Jesus to help care for the whole human family.

≫ Why do Catholics have a special responsibility to help others throughout the world?

≫ What are some ways in which your parish works to help those in need in other countries?

Find Ways to Help

Conduct a group discussion to find ways to support the missions, such as

- Sponsoring a child in another country
- Gathering and sending needed supplies to missionaries
- Inviting missionaries to the school to share their experiences
- Writing to the children of missionaries throughout the world

In the space below, write one thing you can do and invite others to participate.

_____

_____

_____

Care for God's Creation

When God created the world—the animals, plants, and all natural things, he looked upon what he had made and called it "very good" (Genesis 1:31). God made people the *stewards* of the "fish of the sea, the birds of the air, and all the living things that crawl on the earth" (Genesis 1:28). That means humans have a special responsibility to care for all of God's creation.

Catholic Tradition teaches us that God created the Earth and all living things for the common good—the good of everyone. We should work to take care of the environment and all living things, so they can be enjoyed by everyone today and in future generations. The *Catechism* teaches us that we owe animals kindness, because they give glory to God just by being what they were made to be.

Care for Creation

God calls you to protect and preserve all that he has created. He gives you the responsibility of stewardship. You are trusted not to upset or destroy the balance in nature. The Earth is for your use today, but you must care for it so that future generations will be able to enjoy life.

The universe provides energy. Without natural gas, coal, oil, and the energy from the sun, wind, and water, our world would be a dark, cold, and isolated place. In the past, industrialized nations used a tremendous amount of energy with little regard for its replacement. Humans must not waste energy and must work to find new sources.

Catholics are called to take an active role in programs and projects that protect and preserve creation.

≫ Why is it important to be involved in caring for natural resources?

Wind farms provide renewable energy for several areas in the United States.

Design a Project

Small changes can make a big difference in preserving resources. With a partner, respond to the following items. Then plan a project together.

1. What are some of the ways your school may be wasting energy or resources? Write one way of wasting energy that you would change.

   _____

   _____

2. What would have to happen at school to stop this problem? What would it take to make students and teachers want to take the action needed? How would you organize the class to make this happen?

   _____

   _____

   _____

Scripture and the Sacraments

Because Christ is truly present in the Word, the Church gives special honor to the Bible. The Book of Gospels is carried in procession at Mass and placed on the altar until the Gospel reading. After reading the Gospel, the priest or deacon kisses the book out of respect. Every celebration of the Sacraments includes Scripture. Each begins with a Liturgy of the Word. Even if the Sacrament is celebrated for only one person, such as in the Anointing of the Sick, the priest begins with a Scripture passage. The Church encourages the use of God's Word at all gatherings of the faithful.

The Lectionary

The Lectionary contains the Scripture readings for every Sunday, feast day, and special occasion. These readings were chosen to suit the feasts and seasons of the liturgical year.

The Lectionary readings for Sunday Mass follow a three-year cycle:

- Year A uses the Gospel according to Matthew.

- Year B presents the Gospel according to Mark.

- Year C highlights the Gospel according to Luke.

The Gospel according to John appears at special times in each of the three years. The passages from John are read for special celebrations, such as Christmas, Holy Thursday, and Good Friday.

The Readings

The first reading at Sunday Mass is from the Old Testament, except during the Easter Season. At that time, the first reading comes from the Acts of the Apostles. The responsorial psalm is from the Book of Psalms. The psalm is called responsorial because the assembly sings a response after each verse.

The second reading is from one of the New Testament letters or from the Book of Revelation. The Gospel reading is from Matthew, Mark, Luke, or John.

The weekday Lectionary is also arranged according to the seasons of the liturgical year. However, the weekday readings follow a two-year cycle: Year I and Year II. On weekdays, only one reading and a psalm are spoken before the Gospel.

Sacramental Symbols in Scripture

Water and light are central symbols that reflect the power of God the Creator, who gives life to all. In Baptism, light and water are used to show God's gift of new life. The words and the symbols of water and light recall creation, the flood, and the crossing of the Red Sea. These prayers also recall Jesus' baptism in the Jordan River and the water that flowed from his side as he hung on the Cross. The newly baptized hold lighted candles to show that they will "keep the flame of faith alive" in their hearts. They will be ready to meet Christ when he returns.

Oil was used to anoint great leaders. It was also used for healing. Oil is used in the Sacraments of Baptism, Confirmation, Holy Orders, and the Anointing of the Sick.

Unleavened bread and wine are the symbols used in the celebration of the Eucharist. These fruits of the Earth were and are used in the Seder or Passover meal. Jesus gave new meaning to these symbols when he blessed them and gave them to his friends at the Last Supper—now his Body and Blood.

Creed

A creed is a summary of the Christian faith. The word *creed* means "I believe." There are two main creeds in the Church: the Apostles' Creed and the Nicene Creed.

Both the Apostles' Creed and the Nicene Creed are Trinitarian in structure and flow from the baptismal formula: Father, Son, and Holy Spirit.

Apostles' Creed

The Apostles' Creed received its name because it is a summary of the Apostles' faith. However, the earliest reference to this creed appears in fourth-century writings, and the earliest text dates from the eighth century. The Apostles' Creed is used in the celebration of Baptism and is often used at Mass during the Season of Easter and in Masses with children. This creed is part of the Rosary.

I believe in God,
the Father almighty,
Creator of heaven and earth,
and in Jesus Christ, his only Son, our Lord,

At the words that follow, up to and including the Virgin Mary, all bow.

who was conceived by the Holy Spirit,
born of the Virgin Mary,
suffered under Pontius Pilate,
was crucified, died and was buried;
he descended into hell;
on the third day he rose again from the
   dead;

he ascended into heaven,
and is seated at the right hand
   of God the Father almighty;
from there he will come to judge
   the living and the dead.
I believe in the Holy Spirit,
the holy catholic Church,
the communion of saints,
the forgiveness of sins,
the resurrection of the body,
and life everlasting. Amen.

Nicene Creed

The Nicene Creed appeared after the Council of Nicaea in 325 and the Council of Constantinople in 381. These councils discussed the divine nature of Christ. The creed became part of the liturgy of the Church in Rome in 1014 and remains part of the liturgy today.

I believe in one God,
the Father almighty,
maker of heaven and earth,
of all things visible and invisible.

I believe in one Lord Jesus Christ,
the Only Begotten Son of God,
born of the Father before all ages.
God from God, Light from Light,
true God from true God,
begotten, not made, consubstantial with
    the Father;
through him all things were made.
For us men and for our salvation
he came down from heaven,

At the words that follow up to and including
and became man, *all bow.*

and by the Holy Spirit was incarnate of
    the Virgin Mary,
and became man.

For our sake he was crucified under
    Pontius Pilate,
he suffered death and was buried,
and rose again on the third day
in accordance with the Scriptures.
He ascended into heaven
and is seated at the right hand of
    the Father.
He will come again in glory
to judge the living and the dead
and his kingdom will have no end.

I believe in the Holy Spirit, the Lord,
    the giver of life,
who proceeds from the Father and
    the Son,
who with the Father and the Son is adored
    and glorified,
who has spoken through the prophets.

I believe in one, holy, catholic and
    apostolic Church.
I confess one Baptism for the
    forgiveness of sins
and I look forward to the resurrection
    of the dead
and the life of the world to come.
Amen.

The crucifix is a cross on which Jesus may be shown either in his suffering or as Risen Lord. The letters INRI stand for the Latin words *Iesus Nazarenus, Rex Iudaeorum,* meaning "Jesus of Nazareth, King of the Jews." Pontius Pilate ordered the words to be placed on Jesus' Cross.

The Holy Trinity

God is a communion of three Divine Persons: Father, Son, and Holy Spirit. God the Father is the Creator and source of all things. God the Son, Jesus, is the Savior of all people. God the Holy Spirit guides and makes holy all people and the Church.

The Holy Trinity is honored in the Sign of the Cross and in the Doxology, and particularly in the liturgy of the Church. Christians are baptized "In the name of the Father, and of the Son, and of the Holy Spirit." In the opening and final blessing and in the Eucharistic Prayer, prayers are directed to God the Father, through the Son, in the Holy Spirit.

God the Father

The First Person of the Blessed Trinity, God the Father, is Creator of all that is. He is all-powerful and all-knowing. He is the one who journeys with you, as he did with Abraham. He is the faithful and compassionate God who freed his chosen people from slavery. He is as revealed to Moses, "I am who I am." God is gracious and merciful and steadfast in his love.

He is a God whom you can call Father, as Jesus taught in the Lord's Prayer. And, as he also taught, God is love.

God the Son

Through the power of the Holy Spirit, the Second Person of the Trinity took on human nature and was born of the Virgin Mary. Jesus' life can be said to be a Sacrament, a sign of God and his salvation and love. At the Last Supper, Jesus said, "Whoever has seen me has seen the Father …Believe me that I am in the Father and the Father is in me…" (John 14:9, 11).

In each Sacrament, Jesus is priest. For example, in the Eucharist, Jesus brings the people's prayers to God and offers himself as a sacrifice. Jesus is also prophet because he speaks for God. Jesus announced the Good News of God's mercy and forgiveness. Jesus is king, the judge of everything in Heaven and on Earth. His judgments are merciful and just.

God the Holy Spirit

The Third Person of the Trinity, the Holy Spirit, is the guide who opens the minds and hearts of people to know God as he is revealed in his Word—Scripture, and in the living Word—Jesus. It is through the power of the Spirit that you come to know the Father and the Son.

It is the Spirit who makes the Paschal Mystery real and present in the Sacraments and the Mass. In the sharing of the Eucharist, the Holy Spirit unites the faithful with one another and with God in Christ. The Spirit brings joy, peace, and reconciliation into the lives of the faithful.

The Church

The church is a building in which God's people come together to worship. The Church is also the community of people. It was the plan of God the Father to call together those who believe in Christ. The Church is a gift from God, brought into being by the Holy Spirit to serve the mission of Jesus. The Church, in Christ, can be called a Sacrament, a sign of the communion of the Trinity, the union of all people with God, and the unity among people that will reach completion in the fullness of the Kingdom of God.

The Catholic Church is united in her faith, leadership structure, and Seven Sacraments. She is made up of Eastern Rite Catholics (Middle East and Eastern Europe) and Latin Rite Catholics (Rome and Western Europe).

The Church is governed by the Pope in union with the bishops. Through the Sacrament of Holy Orders, bishops, priests, and deacons are ordained to serve the Church. After the death or resignation of a Pope, the cardinals who are under the age of 80 meet in the Sistine Chapel in Rome to vote for a new Pope. Each cardinal writes on a sheet of paper the name of the man (usually a cardinal) he wishes to elect. If a candidate does not receive a majority of votes, the papers are burned with straw to produce black smoke. If a new Pope has been chosen, the papers alone are burned, producing white smoke.

The resignation of Pope Benedict XVI in 2013 was the first papal resignation in nearly 600 years. Following his resignation, Benedict XVI's official title became Pope Emeritus (a word that means retired but retaining a title). His successor, Cardinal Jorge Maria Bergoglio, took the name Pope Francis. Because he was the Cardinal Archbishop of Buenos Aires, Argentina, Pope Francis became the first Pope from the New World.

A diocesan, or secular, priest may own private property. He promises to obey the bishop of his diocese. Celibacy has been required of Latin Rite priests since the thirteenth century; exceptions are made for married men who have been ministers or priests in some other Christian Churches and seek ordination after becoming Catholic. Eastern Rite Catholic priests may marry unless they live where celibacy is the rule (such as in the United States).

Religious order priests belong to religious communities and make vows of poverty, chastity, and obedience. They obey a superior and do not own private property.

Everlasting Life

The greatest hope of Christians is that after death they will live in eternal happiness with God. In the Bible, Heaven is pictured as a house with many rooms, a city shining with light, and a joy-filled place where everyone praises God. A familiar scriptural image of Heaven is the banquet, or feast. Christ is the host and his people are the guests. When the Church celebrates the Eucharistic meal, it glimpses the banquet feast of Heaven.

When a person is near death, special prayers are offered. The person receives the Sacrament of the Anointing of the Sick and is given Communion for the last time. This Eucharist is called viaticum (Latin for "food for the journey"). After a death, the Church honors the person and ministers to the family and friends through a series of rites found in the *Order of Christian Funerals:* prayers when the family first views the body, Liturgy of the Word at the wake or prayer service, prayers for a procession taking the body to church, the funeral liturgy (which may be a Mass), and a graveside service.

The Saints

The Saints are holy people, heroes of the Church who loved God very much, did his work on Earth, cooperated with his grace, and are now with him in Heaven. Catholics honor the Saints for their heroic virtue and try to imitate them. They also ask that the Saints join with them in praying to God for special blessings. Saints are remembered in the Eucharistic Prayer and in the Litany of the Saints at Baptisms. Statues and images of the Saints on medals and holy cards are reminders that these "friends of God" can help believers grow in their own friendship with God.

Mary is honored above all other Saints. She is the Mother of God because she is the mother of the Son of God who became a human being. When the Angel Gabriel told Mary that she would be the mother of the Son of God, Mary believed and accepted God's plan. Her "yes" sets the example for all believers. Throughout the liturgical year, the Church celebrates Mary's place in Christian history. Among different cultures and traditions, devotion to Mary takes many forms.

The Liturgy of the Church

The term *liturgy* refers to the public prayer of the Church. The word means "the work of the people." It includes the Seven Sacraments and a form of daily prayer known as Liturgy of the Hours.

The Seven Sacraments

Jesus is sometimes called the Sacrament of God because his life, Death, and Resurrection make him the sign of God's love in the world. The Seven Sacraments—Baptism, Confirmation, Eucharist, Reconciliation, Anointing of the Sick, Matrimony, and Holy Orders—have their origins in the life and teachings of Jesus. The Sacraments are signs of the new covenant between God and humans.

Signs and symbols of the Sacraments can be understood through human senses. They point to the invisible qualities of God. The matter of a Sacrament consists of its material elements, such as the water of Baptism. The form of a Sacrament consists of its words. Correct matter and form must be present for the Sacrament to be real and true.

The Liturgy of the Hours

The Liturgy of the Hours is the Church's public prayer to make each day holy. This liturgy is offered at set times throughout the day and night. In monasteries, monks and nuns gather as many as ten times each day and night to pray the Liturgy of the Hours. Parishes that celebrate the Liturgy of the Hours do so less frequently, perhaps once or twice each day. The most common celebrations of the Liturgy of the Hours are Morning Prayer and Evening Prayer.

The Sacraments of Initiation

The Sacraments of Initiation—Baptism, Confirmation, and Eucharist—celebrate membership into the Catholic Church.

Through the words and waters of **Baptism**, God forgives all sin and gives new life in Christ. In emergencies and other times of necessity, anyone can baptize another person. The person baptizing must intend to do what the Church does in this Sacrament. He or she needs to pour water over the head of the person being baptized while saying, "I baptize you in the name of the Father, and of the Son, and of the Holy Spirit."

Confirmation completes the baptismal grace and strengthens a person to be a witness to the faith through the power of the Spirit. Catholics in different dioceses in the United States receive the Sacrament of Confirmation at different ages. In the Roman, or Latin, Rite, candidates for Confirmation must meet certain criteria. They must believe in the faith of the Church, be in a state of grace, and want to receive the Sacrament. Candidates must be prepared and willing to be a witness to Christ in their daily lives and take part in the life of the Church.

Eucharist completes the Sacraments of Initiation, nourishing the baptized with Christ's own Body and Blood and uniting the new Catholics with God and one another in Jesus.

The Eucharist is also known as the Blessed Sacrament, Holy Communion, the Bread of Heaven, Breaking of Bread, the Lord's Supper, Holy Sacrifice, Holy Mass, and the Body of Christ.

The Sacraments of Healing

In the Sacraments of Healing—Penance and Reconciliation and Anointing of the Sick—God's forgiveness and healing are given to those suffering physical and spiritual sickness.

In **Penance and Reconciliation,** through the words of absolution, personal sins are forgiven and relationships with God and the Church are healed.

In the **Anointing of the Sick,** one who is sick or dying is anointed with oil and with the laying on of hands. The person unites his or her suffering with that of Jesus. The Sacrament gives spiritual strength and God's grace. Physical healing also may take place.

The Sacraments at the Service of Communion

The Sacraments at the Service of Communion—Holy Orders and Matrimony—celebrate commitments to serve God and the community and build up the People of God.

In **Holy Orders**, the bishop lays hands on a man and anoints him with Sacred Chrism. The man is empowered to serve the Church as deacon, priest, or bishop.

In **Matrimony**, a baptized man and a baptized woman, through their words of consent, make a covenant with God and one another. Marriage is for the sake of their love and any children God blesses them with.

Order of Mass

Introductory Rites

Entrance Chant

Greeting

Rite for the Blessing and Sprinkling of
Water

Penitential Act

Kyrie

Gloria

Collect

Liturgy of the Word

First Reading

Responsorial Psalm

Second Reading

Gospel Acclamation

Dialogue at the Gospel (or Gospel
Dialogue)

Gospel Reading

Homily

Profession of Faith (or Creed—Nicene
Creed or Apostles' Creed)

Prayer of the Faithful

Liturgy of the Eucharist

Preparation of the Gifts

Invitation to Prayer

Prayer over the Offerings

Eucharistic Prayer

Preface Dialogue

Preface

Preface Acclamation

Consecration

Mystery of Faith

Concluding Doxology

Amen

Communion Rite

The Lord's Prayer

Sign of Peace

Lamb of God

Invitation to Communion

Communion

Prayer after Communion

Concluding Rites

Solemn Blessing or Prayer over the People

Final Blessing

Dismissal

Liturgical Year

The liturgical year celebrates Jesus' life and work for the salvation of the world. During Advent and Christmas, the Church celebrates the Incarnation. The Seasons of Lent, Triduum, and Easter explore the Paschal Mystery. Easter is the high point of the liturgical year because it is the greatest celebration of the Resurrection. The life and ministry of Jesus are the focus of Ordinary Time. Mary and the Saints are also remembered throughout the year in what is known as the sanctoral cycle.

Holy Days of Obligation

Catholics must attend Mass on Sunday unless a serious reason prevents their doing so. They must also go to Mass on certain holy days. United States Holy Days of Obligation are

- Mary, Mother of God (January 1)
- Ascension (forty days after Easter or the Sunday nearest the end of the forty-day period)
- Assumption (August 15)
- All Saints Day (November 1)
- Immaculate Conception (December 8)
- Christmas (December 25)

Fasting and Abstinence

To help prepare spiritually for the Eucharist, Catholics fast for one hour before Communion. They take no food or drink except water. (Exceptions can be made for those who are sick and for those of advanced age.)

To fast means to eat only one full meal and two smaller meals during the course of a day. All Catholics, from their eighteenth birthday until their fifty-ninth birthday, are required to fast on Ash Wednesday and Good Friday unless a serious reason prevents them from doing so. Another discipline of self-denial is abstinence. Catholics who are fourteen years of age or older are expected to abstain from eating meat on Ash Wednesday, Good Friday, and, in the United States, on all of the Fridays in Lent.

The Liturgical Environment

Each part of the church has a name:

narthex or vestibule—the lobby of a church

nave—the main body of the church

baptistry—the place for Baptism

ambry—the place where holy oils are kept

sanctuary—the area around the altar where the priest and ministers perform their functions

reconciliation chapel—may be used for celebrating the Sacrament of Penance

Eucharistic chapel—used for prayer and adoration of the Eucharist

sacristy—room where priests put on their vestments and where materials and vessels for the liturgy are prepared

Each item of furniture in a church also has a name:

altar—the table of the Eucharist

font—the pool or basin of water for Baptism

ambo—the reading stand where Scripture is proclaimed

presider's chair—the chair from which the presider leads prayer

Tabernacle—the box in which the Consecrated Host is kept

sanctuary lamp—light kept lit near the Tabernacle

Liturgical Vestments

Some ministers of the liturgy wear special clothing to mark their roles in the celebration. The alb, symbolizing Baptism, is a long white garment with sleeves. Both ordained and lay ministers may wear the alb. A cincture is a cloth belt or cord tied at the waist around the alb. The stole is a long, narrow piece of fabric that signifies ordination. A priest wears the stole over his alb, draping it from his shoulders so that both ends hang down in front. A deacon wears a stole diagonally across his chest, over his left shoulder.

At Mass, the priest wears a chasuble, a long, poncho-like garment. The chasuble is worn over the alb and the stole. When a priest leads an outdoor procession or presides at a solemn liturgy that is not a Mass, he may wear a cope, a long cape that fastens at the collar, over his alb and stole. A bishop wears a hat called a miter. A bishop may also carry a staff, or crosier, modeled on a shepherd's crook. The stole, chasuble, cope, and miter are made from fabric whose color represents the liturgical season. The color for Advent and Lent is violet. For Christmas and Easter, the color is white or gold. Green is worn during Ordinary Time. On Palm Sunday, Good Friday, Pentecost, and the feasts of martyrs, red is worn.

Law

Divine law is the eternal law of God. It includes:

physical law: the law of gravity is an example of physical law.

moral law: a moral law is one that humans understand through reasoning (stealing is wrong) and through Divine Revelation (keep holy the Lord's Day).

Natural moral law is present in every heart. It includes the principles that all humans accept as right. For example, people everywhere understand that no person may kill another unjustly. Everyone must obey natural moral law because everyone is created by God. God's Commandments are based on natural moral law.

The Ten Commandments

1. I am the LORD your God: you shall not have strange gods before me.
2. You shall not take the name of the LORD your God in vain.
3. Remember to keep holy the LORD's Day.
4. Honor your father and your mother.
5. You shall not kill.
6. You shall not commit adultery.
7. You shall not steal.
8. You shall not bear false witness against your neighbor.
9. You shall not covet your neighbor's wife.
10. You shall not covet your neighbor's goods.

Precepts of the Church

1. Take part in the Mass on Sundays and holy days. Keep these days holy and avoid unnecessary work.
2. Celebrate the Sacrament of Penance and Reconciliation at least once a year if there is serious sin.
3. Receive Holy Communion at least once a year during the Easter Season.
4. Fast and/or abstain on days of penance.
5. Give your time, gifts, and money to support the Church.

The Great Commandment

"You shall love the Lord, your God, with all your heart, with all your being, with all your strength, and with all your mind, and your neighbor as yourself." Luke 10:27

The New Commandment

"Love one another. As I have loved you, so you also should love one another." John 13:34

The Beatitudes

Blessed are the poor in spirit,
for theirs is the kingdom of heaven.
Blessed are they who mourn,
for they will be comforted.
Blessed are the meek,
for they will inherit the land.
Blessed are they who hunger and thirst
    for righteousness,
for they will be satisfied.
Blessed are the merciful,
for they will be shown mercy.
Blessed are the clean of heart,
for they will see God.
Blessed are the peacemakers,
for they will be called children of God.
Blessed are they who are persecuted for
    the sake of righteousness,
for theirs is the kingdom of heaven.

Works of Mercy

Corporal (for the body)	Spiritual (for the spirit)
Feed the hungry.	Warn the sinner.
Give drink to the thirsty.	Teach the ignorant.
Clothe the naked.	Counsel the doubtful.
Shelter the homeless.	Comfort the sorrowful.
Visit the sick.	Bear wrongs patiently.
Visit the imprisoned.	Forgive injuries.
Bury the dead.	Pray for the living and the dead.

Gifts of the Holy Spirit

Wisdom
Right judgment (Counsel)
Knowledge
Wonder and awe (Fear of the Lord)

Understanding
Courage (Fortitude)
Reverence (Piety)

Fruits of the Holy Spirit

Charity
Joy
Peace

Kindness
Goodness
Generosity

Faithfulness
Modesty
Self-control

Patience
Gentleness
Chastity

Grace and Sin

Sanctifying grace allows you to share in God's own life. It is a permanent gift that builds your friendship with God and assures you of eternal life.

Actual grace is a temporary gift that helps you think or act according to God's will for you in a particular situation. Actual grace helps you understand what is right and strengthens you to turn away from sin.

Sacramental grace is the gift that comes from the Sacraments. Each Sacrament gives its own particular grace.

Sin

Original Sin is the sin that our first parents, Adam and Eve, committed by choosing to disobey God. This sin describes the fallen state that caused the human condition of weakness and tendency toward sin. Baptism restores the relationship of loving grace in which all people were created by God.

Personal sin is any thought, word, act, or failure to act that goes against God's law. Sin is a choice, not a mistake.

Mortal sin breaks your relationship with God. For a sin to be mortal, it must be a serious matter done with full knowledge and complete consent.

Venial sin weakens or wounds your relationship with God. Continual venial sin can lead to mortal sin.

Social sin results from the effect that personal sin has on a community. People who have been sinned against may sin in return. Violence, injustice, and other wrongs may develop within the community. God created humans in his image and likeness. Because of this, you have human dignity and therefore need to respect your dignity and that of others.

Asking forgiveness, accepting punishment, and resolving not to sin again helps a person develop as a Catholic. However, one who habitually sins neglects moral development, sets a poor example, and harms others. When individuals disobey God's law and just civil laws, the entire community suffers.

Virtue

The Theological Virtues of faith, hope, and charity (love) are gifts from God. These virtues help you live in a loving relationship with God.

Cardinal Virtues are the principal moral virtues that help you lead a moral life. These virtues are prudence (careful judgment), fortitude (courage), justice (giving God and people their due), and temperance (moderation, balance).

Conscience Formation

Conscience is the God-given ability that helps us judge right from wrong and choose what is right. Having an informed conscience is a lifelong task. The following steps will help you in this task: pray for the guidance of the Spirit, educate and develop your conscience through constant use and examination, know the Church's teachings, and seek advice from good moral people.

Examination of Conscience

Examining your conscience should be done daily and especially in preparation for the Sacrament of Penance and Reconciliation.

1. Pray to the Holy Spirit to help you examine your conscience.

2. Look at your life in light of the Beatitudes, the Ten Commandments, the Great Commandment, and the Precepts of the Church.

3. Ask yourself: Where have I fallen short of what God wants for me?

   Whom have I hurt?

   What have I done that I knew was wrong?

   Have I done penance and tried as hard as I could to make up for past sins?

   Am I working to change my bad habits?

   With what areas am I still having trouble?

   Am I sincerely sorry for all my sins?

4. In addition to confessing your sins, you may wish to talk with the priest about one or more of the above questions.

Basic Prayers

These are essential prayers that every Catholic should know. Latin is the official, universal language of the Church. As members of the Catholic Church, we usually pray in the language that we speak, but we sometimes pray in Latin, the common language of the Church.

Sign of the Cross

In the name of the Father,
and of the Son,
and of the Holy Spirit.
Amen.

Signum Crucis

In nómine Patris,
et Fílii,
et Spíritus Sancti.
Amen.

The Lord's Prayer

Our Father, who art in heaven,
hallowed be thy name;
thy kingdom come,
thy will be done
on earth as it is in heaven.
Give us this day our daily bread,
and forgive us our trespasses,
as we forgive those who trespass
   against us;
and lead us not into temptation,
but deliver us from evil. Amen.

Pater Noster

Pater noster qui es in cælis:
santificétur Nomen Tuum;
advéniat Regnum Tuum;
fiat volúntas Tua,
sicut in cælo, et in terra.
Panem nostrum
cotidiánum da nobis hódie;
et dimítte nobis débita nostra,
sicut et nos
dimíttus debitóribus nostris;
et ne nos indúcas in tentatiónem;
sed líbera nos a Malo.

Glory Be

Glory be to the Father
and to the Son
and to the Holy Spirit
as it was in the beginning
is now,
and ever shall be world without end.
Amen.

Gloria Patri

Gloria Patri
et Filio
et Spíritui Sancto.
Sicut erat in princípio,
et nunc et semper
et in sæ´cula sæ´culorem.
Amen.

The Hail Mary

Hail, Mary, full of grace,
the Lord is with thee.
Blessed art thou among women
and blessed is the fruit of thy
   womb, Jesus.
Holy Mary, Mother of God,
pray for us sinners,
now and at the hour of our death.
Amen.

Ave Maria

Ave, María, grátia plena,
Dóminus tecum.
Benedícta tu in muliéribus,
et benedíctus fructus ventris
   tui, Iesus
Sancta María, Mater Dei,
ora pro nobis peccatóribus,
nunc et in hora mortis nostræ.
Amen.

Prayer to the Holy Spirit

Come, Holy Spirit, fill the hearts of your faithful.
And kindle in them the fire of your love.
Send forth your Spirit and they shall be created.
And you will renew the face of the earth.

Let us pray.

Lord, by the light of the Holy Spirit you have taught the hearts
of your faithful. In the same Spirit help us to relish what is right
and always rejoice in your consolation.

We ask this through Christ our Lord. Amen.

Memorare

Remember, most loving Virgin Mary,

never was it heard that anyone who turned to you for help was
left unaided.

Inspired by this confidence, though burdened by my sins, I run to
your protection for you are my mother.

Mother of the Word of God, do not despise my words of
pleading but be merciful and hear my prayer. Amen.

Prayers from the Liturgy

Holy, Holy, Holy Lord

Holy, Holy, Holy Lord God of hosts.
Heaven and earth are full of your glory.
Hosanna in the highest.
Blessed is he who comes in the name of
    the Lord.
Hosanna in the highest.

Sanctus, Sanctus, Sanctus

Sanctus, Sanctus, Sanctus
Dominus Deus Sabaoth.
Pleni sunt coeli et terra gloria tua.
Hosanna in excelsis.
Benedictus qui venit in nomine Domini.
Hosanna in excelsis

Lamb of God

Lamb of God, you take away the
    sins of the world,
        have mercy on us.
Lamb of God, you take away the
    sins of the world,
        have mercy on us.
Lamb of God, you take away the
    sins of the world,
        grant us peace.

Agnus Dei

Agnus Dei, qui tollis peccata mundi:
miserere nobis.
Agnus Dei, qui tollis peccata mundi:
miserere nobis.
Agnus Dei, qui tollis peccata mundi:
dona nobis pacem

Gloria

Glory to God in the highest,
and on earth peace to people of good will.

We praise you,
we bless you,
we adore you,
we glorify you,
we give you thanks for your great glory,
Lord God, heavenly King,
O God, almighty Father.

Lord Jesus Christ, Only Begotten Son,
Lord God, Lamb of God, Son of the
    Father,
you take away the sins of the world,
    have mercy on us;

you take away the sins of the world,
    receive our prayer;
you are seated at the right hand of the
Father,
    have mercy on us.

For you alone are the Holy One,
you alone are the Lord,
you alone are the Most High,
Jesus Christ,
with the Holy Spirit,
in the glory of God the Father.
Amen.

I Confess/Confiteor

I confess to almighty God
and to you, my brothers and sisters,
that I have greatly sinned,
in my thoughts and in my words,
in what I have done and in what I have
failed to do,

Gently strike your chest with a closed fist.

through my fault, through my fault,
through my most grievous fault;

Continue:

therefore I ask blessed Mary ever-Virgin,
all the Angels and Saints,
and you, my brothers and sisters,
to pray for me to the Lord our God.

Personal and Family Prayers

Morning Prayer

God be in my head, and in my
    understanding;
God be in my eyes, and in my looking;
God be in my mouth, and in my speaking;
God be in my heart, and in my thinking;
God be at my end, and at my departing.
Amen.

Evening Prayer

Lord, from the rising of the sun to its
setting, your name is worthy of all praise.
Let our prayer come like incense before
you. May the lifting up of our hands be
as an evening sacrifice acceptable to you,
Lord our God. Amen.

Act of Faith

O God, we firmly believe that you are
one God in three divine Persons, Father,
Son, and Holy Spirit; we believe that your
divine Son became man and died for
our sins, and that he will come to judge
the living and the dead. We believe these
and all the truths that the holy Catholic
Church teaches because you have revealed
them, and you can neither deceive nor be
deceived.

Act of Hope

O God, relying on your almighty power
and your endless mercy and promises, we
hope to gain pardon for our sins, the help
of your grace, and life everlasting, through
the saving actions of Jesus Christ, our Lord
and Redeemer.

Act of Love

O God, we love you above all things, with
our whole heart and soul, because you are
all-good and worthy of all love. We love
our neighbor as ourselves for the love
of you. We forgive all who have injured
us and ask pardon of all whom we have
injured.

Act of Contrition

My God, I am sorry for my sins with all
my heart. In choosing to do wrong and
failing to do good, I have sinned against
you whom I should love above all things.
I firmly intend, with your help, to do
penance, to sin no more, and to avoid
whatever leads me to sin. Our Savior Jesus
Christ suffered and died for us. In his
name, my God, have mercy.

Devotional Practices

When we pray with the Saints, we ask them to pray to God for us and to pray with us. The Saints are with Christ. They speak for us when we need help. As the Mother of Jesus, the Son of God, Mary is called the Mother of God, the Queen of all Saints, and the Mother of the Church. There are many prayers and practices of devotion to Mary. One of the most revered is the Rosary. It focuses on the twenty mysteries that describe events in the lives of Jesus and Mary.

How to Pray the Rosary

1. Pray the Sign of the Cross and say the Apostles' Creed.
2. Pray the Lord's Prayer.
3. Pray three Hail Marys.
4. Pray the Glory Be.
5. Say the first mystery; then pray the Lord's Prayer.
6. Pray ten Hail Marys while meditating on the mystery.
7. Pray the Glory Be.
8. Say the second mystery; then pray the Lord's Prayer. Repeat 6 and 7 and continue with the third, fourth, and fifth mysteries in the same manner.
9. Pray the Hail, Holy Queen.

Hail, Holy Queen

Hail, holy Queen, Mother of mercy,
hail, our life, our sweetness, and our hope.
To you we cry, the children of Eve;
to you we send up our sighs,
mourning and weeping in this land of exile.
Turn, then, most gracious advocate,
your eyes of mercy toward us;
lead us home at last
and show us the blessed fruit of your womb,
Jesus:
O clement, O loving, O sweet Virgin Mary.
    Salve, Regina

The Mysteries of the Rosary

The Joyful Mysteries
The Annunciation
The Visitation
The Nativity
The Presentation in the Temple
The Finding in the Temple

The Luminous Mysteries
The Baptism of Jesus
The Wedding at Cana
The Proclamation of the Kingdom
The Transfiguration
The Institution of the Eucharist

The Sorrowful Mysteries
The Agony in the Garden
The Scourging at the Pillar
The Crowning with Thorns
The Carrying of the Cross
The Crucifixion and Death

The Glorious Mysteries
The Resurrection
The Ascension
The Descent of the Holy Spirit
The Assumption of Mary
The Coronation of Mary in Heaven

Angelus

V. The angel spoke God's message to Mary,
R. and she conceived of the Holy Spirit.
Hail, Mary…
V. "I am the lowly servant of the Lord:
R. let it be done to me according to your word."
Hail, Mary…
V. And the Word became flesh,
R. and lived among us.
Hail, Mary…
V. Pray for us, holy Mother of God,
R. that we may become worthy of the promises of Christ.
Let us pray.
Lord,
fill our hearts with your grace:
once, through the message of an angel
you revealed to us the incarnation of your Son;
now, through his suffering and death
lead us to the glory of his Resurrection.
We ask this through Christ our Lord.
R. Amen.

Litany of St. Joseph

Lord, have mercy.	Lord, have mercy.
Christ, have mercy.	Christ, have mercy.
Lord, have mercy.	Lord, have mercy.
Good Saint Joseph,	pray for us.
Descendant of the House of David	pray for us.
Husband of Mary,	pray for us.
Foster father of Jesus,	pray for us.
Guardian of Christ,	pray for us.
Support of the holy family,	pray for us.
Model of workers,	pray for us.
Example to parents,	pray for us.
Comfort of the dying,	pray for us.
Provider of food to the hungry,	pray for us.
Companion of the poor,	pray for us.
Protector of the church,	pray for us.

The Way of the Cross

In the devotion known as the Way of the Cross, "stations" represent stops along the way of Jesus' journey from Pilate's court all the way to the tomb. Walking in a church from one station to the next and really focusing on each picture or image of the Passion of Christ can inspire prayer from the heart.

The First Station: Jesus is condemned to death. John 3:16
"For God so loved the world that he gave his only Son, so that everyone who believes in him might not perish but might have eternal life."

The Second Station: Jesus bears his Cross. Luke 9:23
"Then he said to all, 'If anyone wishes to come after me, he must deny himself and take up his cross daily and follow me.'"

The Third Station: Jesus falls the first time. Isaiah 53:6
"We had all gone astray like sheep, all following our own way; but the LORD laid upon him the guilt of us all."

The Fourth Station: Jesus meets his mother. Lamentations 1:12
"Come, all who pass by the way, pay attention and see: Is there any pain like my pain, …"

The Fifth Station: Simon of Cyrene helps Jesus carry his Cross. Matthew 25:40
"And the king will say to them in reply, 'Amen, I say to you, whatever you did for one of these least brothers of mine, you did for me.'"

The Sixth Station: Veronica wipes the face of Jesus. John 14:9
"… 'Whoever has seen me has seen the Father'…"

The Seventh Station: Jesus falls a second time. Matthew 11:28
"Come to me, all you who labor and are burdened, and I will give you rest."

The Eighth Station: Jesus meets the women of Jerusalem. Luke 23:28
"Jesus turned to them and said, 'Daughters of Jerusalem, do not weep for me; weep instead for yourselves and for your children …'"

The Ninth Station: Jesus falls a third time. Luke 14:11

"For everyone who exalts himself will be humbled, but the one who humbles himself will be exalted."

The Tenth Station: Jesus is stripped of his garments. Luke 14:33

"In the same way, everyone of you who does not renounce all his possessions cannot be my disciple."

The Eleventh Station: Jesus is nailed to the Cross. John 6:38

… I came down from heaven not to do my own will but the will of the one who sent me."

The Twelfth Station: Jesus dies on the Cross. Philippians 2:7–8

"… And found human in appearance, he humbled himself, becoming obedient to death, even death on a cross."

The Thirteenth Station: Jesus is taken down from the Cross. Luke 24:26

"Was it not necessary that the Messiah should suffer these things and enter into his glory?"

The Fourteenth Station: Jesus is placed in the tomb. John 12:24

"Amen, amen, I say to you, unless a grain of wheat falls to the ground and dies, it remains just a grain of wheat; but if it dies, it produces much fruit."

Catholic **Faith Words**

A

absolution words spoken by the priest during the Sacrament of Penance and Reconciliation to grant forgiveness of sins in God's name **(210)**

Annunciation the Angel Gabriel's announcement to Mary that she was called to be the Mother of God **(178)**

Assumption the teaching that after her earthly life, Mary was taken into Heaven, body and soul, to be with Jesus **(178)**

B

beatification the second step in the process of becoming a Saint, in which a venerable person is recognized by the Church as having brought about a miracle through his or her prayers of intercession **(179)**

Blessed Sacrament the Holy Eucharist, especially the Body of Christ, reserved in the Tabernacle **(246)**

Body of Christ a name for the Church of which Christ is the head. All the baptized are members of the body. **(158)**

Book of Gospels the book containing the Gospel readings from which the priest or deacon proclaims the Gospel during Mass **(236)**

C

canonization a declaration by the Pope naming a person a Saint. Canonized Saints have special feast days or memorials in the Church's calendar. **(179)**

Cardinal Virtues the four principal moral virtues—prudence, temperance, justice, and fortitude—that help us live as children of God and from which the other moral virtues flow. We strengthen these good habits through God's grace and our own efforts. **(108)**

catechumen a "learner," or person preparing to celebrate the Sacraments of Initiation **(202)**

Communion of Saints everyone who believes in and follows Jesus: people on Earth, and people who have died and are in Purgatory or Heaven **(224)**

confession another name for the Sacrament of Penance and Reconciliation; an essential element of the Sacrament when you tell your sins to the priest **(210)**

Confirmation the Sacrament that seals us with a special outpouring of the Gifts of the Holy Spirit, deepens the grace of Baptism, and strengthens us to give witness to Christ in the world **(201)**

consecrated religious life a state of life lived in community and characterized by the vows of poverty, chastity, and obedience **(260)**

consecration the part of the Eucharistic Prayer in which the priest prays the words of Jesus over the bread and wine, and these elements become the Body and Blood of Christ **(246)**

contrition being sorry for your sins and wanting to live better **(210)**

conversion the continual process of becoming the people God intends us to be through change and growth. It is a response to God's love and forgiveness. **(135)**

Corporal Works of Mercy actions that show care for the physical needs of people **(280)**

covenant a sacred promise or agreement between God and humans **(76)**

Creed a formal statement of what we believe about the Holy Trinity and the Church. The word *creed* comes from the Latin for "I believe." **(236)**

Divine Revelation the way God makes himself, and his plan for humans, known to us **(54)**

eternal life life forever with God for all who die in his friendship **(269)**

evangelization giving witness to the faith by proclaiming the Good News of Jesus to the world through words and deeds in a way that invites people to accept the Gospel **(280)**

faith the Theological Virtue that makes it possible for us to believe in God and the things that he has revealed to us. Faith leads us to obey God. It is both a gift from him and something we choose. **(67)**

free will the God-given freedom and ability to make choices. God created us with free will so we can have the freedom to choose good. **(124)**

Fruits of the Holy Spirit the qualities that can be seen in us when we allow the Holy Spirit to work in our hearts **(176)**

Gifts of the Holy Spirit seven powerful gifts God gives us to follow the guidance of the Holy Spirit and live the Christian life. We are sealed with the Gifts of the Holy Spirit at Confirmation. **(279)**

grace God's free, loving gift of his own life and help to do what he calls us to do. It is participation in the life of the Holy Trinity. **(67)**

Heaven the full joy of living eternally in God's presence **(269)**

Hell eternal separation from God because of a choice to turn away from him and not seek forgiveness **(269)**

holy unique and pure; set apart for God and his purposes **(176)**

Holy Trinity the mystery of one God in three Divine Persons: Father, Son, and Holy Spirit **(90)**

Incarnation the mystery that the Son of God took on human nature in order to save all people **(124)**

infallibility a gift of the Holy Spirit to the Church by which the Pope and the bishops in union with him may declare definitively that a matter of faith or morals is free from error and must be accepted by the faithful **(168)**

Kingdom of God God's rule of peace, justice, and love that exists in Heaven, but has not yet come in its fullness on Earth **(132)**

laity all of the baptized people in the Church who share in God's mission but are not priests or consecrated sisters or brothers; sometimes called lay people **(260)**

liturgical year the feasts and seasons of the Church calendar that celebrate the Paschal Mystery of Christ **(144)**

liturgy the public prayer of the Church. It includes the Sacraments and forms of daily prayer. **(100)**

Magisterium the teaching office of the Church, which is all of the bishops in union with the Pope. The Magisterium has the teaching authority to interpret the Word of God found in Scripture and Tradition. **(168)**

Marks of the Church the essential characteristics that distinguish Christ's Church and her mission: one, holy, catholic, and apostolic **(158)**

Messiah the promised one who would lead his People. The word *Messiah* means "God's anointed," or "God's chosen one." Jesus is the Messiah. **(67)**

miracle an event that cannot be explained by science because it happened by the power of God **(135)**

missionaries people who answer God's call to bring the message of Jesus and announce the Good News of his Kingdom to people in other places **(279)**

mortal sin the most serious form of personal sin, through which a person breaks his or her relationship with God **(193)**

Mother of God a title given to Mary because she is the Mother of the Son of God who became man **(178)**

mystery a spiritual truth that is difficult to perceive or understand with our senses, but is known through faith and through signs **(88)**

Original Holiness the state of goodness that humanity enjoyed before our first parents, Adam and Eve, chose to sin against God **(190)**

Original Sin the sin of our first parents, Adam and Eve, which led to the sinful condition of the human race from its beginning **(143)**

parable a story Jesus used to describe the Kingdom of God, using examples from everyday life **(133)**

Particular Judgment the individual judgment by God at the time of a person's death; when God decides, after a person's death, where that person will spend eternity according to his or her faith and works **(269)**

Paschal Mystery Christ's work of redemption through his suffering, Death, Resurrection, and Ascension **(144)**

Pope the successor of Peter, the Bishop of Rome, and the head of the entire Catholic Church **(167)**

providence God's loving care for all things; God's will and plan for creation **(56)**

psalms poems and hymns that were first used in the liturgy of the Israelites. Today, the psalms are also prayed and sung in the public prayer of the Church. **(236)**

Purgatory a state of final cleansing after death and before entering into Heaven **(269)**

Real Presence the phrase used to describe that Jesus Christ is really and truly with us in the Eucharist—Body, Blood, Soul, and Divinity **(224)**

religion a group of beliefs, prayers, and practices through which people express longing for God **(65)**

reparation the action taken to repair the damage done from sin **(210)**

reverence the care and respect you show to God and holy persons and things **(99)**

Rite of Christian Initiation of Adults (RCIA) the process by which adults and some children become members of the Catholic Church through the Sacraments of Initiation **(202)**

Sacred Chrism perfumed oil used for anointing in the Sacraments of Baptism, Confirmation, and Holy Orders. In Eastern Rite Churches, Confirmation takes its name from this word and is known as Chrismation. **(201)**

Sacred Scripture another name for the Bible; Sacred Scripture is the inspired Word of God written by humans **(4, 54)**

Sacred Tradition God's Word to the Church, safeguarded by the Apostles and their successors, the bishops, and handed down verbally—in her Creeds, Sacraments, and other teachings—to future generations **(54)**

sacrifice giving up something out of love for someone else or for the common good (the good of everyone). Jesus sacrificed his life for all people. **(144)**

salvation the loving action of God's forgiveness of sins and the restoration of friendship with him brought by Jesus **(176)**

Savior a title for Jesus, who came into the world to save all people who were lost through sin and to lead them back to God his Father **(124)**

Seven Sacraments effective signs of God's life, instituted by Christ and given to the Church. In the celebration of each Sacrament, there are visible signs and Divine actions that give grace and allow us to share in God's work. **(3, 76)**

sin a deliberate thought, word, deed, or omission contrary to the law of God. Sin hurts our relationship with God and other people. **(193)**

soul the spiritual part of a human that lives forever **(124)**

Spiritual Works of Mercy actions that address the needs of the heart, mind, and soul **(280)**

sponsor a representative of the Church community who supports a catechumen celebrating the Sacraments of Initiation **(202)**

stewardship the way we appreciate and use God's gifts, including our time, talent, and treasure, and the resources of creation **(56)**

T–V

transubstantiation the process by which the power of the Holy Spirit and the words of the priest transform the bread and wine into the Body and Blood of Jesus **(246)**

venial sin a sin that weakens a person's relationship with God but does not destroy it **(193)**

viaticum the Eucharist given to a person who is near death to sustain him or her on the journey to eternity **(270)**

virtues good spiritual habits that strengthen you and enable you to do what is right and good. They develop over time with our practice and openness to God's grace. **(90)**

vocation a particular way to answer God's call, whether as a lay person (married or single), a religious, or a member of the ordained ministry **(258)**

vows solemn promises that are made to or before God **(260)**

worship to adore and praise God, especially in the liturgy and in prayer **(100)**

Index

presider's chair 315
priest 89, 101, 135, 167, 170, 200, 202, 211, 213, 225, 227, 228, 235, 237, 247, 261, 304, 308, 309, 312, 315, 319
Prophetic Books 5
providence **56**, 57, 142, 330
prudence (careful judgment) 109, 319
psalms **236**, 330
Purgatory 268, **269**, 330
pyx 270

Real Presence **224**, 225, 330
reconciliation 210, 211, 312
reconciliation chapel 315
Redeemer 144
Reign of God 132, 158, 258, 280, 281
   see also Kingdom of God
"The Rejection at Nazareth" 279
religion **65**, 331
reparation **210**, 211, 331
repentance 26, 102, 209, 270
respect 21, 55, 58, 102, 109, 193, 282, 294, 295, 298, 299, 304, 318
responsibility 40, 227, 228, 248, 258, 260, 281, 282, 293, 294, 302, 303
Resurrection 11, 30, 33, 34, 76, 100, 144, 145, 146, 178, 188, 192, 201, 225, 226, 256, 267, 270, 271, 311, 314
"The Resurrection of Jesus" 144
"Return to the Lord" 223
reverence 25, **99**, 237, 331
Rights and Responsibilities 294–295
Rite of Christian Funerals 270
Rite of Christian Initiation of Adults (RCIA) **202**, 331
Robert Bellarmine, Saint 161
Rosary, the 9, 10, 11, 180, 224, 306, 324
   how to pray 180, 324
   Mysteries of 180, 181, 324
Rose of Lima, Saint 296

sacramental 180
sacramental grace 318
Sacred Chrism 77, 200, **201**, 312, 331
Sacred Scripture 2, **4**, 5, 6, 16, 34, 35, 41, 52, **54**, 67, 68, 92, 98, 99, 122, 135, 136, 160, 179, 190, 194, 236, 238, 239, 271, 298, 304, 305, 309, 310, 315, 331
Sacred Tradition 6, 52, **54**, 168, 236, 298, 302, 331
sacrifice 21, 26, 30, **144**, 177, 191, 246, 308, 331
"The Sacrifice of Jesus" 191
sacristy 315
Saint 2, 6, 10, 11, 12, 176, 177, 178, 179, 181, 234, 235, 310, 314, 324
   Athanasius 93
   Augustine 63, 69
   Benedict 79
   Catherine of Siena 137
   Cecilia 103
   Clare of Assisi 249
   Cyril of Jerusalem 205
   Damien de Veuster 212, 213
   Frances Xavier Cabrini 176, 278, 279
   Francis Xavier 263
   Gemma Galgani 195
   Hildegard of Bingen 59

Ignatius of Loyola 234, 235
Isidore 259, 260
Jerome 239
John Paul II 143, 171, 297
John XXIII 143, 156
John Vianney 215
Joseph 21, 325
Juan Diego 176
Kateri Tekakwitha 177
Louis de Montfort 229
Maria 259, 260
Patrick 88, 89
Paul 201, 226
Paul Miki 147
Peter 166, 168
Pio of Pietrelcina 177
Robert Bellarmine 161
Rose of Lima 296
Stephen 273
Teresa of Ávila 176
Thomas More 113
Vincent de Paul 283
salvation 1, 3, 25, 30, **176**, 177, 188, 191, 246, 270, 308, 314, 331
"The Parable of the Samaritan Woman" 66
sanctifying grace 318
sanctoral cycle 10, 314
sanctuary 315
sanctuary lamp 315
Savior **124**, 126, 146, 245, 277, 308, 331
scribes 108, 122, 209
Second Coming 16, 256, 268
Second Vatican Council 156, 157, 158
sense of the faithful 169
Service of Communion, Sacraments at the 256, 260, 261, 312
serving 46, 145, 227, 228, 258, 260, 261, 262, 312
Seven Sacraments 3, 6, 35, 41, 52, 57, **76**, 77, 120, 135, 145, 159, 170, 180, 201, 228, 304, 309, 311, 331
Sign of the Cross 90, 91, 92, 101, 308, 320, 324
signs 46, 74, 75, 76, 77, 122, 125, 134, 135, 159, 176, 192, 308, 311
sin 124, 135, 144, 145, 178, 188, 190, 191, 192, **193**, 201, 211, 214, 246, 269, 312, 316, 318, 331
social justice 281, 282
social sin 318
Solemnity of the Epiphany 20
Son of God 3, 20, 21, 77, 90, 93, 101, 124, 167, 178, 192, 203, 308, 310, 324
Son of Man, the 126
soul 39, 63, 108, **124**, 125, 178, 225, 267, 269, 270, 331
"The Parable of the Sower" 133
Spiritual Works of Mercy 272, **280**, 281, 317, 331
sponsor **202**, 203, 301, 331
Stephen, Saint 273
stewardship **56**, 57, 58, 303, 331
stole 315
"The Story of Creation" 121
Sunday Mass 304
synagogue 131, 258, 279

Tabernacle 247, 315
talents 40, 57, 103, 228, 299
temperance 109, 111, 319
Temple 21, 273

Ten Commandments 86, 91, 100, 112, 204, 214, 291, 316, 319
Teresa of Ávila, Saint 176
Theological Virtues 91, 92, 319
   see also faith, hope, and charity (love)
Thomas More, Saint 113
transubstantiation **246**, 247, 331
Triduum 29, 30, 314
"True Blessedness" 233
"Trust in God the Creator and Redeemer" 277

unity 3, 21, 155, 156, 159, 161, 309, 312

Venerable 6
venial sin 192, **193**, 318, 331
viaticum **270**, 310, 331
Vincent de Paul, Saint 283
virtues 86, **90**, 91, 107, 110, 176, 319, 331
"The Visit of the Magi" 122
vocation 142, **258**, 260, 262, 263, 331
vows **260**, 262, 309, 331

"The Washing of the Disciples Feet" 29
Way of the Cross 326
Wisdom Books 5
witness 39, 142, 158, 167, 204, 312
Word of God 2, 4, 34, 54, 133, 135, 168, 200, 225, 228, 235, 236, 237, 238, 239, 278, 304
worship 20, 52, 57, 86, 99, **100**, 101, 102, 109, 159, 179, 222, 227, 228, 260, 273, 291, 309, 331